NEW YORK'S
GRAND EMANCIPATION JUBILEE

NEW YORK'S
GRAND EMANCIPATION JUBILEE

Essays on Slavery, Resistance, Abolition, Teaching, and Historical Memory

ALAN J. SINGER

SUNY
PRESS

Cover engraving: Schomburg Center for Research in Black Culture, Photographs and Prints Division, The New York Public Library. "Reading the Emancipation Proclamation," New York Public Library Digital Collections.

Published by State University of New York Press, Albany

For information, contact State University of New York Press, Albany, NY
www.sunypress.edu

Library of Congress Cataloging-in-Publication Data

Names: Singer, Alan J., author
Title: New York's Grand Emancipation Jubilee : Essays on Slavery, Resistance, Abolition, Teaching, and Historical Memory / Alan J. Singer, author.
Description: Albany : State University of New York Press, [2018] |
Includes bibliographical references and index.
Identifiers: ISBN 9781438469713 (hardcover : alk. paper) | ISBN 9781438469720 (e-book) | ISBN 9781438469706 (paperback : alk. paper)
Further information is available at the Library of Congress.

10 9 8 7 6 5 4 3 2 1

DEDICATION

At a time when candidates for public office garner support
with not-so-veiled racist rhetoric and activists are compelled
to conduct a campaign based on the radical idea that black lives matter,
the words and warning of Frederick Douglass of Rochester, New York,
in his 1862 essay on "The Work of the Future" continue to ring true.

This book is dedicated to Douglass and his belief that
"if there is no struggle, there is no progress" and that
"the work does not end with the abolition of slavery but only begins."
Ironically Douglass received recent attention when, at a 2017
Black History Month event, President Donald Trump seemed to imply
that the abolitionist and human rights activist was still alive and active.
According to the President, "Frederick Douglass is an example
of somebody who's done an amazing job and is getting recognized
more and more," credit that Douglass, although definitely deceased,
definitely deserves (Wootson 2017).

Douglass, his work, and his words play a central role in many of
the chapters in this book, particularly the concluding chapter
on "Politics of Historical Memory."

CONTENTS

PREFACE

THE WORK OF THE FUTURE
—*Frederick Douglass*

ALREADY IT SEEMS WELL TO LOOK FORWARD TO THE FUTURE TO WHICH WE ARE HAS-tening. No nation was ever called to the contemplation of a destiny more important and solemn than ours. Great duties and responsibilities are devolved upon us. Liberty, order, and civilization are staked against a slaveholding despotism, and social anarchy. To-day we have to put down a stupendous rebellion. To-morrow we shall have to reconstruct the whole fabric of Southern society, and bring order out of anarchy. It is a tremendous undertaking.... It would be absurd and ridiculous to expect that the conquered traitors will at once cordially cooperate with the Federal Government. They must be set aside for a new class of men, men who have hitherto exercised but little influence in the State. For this, we shall have to educate the people. The arduous task of the future will be to make the Southern people see and appreciate Republican Government, as a blessing of inestimable value, and to be maintained at any and every cost. They have got to be taught that slavery which they have valued as a blessing has ever been their direct calamity and curse.—The work before us is nothing less than a radical revolution in all the modes of thought which have flourished under the blighting slave system. The idea that labor is an evil, that work is degrading and that idleness is respectable, must be dispelled and the idea that work is honorable made to take its place.—Above all they must be taught that the liberty of a part is never to be secured by the enslavement or oppression of any. Neither the slave or the slaveholder can instantly throw off the sentiments inspired and ground into them by long years of tyranny on the one hand and of abject and cringing submission on the other. The master will carry into the new relation of liberty much of the insolence, caprice and pretention exercised by him while the admitted lord of the lash. The slave in his turn will be bound in the invisible chains of slavery long after his iron chains are broken and forever buried out of sight. There is no such thing as immediate Emancipation either for the master or for the slave. Time, experience and culture must gradually bring society back to the normal condition from which long years of slavery have carried all under its iron sway.... It is not likely however, that at the outset, the Southern people will consent to an absolutely just and humane policy towards the newly emancipated black people so long enslaved and degraded.... Men full of faith in the race, and of the sacred fire of love, must walk among these slavery-smitten columns of humanity and lift their forms towards Heaven. Verily, the work does not end with the abolition of slavery but only begins.

Source: *Douglass' Monthly*, November 1862. http://rbscp.lib.rochester.edu/4405 (accessed online January 4, 2016).

ACKNOWLEDGMENTS

WHEN HE READ A DRAFT OF THIS MANUSCRIPT, EUSTACE THOMPSON, A COLLEAGUE AT Hofstra University and a former school and district administrator, argued that race and racism were so deeply embedded in the fabric of American society that they were always present, even when unseen. As an educator, but also as an African American man, he could not imagine American society where race was not a factor. I thank him for his insights.

This book should be viewed as a sequel to *New York and Slavery: Time to Teach the Truth*, published by SUNY Press in 2008. As with that book, it is a hybrid. It primarily comments on history and historical debates rather than presenting new research. Its audience is general readers, teachers, and, hopefully, also secondary and college students rather than just historians.

I received important advice and assistance from professional historians, teachers, and also ordinary people with an interest in history. Ideas presented in this book evolved as part of panels and presentations at conferences sponsored by the Capital District Underground Railroad History Project (UGRRHP) and Hofstra University. Participants in these conferences included Andor Skotnes of Russell Sage College, Jonathan Lightfoot, Michael D'Innocenzo, and Athlene Collins of Hofstra University, Gloria Browne-Marshall of John Jay College-CUNY, and Paul and Mary Liz Stewart of the UGRRHP. Colleagues, teachers, and friends Felicia Hirata, Maureen Murphy, William Katz, Michael Pezone, John Staudt, Cecelia Goodman, Andrea Libresco, Pearlita King, Adeola Tella-Williams, Justin Williams, April Francis, Bill Hendricks, and Pablo Muriel were part of ongoing discussions about the issues presented in this book. They also read and commented on sections. Without them as partners, my work would never have reached this point. Errors of fact and interpretation, of course, are my own.

A number of social studies teachers affiliated with the Hofstra University New Teachers Network helped research material discussed in this book. Their work was published in theme issues of *Social Science Docket*, a joint publication of the New York and New Jersey Councils for the Social Studies. Support staff in the Hofstra University library and in the office of the Department of Teaching, Learning and Technology were of invaluable assistance.

As with all historians writing about African American history, I am indebted to researchers who pioneered this field of study, especially Herbert Aptheker and John Hope

Franklin. I was first introduced to their work in an undergraduate "American Negro History" course at the City College of New York taught by Milton Borome in 1970. I am also indebted to the staff at SUNY Press and anonymous readers for their support.

Two of my intellectual partners died during the development of this book, Martin Eisenberg and Mary Kennedy Carter, and they deserve special recognition. Martin and I worked together as community organizers for decades and our ongoing discussions, as well as actions and shared experiences, contributed greatly to my understanding of social movements. Mary was a social studies teacher and Hofstra University student teaching field supervisor, as well as an activist and an organizer. She was on the committee that developed the award winning "New York and Slavery: Complicity and Resistance" curriculum and worked for its implementation as part of the state's Amistad Commission. Mary believed that all students should know the history of Africa and Egypt and the contributions they made to world history. This is not just something to be taught to black children. They also all need to understand that many white people played important roles in the struggles for minority rights. Martin Eisenberg and Mary Kennedy Carter, teachers and political activists, will be missed. Judith Singer, who partnered on much of my earlier work, was gravely ill during the completion of this book. Her contributions were missed.

An earlier version of chapter 2 was originally published as A. Singer, "New York State's Radical Black Abolitionists," *Social Science Docket* 12(2) (Summer/Fall 2012).

An earlier version of chapter 5 was originally published as A. Singer, "We May never Know the Real Harriet Tubman," *Afro-Americans in New York Life and History* 36(1) (January 2012).

A version of chapter 10 is scheduled for publication in *New York History*.

Material in chapter 11 was originally published as A. Singer, "Myths and Movies," *Social Science Docket* 13(2) (Summer/Fall 2013).

CENTRALIZING THE HISTORY OF SLAVERY, RACISM, AND RESISTANCE

Why Race Still Matters

IN THE PREFACE TO *THE SOULS OF BLACK FOLK* (1903/2007, 9), W. E. B. DUBOIS DESCRIBED the "problem of the Twentieth Century" as the "problem of the color-line." The more research and reading I did for this book and the more discussion and teaching I engaged in on the legacy of slavery, race, and racism in the United States, it became clearer that if DuBois were alive today he would amend this statement. It has become increasingly apparent that the "problem of the color-line" in the United States was not just the "problem of the Twentieth Century," but is also the "problem" of the eighteenth, nineteenth, and early twenty-first centuries. This book, written just before and after the election of Donald Trump as president of the United States, builds on DuBois's claim to place slavery, racism, and resistance to oppression at the center of American history.

During the last three decades, sociologist William Julius Wilson, who is African American, has been one of the principle researchers and writers about race in the United States. In *The Declining Significance of Race* (1978), he argued that race played a diminished role in determining opportunity in American society and that problems faced by African Americans were increasingly related to economic issues and social class. This was a controversial position at the time, lauded by conservatives, and some liberals, who saw it as a justification for abandoning, or at least retreating on, federal Great Society and civil rights initiatives from the 1960s. President Ronald Reagan invited Wilson to a White House–sponsored meeting of black conservatives, a meeting that Wilson declined to attend (Ondaatje 2011, 161).

Wilson continually argued that his position on race was misrepresented. In *The Truly Disadvantaged* (1987), *When Work Disappears* (1996), and *More than Just Race* (2009), he responded to both critics and misguided supporters arguing that the impact of race and racism on the African American community had never ended. For Wilson, while economic opportunity was the major factor in determining life possibilities for individuals and groups, government action, institutional bias, and private behavior had created the historic racial impediments that trapped many African Americans in poverty, unemployment, and declining ghetto neighborhoods as industry, urban areas, and American society as a whole underwent enormous demographic, economic, and structural change at the end of the twentieth century. In a very real sense, the willingness of powerful whites, conservatives and liberals, to endorse what they thought of as the main thesis of *The Declining Significance of Race* represents the continuing significance of race in American society.

There were a number of occasions in the past when it appeared that the United States might resolve the racial hostilities rooted in the enslavement of Africans, but in each case it failed to happen. The Declaration of Independence declared that "all men are created equal," but after some initial movement toward emancipation in the North and West, the invention of the cotton gin, new demand for cotton from the industrializing North and Europe, in combination with the expansion of slavery west into Alabama, Mississippi, Louisiana, and Texas, led to the growth of a Cotton Kingdom dependent on the labor of enslaved Africans (Beckert 1915).

Historian Carl Degler (1983) argued that the racism that accompanied the enslavement of Africans was so deeply rooted in American society, both in the North and the South, that post–Civil War Reconstruction, which initially appeared to promise steps toward change and equality, can best be described as a "Dawn Without Noon." For Dubois (1903), the failure to address racism and resolve racial inequality at the end of the Civil War, along with the subsequent emergence of Jim Crow segregation and the reemergence of white rule in the South, were what made the problem of the twentieth century "the problem of the color-line."

The Great Migration of the 1920s, the New Deal of the 1930s, the African American civil rights movement of the 1950s and 1960s, and Great Society legislation in the 1960s, again promised to transform race relations in the United States. But as historian Ira Katznelson (2005) demonstrates, Franklin Roosevelt was able to secure Southern Democratic Congressional support for New Deal legislation by allowing local administration of federal programs, which meant support was denied to Southern blacks. The Pentagon, which opened in 1943, had racially separate bathrooms, and American army units remained segregated during World War II (Staples 2014).

In the 1960s, Lyndon Johnson's Great Society finally outlawed many Jim Crow practices, but it clearly failed to create a Great Society. From 1970 to 2011, the income of the lowest 20 percent of black households declined in real dollars from $6,465 to $6,379 as large portions of America's black community remained impoverished. In 2009, four decades after the Johnson presidency, the net worth of white families was nineteen times the net worth of black families (MacEwan 2013, 26). United States history can perhaps be best read as a series of dawns without noons.

In a 1967 speech to the Southern Christian Leadership Conference, Reverend Martin Luther King Jr. commented on the failures of Lyndon Johnson's legislative program (Pohlmann 2003, 87). According to King:

> When the Constitution was written, a strange formula to determine taxes and representation declared that the Negro was sixty percent of a person. Today another curious formula seems to declare that he is fifty percent of a person. Of the good things in life, the Negro has approximately one half those of whites. Of the bad things of life, he has twice those of whites. Thus half of all Negroes live in substandard housing. And Negroes have half the income of whites. When we view the negative experiences of life, the Negro has a double share. There are twice as many unemployed. The rate of infant mortality among Negroes is double that of whites and there are twice as many Negroes dying in Vietnam as whites in proportion to their size in the population.

Race, myth, and politics in the United States are an explosive mix. They were in the past; they are in the present. In 2005, *New York Times* columnist Bob Herbert reported on a 1981 interview with Lee Atwater, Republican Party consultant and confidant of presidents Reagan and Bush in which Lee Atwater discussed politics in the American South and the United States as a whole. According to Atwater, "You start out in 1954 by saying, 'Nigger, nigger, nigger.' By 1968 you can't say 'nigger'—that hurts you. Backfires. So you say stuff like forced busing, states' rights and all that stuff. You're getting so abstract now [that] you're talking about cutting taxes, and all these things you're talking about are totally economic things and a byproduct of them is [that] blacks get hurt worse than whites. And subconsciously maybe that is part of it. I'm not saying that. But I'm saying that if it is getting that abstract, and that coded, that we are doing away with the racial problem one way or the other. You follow me—because obviously sitting around saying, 'We want to cut this,' is much more abstract than even the busing thing, and a hell of a lot more abstract than 'Nigger, nigger' " (Herbert 2005, 37).

Atwater successfully employed this racial electoral strategy during the 1988 presidential campaign when a television attack advertisement was used to identify the Democratic candidate Michael Dukakis, the governor of Massachusetts, with a black prisoner from Massachusetts who escaped while on a weekend furlough for good behavior and then raped a white woman in Maryland (Simon 1915). In the lead-up to the 2016 presidential race the Republican strategy seemed to be to mobilize disaffected white male voters (and ignore the rest) with attacks on immigrants, Muslims, and affirmative action, a code word for blacks (Nesbit 2015).

In 1993, activist and scholar Cornel West could still argue, "Race is the most explosive issue in American life precisely because it forces us to confront the tragic facts of poverty and paranoia, despair and distrust. In short, a candid examination of race matters takes us to the core of the crisis of American democracy" (West 1993, 155–56). West warned, "We simply cannot enter the twenty-first century at each other's throats, even as we acknowledge the weighty forces of racism, patriarchy, economic inequality, homophobia, and ecological abuse on our necks. We are at a crucial crossroad in the history of this nation—and we either hang together by combating these forces that divide and degrade us or we hang separately" (ibid., 159).

There was some hope that the election of Barack Obama, a biracial man who identifies as African American, as president in 2008, signaled a new era in race relations in the United States, but that remains unclear. Direct and open expressions of racism appear to no longer be acceptable to most Americans; racist statements cost Donald Sterling ownership of the Los Angeles Clippers basketball team, although he was rewarded with a billion dollar buyout. More subtle forms of racism clearly continue. Ta-Nehisi Coates describes

the persistence of an "elegant racism" that avoids more incendiary language and crude stereotypes (Coates 2014). A study by the Public Religion Research Institute revealed deep anxiety among non-Hispanic white Americans about the possibility that the nonwhite population of the country would soon be in a majority (Jones et al. 2014, 14–15). This anxiety definitely contributed to the election of Donald Trump in 2016.

After his election, President Obama rarely spoke in public about racial division in the United States, perhaps because he did not want to be seen as the black president. However, he was deeply moved by the killing of a black Florida teenager in 2012 and the acquittal of his assailant. In an impromptu speech in the White House briefing room in July 2013 he told reporters, "Trayvon Martin could have been me 35 years ago" (Landler and Shear 2013, A1). Obama wanted Americans to recognize that the African American community looks at this issue through a "set of experiences and a history that doesn't go away." He explained that "very few African American men in this country," including the president himself, had not experienced "being followed when they were shopping in a department store," having women clutch their bags when they walk by, or drivers lock their doors. He emphasized "those sets of experiences inform how the African American community interprets what happened one night in Florida." He felt the situation grows even worse, adding to the frustration of the black community, when the lingering effect of racism goes unacknowledged.

While the death of Trayvon Martin and the acquittal of his assailant unleashed deeply felt personal reactions and a series of major political demonstrations, and helped launch the Black Lives Matter movement, United States Supreme Court majority decisions will probably have a more lasting impact on American society. In 2007, the Supreme Court narrowly overturned public school choice plans in Louisville, Kentucky and Seattle, Washington, because race was one of the factors used in the assignment of students. In a majority opinion destructive of efforts to promote racial equality, Chief Justice John

Roberts declared that school integration plans perpetuated racism in the United States. According to Roberts, "The way to stop discrimination on the basis of race is to stop discriminating on the basis of race" (Roberts 2007, 91). Roberts argued, "Before Brown, schoolchildren were told where they could and could not go to school based on color of their skin. The school districts in these cases have not carried the heavy burden of demonstrating that we should allow this once again—even for very different reasons" (ibid., 47). With this decision, acknowledging the impact of race was made tantamount to promoting racism.

Continuing this trend, in *Schuette v. Bamn* (2014), the Supreme Court majority endorsed a Michigan ban on affirmative action. In a powerful and openly angry dissent, Associate Justice Sonia Sotomayor, a Latina who grew up in tenements and public housing projects in the South Bronx neighborhood of New York City, argued that "race matters" (Sotomayor 2014, 45) and "to know the history of our Nation is to understand its long and lamentable record of stymieing the right of racial minorities to participate in the political process" (ibid., 51).

Sotomayor continued:

> Race matters in part because of the long history of racial minorities being denied access to the political process.... Race also matters because of persistent racial inequality in society—inequality that cannot be ignored and that has produced stark socioeconomic disparities.... Race matters because of the slights, the snickers, the silent judgments that reinforce that most crippling of thoughts: "I do not belong here" (ibid., 45).

In an unusual direct rebuttal to the majority opinion issued by Chief Justice John Roberts, Sotomayor wrote:

> In my colleagues' view, examining the racial impact of legislation only perpetuates racial discrimination. This refusal to accept the stark reality that race matters is regrettable. The way to stop discrimination on the basis of race is to speak openly and candidly on the subject of race, and to apply the Constitution with eyes open to the unfortunate effects of centuries of racial discrimination.... It is this view that works harm, by perpetuating the facile notion that what makes race matter is acknowledging the simple truth that race does matter (ibid., 46).

This book draws on and extends the work of recent histories of slavery and the struggle for emancipation by Ira Berlin (2015), Eric Foner (2006 and 2015), and Manisha Sinha (2106). These historians highlight the role African Americans played in the campaign to end slavery. Berlin favorably quotes Major Martin Delany, the highest-ranking black officer in the United States Army during the Civil War. In a speech to approximately five hundred formerly enslaved men and women on South Carolina's St. Helena Island during Summer 1865, Delany told his audience "We would not have become free, had we not armed ourselves and fought out our independence" (Berlin 2015, 3–4).

According to both Berlin and Foner, enslaved Southern blacks who sought freedom via the Underground Railroad made personal choices that directly challenged the legitimacy of the slavery regime and the right that people could be held as property. In addition, free Northern black abolitionists who were engaged in a political struggle for both emancipation and equal rights as full citizens and human beings were central to the campaign that brought about the ultimate destruction of slavery in the United States. Both groups, by standing against slavery, placing their lives and freedom at risk, and openly resisting slavecatchers and pro-Southern legal officials and laws, created hysteria in the South that helped propel the nation toward a Civil War and the end of chattel slavery. Through their actions, African Americans, many of them working out of New York State, polarized an already divided nation that Abraham Lincoln believed could not "endure, permanently half slave and half free" (Davis and Wilson 2014, 232). Sinha argues that slave resistance, rather than bourgeois liberalism or white abolitionists, was at the core of the antislavery struggle (Sinha 2016, 2–8). While I do not agree with all of her conclusions, the encyclopedic nature of her study creates a new starting point for any discussion of slavery and emancipation in the United States.

Race mattered at the very beginning of the nation. According to the initial census in 1790 (United States Census Bureau), there were approximately seven hundred thousand enslaved Africans in the United States distributed across every state except Massachusetts. However, the founding documents of the United States, the Declaration of Independence, the Constitution, and the Bill of Rights, ignored race and racism and did not mention the words *slave* or *slavery.* The founders were so careful to avoid the term and the issue that charges that the King of England had "waged cruel war against human nature itself" by imposing slavery and the slave trade on Britain's North American colonies were removed from an early draft of the Declaration (Franklin 1974, 88). Article 1 Section 2 of the Constitution, which established the notorious Three-Fifths Compromise, determined representation and direct taxation by adding to the "whole Number of free Persons ... three fifths of all other Persons." It did not mention slaves or slavery. Article 1 Section 9, which prohibited Congress from acting to ban the slave trade until 1808, discussed the "Importation of such Persons," not slaves or slavery. The ban on "cruel and unusual punishment" in the Bill of Rights clearly did not include a ban on the enslavement of Africans.

In *Federalist Papers* no. 54, James Madison, who himself owned more than one hundred enslaved Africans, discussed the logic behind including "our slaves" as people when calculating representation and as property when calculating taxes. He concluded that "[t]he true state of the case is that they partake of both of these qualities: being considered by our laws, in some respects, as persons, and in other respects as property" (Rossiter 1961,

337). In *Federalist Papers* no. 8 and 29 Alexander Hamilton discussed fear of enslavement by either a foreign power or a domestic army. Hamilton and Madison continued the discussion jointly in *Federalist Papers* no. 18, but in each case they were concerned about the possible enslavement of the white population, not enslaved Africans. Only in *Federalist Papers* no. 42 was there any hint that the institution of slavery was a problem for the new country. In this essay Madison argued that the ability of Congress to end the slave trade after 1808 was a "great point gained in favor of humanity" (ibid., 266).

Letters written by Madison, who was secretary of the Constitutional Convention in 1787 and president of the United States from 1809 to 1817, show clear unease with the institution of slavery, particularly toward the end of his life, but he was unable to support abolition because of his own racism and that of his countrymen. In 1825, Madison wrote Francis Wright, an ardent opponent of slavery, that "[t]he magnitude of this evil among us is so deeply felt, and so universally acknowledged: that no merit could be greater than that of devising a satisfactory remedy for it. Unfortunately the task, not easy under other circumstances, is vastly augmented by the physical peculiarities of those held in bondage, which preclude their incorporation with the white population" (Root 2008, 69). In an 1826 letter to the Marquis de Lafayette, Madison argued, "The two races cannot co-exist, both being free & equal. The great sine qua non therefore is some external asylum for the colored race" (Taylor 2012, 222–23).

The general population more than shared Madison's antipathies toward enslaved Africans. Alexis De Tocqueville, a French commentator who visited the United States from 1831 to 1833 and published his observations on the emerging democracy, believed that the young country's democratic institutions worked against the development of racial equality. He wrote, "I do not believe that the white and black races will ever live in any country upon an equal footing.… A despot who should subject the Americans and their former slaves to the same yoke might perhaps succeed in commingling their races; but as long as the American democracy remains at the head of affairs, no one will undertake so difficult a task; and it may be foreseen that the freer the white population of the United States becomes, the more isolated will it remain" (de Tocqueville 1839, 354).

This hostility toward the humanity and potential political and social equality of African Americans continued, even escalated, during the 1850s and 1860s. In March 1857, in the case of *Dred Scott v. Sanford*, Chief Justice Roger B. Taney used the terms *slave*, *slavery*, and *enslaved* repeatedly as he concluded for the majority of the Supreme Court that people of African ancestry were "not included, and were not intended to be included, under the word 'citizens' in the Constitution, and can therefore claim none of the rights and privileges which that instrument provides for and secures to citizens of the United States. On the contrary, they were at that time considered as a subordinate and inferior class of beings, who had been subjugated by the dominant race, and, whether emancipated or not, yet remained subject to their authority, and had no rights or privileges but such as those who held the power and the Government might choose to grant them" (Kommers *et al.* 2008, 908).

On January 27, 2012, *The New York Times* (Rothstein 2012, C27) published a review of two new museum exhibitions on the history of slavery in the United States. Both of the exhibitions focused on Thomas Jefferson, principal author of the Declaration of Independence, an influential member of George Washington's initial cabinet, and the third president of the United States, who was a Virginia planter and slaveholder. One exhibit was temporarily housed at the Smithsonian National Museum of American History in Washington, D.C. The other is a permanent exhibit at the Jefferson homestead in Monticello, Virginia.

Lonnie Bunch III, director of the Smithsonian's National Museum of African American History and Culture, which opened in Washington, D.C., on the National Mall in 2016, emphasized that the Smithsonian's new exhibit was part of an effort by museum staff to figure out exactly how to present the history of slavery in the United States to the public. In another interview, Bunch told *The Washington Post* that the Smithsonian exhibit "allows us to centralize slavery" in American history (Trescott 2012, CO8).

Because this book presents an individual historian and teacher's point of view and does not represent an effort to define a national consensus on the history of slavery in the United States, I do not operate under the same political constraints as Lonnie Bunch and other people involved in creating the Smithsonian's new African American Museum. While I deeply respect what they are doing, I can use my position as an "outsider" to press for a broader and I think sharper understanding of the role slavery played in shaping the United States in the past and present, but also on the crucial role African American resistance to slavery played in precipitating the American Civil War and redefining the nation. My independence also allows me to respond directly to individuals and institutions I believe are misrepresenting the history of slavery in the United States and of African American resistance because of their own political agendas.

Because of the continuing significance of race in the United States and racism that I believe had its roots in the enslavement of Africans in the Americas, I want to state that I am white and consider myself an American historian, rather than a historian of the African American experience. I study and write about the history of slavery in the United States because I agree with Lonnie Bunch on its centrality to the shaping of this country.

Each chapter in this book addresses a different theme in the history of slavery in the United States, with a focus on events and debates in New York. Interspaced throughout the book are Teaching Notes that generally explore primary source documents; however, these sections are not restricted to teachers.

Chapter 1 discusses how, while most of the "founders" of the United States were not abolitionists, influential figures from New York State were. The chapter also examines

TEACHING NOTES

The Language We Use to Describe Slavery

QUESTIONS TO CONSIDER

1. How important is the language used in classrooms, textbooks, and discussions?

2. How should we address language used in the past that is no longer acceptable today?

3. Is choice of language a matter of "political correctness" or social and historical sensitivity?

In 2015 an African American high school student in Texas noticed in his McGraw-Hill geography textbook a map caption that referred to the enslaved Africans in the American South as "workers." The ensuing uproar led to apologizes from the publisher and the promise to revise future editions of the book (Fernandez and Hauser 2015, A10).

The language teachers and textbooks use to describe something shapes the way students think about and understand it. Should unfree Africans in the American South and the Caribbean be described as "slaves" or as "enslaved Africans" or "enslaved people"? Enslavement was something done to them and I think it is important in our language to reject the idea that enslaved Africans, although legally chattel, were less than fully human. I also use *freedom seekers* to describe people escaping from bondage on the Underground Railroad rather than the more traditional terms *fugitives* or *runaway slaves*. In a September 2015 essay posted on the *History News Network*, historian Michael Todd Landis made a persuasive case for the importance of language when describing slavery and the American Civil War. Landis argues that the Civil War should not be described as a battle between the North and the South or the Union and the Confederacy, which grants legitimacy to Confederate claims of a war between equal sovereign powers, but between the United States and rebel forces. In recent work, other historians have made similar points. Edward Baptist (2014) argues that using the term *slaveowners* supports their claim that they were somehow entitled to own other human beings and he wants them called *enslavers*. Paul Finkelman (2012) argues that what teachers and historians refer to as the Compromise of 1850 is better described as the Appeasement of 1850 because Northern politicians made all the compromises. In this book I try to always be cognizant of the impact of language on readers.

the political nature of current debates about the nature of the national founders and their views on slavery and explores the debate among abolitionists about how to understand the Constitution and whether it was a pro-slavery document. It concludes with a Teaching Notes section on the Congressional "Gag Rule" restricting debate over slavery in the House of Representatives.

Chapter 2, "Resistance! Resistance! Resistance! New York State's Radical Black Abolitionists and the Coming of the Civil War," explains how New York State was a hotbed of radical and influential black abolitionism from the American Revolution to the American Civil War. It focuses on resistance to enslavement in New York City, Buffalo, Syracuse, and Troy. The Teaching Notes section focuses on teaching about slavery on Long Island using primary source documents.

Chapter 3 takes a more theoretical approach to understanding social movements, seeking to explain how the national abolitionist movement moved from the margins in American society to ultimate success in ending slavery. This topic is explored again in chapter 8. In the 1830s and 1840s, the abolitionist movement was ignored, seemed doomed, and slavery appeared impregnable and racism was pervasive. The chapter explores the reasons for sudden change after seemingly endless disappointment, marginalization, and sectarian internal conflict and why some movements are successful. The Teaching Notes section examines demands for black suffrage and the demand for full citizenship rights in New York State.

Chapters 4 and 5 discuss two of the more significant New Yorkers in the struggle to end slavery in the United States, Solomon Northup and Harriet Tubman. The absence of work and community and the focus on religious salvation in most runaway slave narratives, as well as the fact that the events recounted took place in the Border States rather than on Deep South cotton and sugar plantations, is what makes Solomon Northup's account of his twelve years of enslavement in Louisiana so important as an exposé of the slave regime and as a historical document. Frederick Douglass recognized the special nature of Northup's account in reviews published in *The Liberator* and *Frederick Douglass' Paper*. The Teaching Notes section for chapter 4 includes excerpts from Northup's memoir. Harriet Tubman was a New Yorker by choice, a self-liberated former slave, a religious evangelical, an Underground Railroad conductor, and a Civil War scout and nurse. However, her life has been so mythologized it is difficult to sort out who the real Harriet Tubman actually was. In keeping with the question of mythologizing, the Teaching Notes section for chapter 5 examines the history of slavery as told in children's books.

New York City and Brooklyn were locations for major celebrations of the Emancipation Proclamation by abolitionists and black communities. A major focus of chapter 6 is on the concerns and response of Frederick Douglass. Teaching Notes discusses debate over the renaming of public places and institutions where names have connections with slavery and racist traditions.

TEACHING NOTES

New York State Curriculum

QUESTIONS TO CONSIDER

1. How much of a focus should there be on slavery, the slave trade, and the abolitionist movement in the elementary, middle-level, and high school curricula?

2. Should State Education Departments and school districts develop a specific curriculum package that focuses on the history of slavery and the struggle to end it in the United States?

In October 1996, the New York State legislature passed legislation calling for the development of a human rights–based social studies curriculum that included the Great Irish Famine and the right of people to food, the European Holocaust and the right of people to life, and slavery and the transatlantic slave trade and the right of people to freedom (Singer 2008, 30). While an official "slavery curriculum" was never adopted, the history of slavery, the slave trade, the abolitionist movement, and the Underground Railroad are prominent in the updated 2016 New York State Social Studies Framework, which offers school districts a guide for instruction with "key ideas, conceptual understandings, and content specifications" (engageNY 2016). These topics are first introduced in fourth grade and their role in the development of British North America and the United States are major themes in middle school (grades 7 and 8). On both levels, students are introduced to prominent opponents of slavery in the United States and connections between New York State and the slave system, although the focus is more heavily on the Underground Railroad. In high school ninth grade, students learn about slavery in the ancient world and the role played by slavery and the transatlantic slave trade in the development of the Americas in the centuries after the Columbian Exchange. The Haitian Revolution led by enslaved Africans and European campaigns to abolish the transatlantic slave trade are part of the tenth grade curriculum and slavery and abolition in the United States are a major focus in the eleventh grade during early units on United States history.

Students also learn about slavery and abolition in English/Language Arts classes. The engageNY recommended reading list for seventh grade includes an edited version of *Narrative of the Life of Frederick Douglass* (1968) and Virginia Hamilton's book of African American folktales *The People Could Fly* (Hamilton 1985; engageNY 2013). In high school ELA classes, students do close reading of major United States documents including the Emancipation Proclamation. A weakness with the ELA readings is that they do not always align with what students are studying in social studies curriculum. (*continues on page 12*)

(continued from page 11)
A more serious problem for social studies and history education in general is the shift in focus in schools to skills-based instruction in response to Common Core and Common Core aligned high-stakes testing. Without a mandated curriculum and the allocation of specific time, an exploration of slavery and its impact on the United States and the world, as well as other important content area topics, are in danger of being marginalized as teachers and schools feel pressured to prepare students for standardized exams (Singer 2014).

Chapter 7 explores Abraham Lincoln's views on slavery, racial equality, the U.S. Constitution, and the postwar era and responses to Lincoln by the New York press. It argues that Lincoln's limitations were partly responsible for the emergence of segregation and Jim Crow in the postwar South. Teaching Topics examines the career and ideas of New York State governor and senator and federal secretary of state, the puzzling William Seward.

Chapter 8 looks at the role New York played in the election of 1864. New York City and New York State, their political leaders and their press, were central to national debates over slavery, racial equality, and the reelection of Abraham Lincoln in 1864. These debates helped establish the next one hundred years of race relations in the United States. The Teaching Notes section focuses on one specific controversy, the miscegenation hoax.

Chapter 9 extends a discussion introduced in chapter 3 on abolition as a social movement and seeks to explain its relatively sudden shift from the political margins and factionalism toward success in pressing for emancipation. The Teaching Notes section focuses on local history, specifically the history of Brooklyn.

Chapter 10 uses minutes from Congressional debates published in the *Congressional Globe* to examine the negative role New York Democratic Party politicians played in debates over a Constitutional Amendment to formally and finally abolish slavery and efforts on their part to obstruct Congressional Reconstruction of the South. While they do not bear total responsibility, their actions contributed to failures to root out racist practices in the South and to establish state governments with at least some commitment to racial justice. The Teaching Notes section reviews the depiction of slavery and abolition in recent fictional books, documentaries, and movies.

Chapter 11 considers the politics of historical memory and reviews efforts by historical societies and historians to define slavery in New York and the United States, and the political nature of historical memory. The final Teaching Notes section examines selections from the speeches and writing of Frederick Douglass, New York State's and the nation's most prominent abolitionist and one of the great writers and thinkers of the nineteenth century.

1

MOST OF THE "FOUNDERS" WERE NOT ABOLITIONISTS, BUT SOME FROM NEW YORK WERE

CRISES AND CONTROVERSIES INVITE HISTORICAL ANALOGIES. THE CONTEMPORARY Tea Party movement fancies itself operating in the tradition of antitax protesters who dumped tea into Boston Harbor in 1773 in defiance of British authority. In an interview with George Stephanopoulos for ABC News, congressional Representative Michele Bachmann (R-MN), a Tea Party movement stalwart and a candidate for the 2012 Republican nomination for president, claimed that the founders of the nation "worked tirelessly" to end slavery. She explained what was "marvelous is that in this country and under our constitution, we have the ability when we recognize that something is wrong to change it. And that's what we did in our country. We changed it. We no longer have slavery" (Stephanopoulos 2011; Singer 2011b).

David Barton, a conservative Texas Republican aligned with the Christian Right made similar points. In "The Founding Fathers and Slavery" (2011), Barton argued that "the historical fact is that slavery was not the product of, nor was it an evil introduced by, the Founding Fathers," and that "[t]he Revolution was the turning point in the national attitude [toward slavery]—and it was the Founding Fathers who contributed greatly to that change." He quoted Henry Laurens, president of the Continental Congress, John Jay, Benjamin Franklin, and Thomas Jefferson to support his case. However, he did not mention that at some point in their lives, each of them was a slaveholder. Laurens, president of the Second Continental Congress from 1777 to 1778, was a partner in the largest slave-trading company in the British colonies and personally "owned" three hundred enslaved Africans who worked on his rice plantation on the Cooper River near Charleston, South Carolina (SCNHC 2014). Historian Paul Finkelman (1994, 193–228) dismissed similar claims about the nation's "founders" and their antislavery stance in an article, "Thomas Jefferson and Antislavery: The Myth Goes On," in the *Virginia Magazine of History and Biography*.

The "founders" were a curious and inconsistent bunch, who like Jefferson, sometimes bemoaned an institution, slavery, that was the basis for their wealth and authority. Patrick Henry, for example, argued for independence from Britain because of British violation of the colonists' personal liberties, yet he enslaved between seventy and eighty Africans on his plantation. In one of the best-known speeches in United States history delivered in 1775 in the Virginia House of Burgesses, Henry declared that the issue of independence was "nothing less than a question of freedom or slavery" and warned Virginians that "there is no retreat but in submission and slavery!" This was the same Patrick Henry who wrote, "Would any one believe that I am master of slaves by my own purchase? I am drawn along by the general inconvenience of living without them. I will not—I cannot justify it, however culpable my conduct" (Basker 2012, n.p.).

The commitment of patriot-aligned Southern planters, at least philosophically, to liberty, combined with their reliance on an enslaved African workforce, coupled with the profit from slave trading and the trade in slave-produced commodities for Northern merchants and financiers, meant that the Declaration of Independence and the United States Constitution were left intentionally vague on the future of slavery in the new country, a vagueness that set the stage for later sectional conflict.

During debate over the initial draft of the Declaration of Independence, the "Founders" removed a clause from the document that denounced King George for promoting the transatlantic slave trade.

During the War for Independence, George Washington refused to enlist enslaved Africans who wanted to secure their freedom by joining the Revolutionary army, and at the end of the war he sent a letter to British commanders demanding that they return runaway slaves as wartime contraband. When Thomas

---

THE DELETED PASSAGE (1776)

QUESTION TO CONSIDER

Why was this passage deleted?

He has waged cruel war against human nature itself, violating its most sacred rights of life and liberty in the persons of a distant people who never offended him, captivating & carrying them into slavery in another hemisphere or to incur miserable death in their transportation thither. This piratical warfare, the opprobrium of infidel powers, is the warfare of the Christian King of Great Britain. Determined to keep open a market where Men should be bought & sold, he has prostituted his negative for suppressing every legislative attempt to prohibit or restrain this execrable commerce. And that this assemblage of horrors might want no fact of distinguished die, he is now exciting those very people to rise in arms among us, and to purchase that liberty of which he has deprived them, by murdering the people on whom he has obtruded them: thus paying off former crimes committed again the Liberties of one people, with crimes which he urges them to commit against the lives of another (Jefferson 2010, 210–11).

[handwritten margin note: Purposely left vague by founders]

Jefferson, the primary author of the Declaration of Independence, was president, he refused to recognize the newly independent government of Haiti because Africans, who had fought a bloody war to end enslavement, governed the former French colony. In letters, Jefferson described Toussaint Louverture and his followers as "cannibals of the terrible republic" (Blackburn 2011, 242).

On the other hand, Representative Bachmann was not entirely wrong, although when asked, she could not provide evidence to support her position. Many founders from New York State were opponents of slavery and did work to bring it to an end. They included Alexander Hamilton, Washington's aide-de-camp during the Revolutionary War, a member of the convention that wrote the U.S. Constitution, and later the secretary of the treasury of the United States. During the War for Independence, Hamilton argued that Africans had the same natural abilities as Europeans and they should be recruited as soldiers and given "their freedom with their muskets" (Chernow 2005, 122). While Washington and the Continental Congress were reluctant to offer freedom to enslaved Africans, New York State passed legislation promising emancipation in exchange for three years of military service, however enlistment did require permission from enslavers, who were compensated with public land (McManus 1966, 157–58).

Prominent opponents of slavery included John Jay, the first Chief Justice of the Supreme Court of the United States and an early governor of New York State, Aaron Burr, United States senator from New York and vice-president of the United States, and Gouverneur Morris and Thomas Tredwell, members of New York's Revolutionary Congress who helped draft the state's first Constitution. Jay, Morris, and Tredwell came from families that owned significant estates and large numbers of enslaved Africans. However, each worked to end slavery in New York State and the United States.

In 1777, Gouverneur Morris proposed a motion, which was defeated, at the state's Constitutional Convention recommending that the Legislatures of the State of New York "take measures consistent with the public safety for abolishing domestic slavery" (McManus 1966, 161). Morris later relocated to Philadelphia, and he represented Pennsylvania at the Federal Constitutional Convention where he opposed constitutional protection for slavery, the slave trade, and the three-fifths compromise. In 1780, while representing the rebelling colonies in Spain, Jay wrote praising Pennsylvania's newly enacted gradual manumission law and declared, "Till America comes into this Measure [abolition], her prayers to Heaven for Liberty will be impious. . . . Were I in [the] Legislature I would prepare a bill for the Purpose with great Care, and I would never cease moving it till it became a Law or I ceased to be a member. I believe God governs this world, and I believe it to be a Maxim in his as in our Court that those who ask for Equity ought to do it" (Flanders 1855, 216).

In 1785, the New York State Legislature debated, but ultimately refused to approve, either immediate or gradual emancipation. During debate in the State Assembly, Aaron

Burr, much maligned in the Broadway musical *Hamilton* for never stating or standing on principles, headed the faction demanding the immediate end of slavery in New York (Miranda 2015). Historian Edgar McManus attributes the failure of these bills to opposition from white New Yorkers to the possibility that emancipation would lead to civil and legal equality, especially the right to vote (McManus 1966, 163–64).

After the American Revolution, New York Manumission Society was headed by John Jay and Alexander Hamilton (McManus 1966, 168–72). It purchased the freedom of persons held in bondage and founded the African Free School. Jay and Hamilton also helped win dozens of legal cases in defense of the freedom of black New Yorkers threatened with kidnapping and being sent to the South as slaves. In 1788, in his capacity as president of the Manumission Society, Jay wrote British abolitionists, "That they who know the value of liberty, and are blessed with the enjoyment of it, ought not to subject others to slavery. . . . The

ALEXANDER HAMILTON TO JOHN JAY, PRESIDENT OF THE CONTINENTAL CONGRESS (1779)

QUESTION TO CONSIDER

Why was Hamilton's advice rejected?

I frequently hear it objected to the scheme of embodying negroes that they are too stupid to make soldiers. This is so far from appearing to me a valid objection that I think their want of cultivation (for their natural faculties are probably as good as ours) joined to that habit of subordination which they acquire from a life of servitude, will make them sooner become soldiers than our White inhabitants. I foresee that this project will have to combat much opposition from prejudice and self-interest. The contempt we have been taught to entertain for the blacks, makes us fancy many things that are founded neither in reason nor experience; and an unwillingness to part with property of so valuable a kind will furnish a thousand arguments to show the impracticability or pernicious tendency of a scheme which requires such a sacrifice. But it should be considered, that if we do not make use of them in this way, the enemy probably will; and that the best way to counteract the temptations they will hold out will be to offer them ourselves. An essential part of the plan is to give them their freedom with their muskets. This will secure their fidelity, animate their courage, and I believe will have a good influence upon those who remain, by opening a door to their emancipation (quoted in Lanning 2005, 68).

x Contradictors

United States are far from being irreproachable in this respect. It undoubtedly is very inconsistent with <u>their declarations on the subject</u> of human rights to <u>permit a single slave to be found within their jurisdiction.</u>" Although disappointed that "local interests, and in some measure local prejudices" prevented the new Constitution from addressing the issue of slavery, Jay was hopeful that "a disposition favourable to our views and wishes prevails more and more, and that it has already had an influence on our laws" (Jay 1833, 234).

Between 1799 and 1827 the legal status of blacks in the State of New York changed radically. In <u>1799</u>, as governor, John Jay signed a <u>gradual emancipation</u> law providing that from July 4 of that year onward, all children born to slave parents in New York State would be free upon reaching adulthood, and in 1801 the law was amended to prevent the export of enslaved

Africans out of the state. In 1809, New York laws permitted marriage between people who were still enslaved, prohibited the separation of spouses, and recognized the right of enslaved people to own and <u>transfer property</u>. An 1813 law ended the prohibition on blacks testifying against whites and ensured enslaved Africans the <u>right to a jury trial when accused of a crime</u>. The final blow to slavery in New York was an <u>1817 act</u> that declared every <u>enslaved person</u> in the state <u>would be freed on July 4, 1827</u> (McManus 1966, 178–79).

Thomas Tredwell was an Anti-Federalist who opposed adoption of the United States Constitution by New York State because of its complicity with the slave system. In 1794, Tredwell relocated his family from Suffolk County to the North Country where he emancipated the people his family had enslaved and established them as free farmers on their own land.

The reality is that the founders, when they wrote the Constitution and created the nation, <u>left the issue</u> of slavery unresolved <u>because they could not agree on the future of</u>

REJECTED MOTION AT THE NEW YORK STATE CONSTITUTIONAL CONVENTION (1777)

QUESTION TO CONSIDER

Why was the Morris motion rejected?

And whereas a regard to the rights of human nature and the principles of our holy religion, loudly call upon us to dispense the blessings of freedom to all mankind: and inasmuch as it would at present be productive of great dangers to liberate the slaves within this State: It is, therefore most earnestly recommended to the future Legislatures of the State of New-York, to take the most effectual measures consistent with the public safety, and the private property of individuals, for abolishing domestic slavery within the same, so that in future ages, every human being who breathes the air of this State, shall enjoy the privileges of a freeman (Kirschke 2005, 62).

[handwritten annotations in top margin: "it wouldn't work in a may it", "was disappeared"]

[handwritten annotation in left margin: "people are reluctant to change"]

AN ACT FOR THE GRADUAL ABOLITION OF SLAVERY (1799)

QUESTION TO CONSIDER

Why did New York State enact gradual rather than immediate emancipation?

Be it enacted ... That any child born of a slave within this state after the fourth day of July next shall be deemed and adjudged to be born free: *Provided nevertheless.* That such child shall be the servant of the legal proprietor of his or her mother until such servant, if a male, shall arrive at the age of twenty-eight years, and if a female, at the age of twenty-five years (Gellman and Quigley 2003, 53).

Africans in the United States. John Jay, who supported adoption of the Constitution, recognized this when he wrote, "When it is considered how many of the legislators in the different States are proprietors of slaves, and what opinions and prejudices they have imbibed on the subject from their infancy, a sudden and total stop to this species of oppression is not to be expected" (Jay 1833, 234).

During the first decades of the nineteenth century, slavery gradually withered away in the northern United States as it lost its economic viability and waves of European immigrants provided for an expanding workforce. New York's gradual emancipation act, passed in 1799 and amended in 1817, finally went into full effect in 1827. On July 4, 1827, Emancipation Day, William Hamilton, a founder of the New York African Society for Mutual Relief, spoke at the African Zion Church in lower Manhattan. Hamilton declared, "This day we stand redeemed from a bitter thraldom. Of us it may be truly said, 'the last agony is o'er,' THE AFRICANS ARE RESTORED! No more shall the accursed name of the slave be attached to us—no more shall *negro* and *slave* be synonymous." But it was not only Africans who were freed from slavery. "This day has the state of NEW-YORK regenerated herself—this day has she been cleansed of a most foul, poisonous and damnable stain" (Gellman and Quigley 2003, 221–22).

The next day two thousand members of New York's African American community paraded through the streets celebrating the end of slavery in New York State. Dr. James McCune Smith, an African American physician who studied medicine in Glasgow, attended the parade as a teenager and later described the procession:

A splendid looking black man, mounted on a milk-white steed, then his aids on horseback, dashing up and down the line; then the orator of the day, also mounted, with a handsome scroll, appearing like a baton in his right hand, then in due order, splendidly dressed in scarfs of silk with gold-edgings, and with colored bands of music and their banners appropriately lettered and painted, followed, the New York African Society for Mutual Relief, the Wilberforce Benevolent Society, and the Clarkson Benevolent Society; then the people five or six abreast from grown men to small boys. The sidewalks were crowded with wives, daughters, sisters, and mothers of the celebrants, representing every state in the Union, and not a few with gay bandanna handkerchiefs, betraying their West Indian birth. Nor was Africa underrepresented. Hundreds who survived the middle passage and a youth in slavery joined in the joyful procession (Hodges 1999, 223–24).

John Jay and New York's other antislavery founders thought, or at least hoped, that slavery in the South would gradually disappear there as it appeared to be doing in the North. What they could not anticipate was that with the invention of the cotton gin in the 1790s, the Industrial Revolution's insatiable hunger for cotton, the rapid growth of cotton production in the South during early nineteenth century, and the expansion of the plantation system west into Alabama, Mississippi, and Louisiana, the need for enslaved African labor and slavery would also grow at an astronomical pace. At the same time, Northern merchants, bankers, and industrialists became an integral part of the slave system and allies of the Slavocracy. They financed, manufactured, and distributed products made from slave-produced commodities and supplied the new plantations with materials and the planters with luxury goods. After the importation of foreign slave labor was outlawed in 1808, the domestic slave trade transporting enslaved blacks from Virginia deep into the Cotton Belt

AN ACT RELATIVE TO SLAVES AND SERVANTS (1817)

QUESTION TO CONSIDER

Why did New York State make the "export" of enslaved people out of state a criminal offense in 1817?

[A]ll marriages contracted, or which may hereafter be contracted, wherein one or both of the parties was, were or may be slaves, shall be considered equally valid as though the parties thereto were free, and the child or children of any such marriage shall be deemed legitimate: *Provided*, that nothing in this section contained, shall be deemed or construed to manumit any such slave or slaves ... if any person shall send to sea, or export, or attempt to export from this state, or send or carry out of, or attempt to send or carry out of this state, except as is by this act provided, any slave or servant ... shall be deemed guilty of a public offence, and forfeit the sum of five hundred dollars (Gellman and Quigley 2003, 69–70).

states expanded to satisfy the planters' craving for labor. According to federal census data, there were fewer than one million enslaved Africans in the Southern states in 1800 and almost four million in 1860 (Beckert 2015, 99–135; Baptiste 2014, 145–69).

Northern politicians assisted in the spread of slavery by repeatedly acquiescing to Southern demands that the slave system go untouched, even unmentioned. The First Amendment to the United States Constitution promises, "Congress shall make no law . . . abridging the freedom of speech, or of the press; or the right of the people peaceably to assemble, and to petition the Government for a redress of grievances." Soon after its founding in 1833, the American Anti-Slavery Society launched a petition drive demanding an end to slavery in Washington, D.C. The campaign rapidly picked up steam and during the Twenty-Fifth Congress (1837–38), abolitionist groups submitted more than 130,000 petitions. The congressional response, starting with the Twenty-Fourth Congress in 1836, was to try to keep the petitions out of the *Congressional Record* by ignoring both the petitioners and the Constitution.

In May 1836, John C. Calhoun in the Senate and Henry Pinckney in the House of Representatives, both from South Carolina, pressed for resolutions that would prevent other members of the bodies from introducing the petitions (*Congressional Globe* 24/1,

---

TREDWELL'S ADDRESS TO THE NEW YORK STATE CONSTITUTIONAL RATIFICATION CONVENTION (1788)

QUESTION TO CONSIDER

Was it legitimate for New York State to reject the new Constitution over the issue of slavery?

There is another clause in this Constitution, which, though there is no prospect of getting it amended, I think ought not to be passed over in silence, lest such a silence should be construed into a tacit approbation of it. I mean the clause which restricts the general government from putting a stop, for a number of years, to a commerce which is a stain to the commerce of any civilized nation, and has already blackened half the plains of America with a race of wretches made so by our cruel policy and avarice, and which appears to me to be already repugnant to every principle of humanity, morality, religion, and good society (Madison 1901, 402).

238–40, 505–506). In Calhoun's twisted logic, the First Amendment guaranteed the right of Americans to send petitions to Congress but did not obligate Congress to receive or recognize the petitions. The original resolution declared that "all petitions, memorials, resolutions, propositions or papers relating in any way, or to any extent whatever, to the subject of slavery, or the abolition of slavery, shall, without being either printed or referred, be laid upon the table, and that no further action whatever shall be had thereon." Former president John Quincy Adams, a congressional representative from Massachusetts, responded, "I hold the resolution to be a direct violation of the constitution of the United States, the rules of this house, and the rights of my constituents" (Von Holst 1888, 236–72).

The tendency is to view support for the "gag rule" and opposition to abolitionists during this period as part of a South versus North and Slave state versus Free state divide. The political reality in 1836 was quite different. A look at the roll call vote in the House, particularly votes cast by representatives from the state of New York, shows strong support for the "gag rule" and opposition to ending slavery in Washington, D.C., among New York State's Jacksonians.

The noninterference with slavery in Washington, D.C., resolution passed in the House by a vote of 132 to 45 and Pinckney's gag rule suppressing antislavery petitions was approved by a vote of 117 to 68. New York State had thirty-three representatives in the House, the largest state delegation to the Twenty-Fourth Congress. Twenty-six members of the state delegation, all members of the Jackson caucus, voted in the affirmative on both resolutions (*Congressional Globe* 1836, 505–506). Without their votes the Pinckney resolution would not have carried.

Among the somewhat prominent New Yorkers who voted for both antiabolitionist resolutions were Samuel Barton, who had family connections to the Vanderbilts and worked for their steamship company, Churchill Cambreleng, a wealthy businessman with commercial ties to John Jacob Astor and political ties to Martin Van Buren, and Gideon Lee, former mayor of New York City. The Jacksonian faction also included Ulysses Doubleday of Cayuga County, whose son Abner Doubleday was a Union Army general during the Civil War and is sometimes credited with the invention of baseball. The anti-Jackson group generally represented counties along the Erie Canal.

The failure to end slavery at the time of the American Revolution or with the writing of the Constitution, the compromises made at that time in an effort to tie together a new nation, the vagaries and inconsistencies in the document itself, set the stage for the implosion of the nation and civil war. For abolitionists, it led to almost incessant internecine debate over how to understand the Constitution and whether it could be utilized in the fight to end slavery. William Lloyd Garrison, writing in *The Liberator*, declared the Constitution "the most bloody and heaven-daring arrangement ever made by men for the continuance and protection of a system of the most atrocious villainy ever exhibited on earth," and at an 1854 July 4th antislavery rally he burned a copy (Lowance 2003, 345, lii).

In response to Garrison's adamant anticonstitutional position, Gerrit Smith was probably the leading advocate for abolitionists deploying the Constitution as a weapon in the war against slavery. Smith was a founder of the antislavery Liberty Party, which was largely based in New York State, and a one-term congressional representative from the Utica area. While the Liberty Party never garnered more than a few thousand votes in presidential campaigns from 1840 to 1852, its members were influential in the founding of the Free Soil and Republican parties, although these parties officially

---

FREDERICK DOUGLASS AND THE CONSTITUTION (1849, 1860)

QUESTION TO CONSIDER

How do we explain the shift in Douglass's position on the meaning of the Constitution from 1849 to 1860?

Frederick Douglass, "The Constitution and Slavery," *The North Star (1849)*

We hold it [the Constitution] to be a most cunningly-devised and wicked compact, demanding the most constant and earnest efforts of the friends of righteous freedom for its complete overthrow. It was "conceived in sin, and shapen in iniquity".... Had the Constitution dropped down from the blue overhanging sky, upon a land uncursed by slavery, and without an interpreter, although some difficulty might have occurred in applying its manifold provisions, yet so cunningly is it framed, that no one would have imagined that it recognized or sanctioned slavery. But having a terrestrial, and not a celestial origin, we find no difficulty in ascertaining its meaning in all the parts which we allege to relate to slavery. Slavery existed before the Constitution, in the very States by whom it was made and adopted.—Slaveholders took a large share in making it. It was made in view of the existence of slavery, and in a manner well calculated to aid and strengthen that heaven-daring crime.... The parties that made the Constitution, aimed to cheat and defraud the slave, who was not himself a party to the compact or agreement. It was entered into understandingly on both sides. They both designed to purchase their freedom and safety at the expense of the imbruted slave (Ashbrook Center, *TeachingAmericanHistory.org*. http://teachingamericanhistory.org/library/index.asp?document=1106).

ignore → sanction?

opposed the extension of slavery into new western territories rather than slavery itself (Sernett 2002, 112–28).

In an 1844 letter that Garrison published in *The Liberator*, Smith argued, "Is the Constitution pro-slavery, because the Government of the United States has, almost from its beginning, been administered for the advantage of slavery? ... The fact, that the nation, in its national capacity, favors and upholds slavery, proves nothing against the Constitution; ... for this it may do, in utter repugnance, and in bold defiance, of the Constitution" (Smith 1844). Nothing to do w/ Const.

Frederick Douglass started out as a Garrisonian but ended up on the pro-constitutional side of the abolitionist debate. In 1849, in a *North Star* editorial on "The Constitution and Slavery," Douglass called the Constitution a "most cunningly-devised and wicked compact, demanding the most constant and earnest efforts of the friends of righteous freedom for its complete overthrow. It was 'conceived in sin, and shapen in iniquity'" (Foner 1999, 130). However, in 1860, Douglass denied that "the Constitution guarantees the right to hold property in man, and believe that the way to abolish slavery

---

Frederick Douglass, Glasgow, Scotland (1860)

I ... deny that the Constitution guarantees the right to hold property in man, and believe that the way to abolish slavery in America is to vote such men into power as will use their powers for the abolition of slavery.... The intentions of those who framed the Constitution, be they good or bad, for slavery or against slavery, are so respected so far, and so far only, as we find those intentions plainly stated in the Constitution.... Where would be the advantage of a written Constitution, if, instead of seeking its meaning in its words, we had to seek them in the secret intentions of individuals who may have had something to do with writing the paper? ... The fact that men go out of the Constitution to prove it pro-slavery ... is an admission that the thing for which they are looking is not to be found where only it ought to be found, and that is in the Constitution itself.... Its language is "we the people;" not we the white people, not even we the citizens ... but we the people.... The constitutionality of slavery can be made out only by disregarding the plain and common-sense reading of the Constitution itself.... My position now is one of reform, not of revolution. I would act for the abolition of slavery through the Government—not over its ruins. If slaveholders have ruled the American Government for the last fifty years, let the anti-slavery men rule the nation for the next fifty years. If the South has made the Constitution bend to the purposes of slavery, let the North now make that instrument bend to the cause of freedom and justice (Ashbrook Center, *TeachingAmericanHistory.org*. http://teachingamericanhistory.org/library/index.asp?document=1128).

in America is to vote such men into power as well use their powers for the abolition of slavery." Douglass based his argument on the language of the document, which declared the United States a country of " 'we the people;' not we the white people, not even we the citizens ... but we the people.... The constitutionality of slavery can be made out only by disregarding the plain and common-sense reading of the Constitution itself" (ibid., 387).

Because the founders failed to address the slavery divide during the struggle for independence and when they created the new national government, it took decades of struggle by free blacks in the Northern states, freedom seekers escaping from bondage, and white abolitionist allies to promote the antislavery cause. Many, such as Frederick Douglass, Henry Highland Garnet, Lewis and Arthur Tappan, Gerrit Smith, and William Seward, were based in New York State. Douglass's shift in position about the Constitution reflected a shift among abolitionists from a sense of isolation to possibility in the campaign to end slavery. The Mexican-American War, U.S. territorial expansion to the Pacific, the Fugitive Slave Law of 1850, Bloody Kansas, and finally the Supreme Court's *Dred Scott* decision ruling that under the Constitution blacks were neither citizens nor entitled to legal rights, supported the idea that the Constitution was pro-slavery. Finally, an aggrieved South, anxious to preserve slavery, afraid its position of power in the national government was threatened, with laws defining blacks as property not people being defied by the abolitionist movement, terrified by the possibility of slave revolts, especially after John Brown and his supporters attacked Harpers Ferry, and with its assumptions about the racial inferiority of Africans challenged by the very existence of educated, articulate, black opponents of slavery, tried to secede from the union. The national division over slavery and human rights meant that from 1861 to 1865 the United States fought a bloody civil war because, as Abraham Lincoln said in 1858, "this government cannot endure, permanently half slave and half free" (Lincoln 1858).

Using Const. as either a way to back slavery or another clever & dangerous device to end the existence of slavery ensuring

TEACHING NOTES

Debating the Congressional "Gag Rule"

QUESTIONS TO CONSIDER

1. Is it ever legitimate to silence debate in a representative body?

2. Why did members of the New York congressional delegation initially support the "gag rule," and how do we explain the later shift?

In January 2017 the antebellum congressional "gag rule" that prevented Northern representatives from presenting antislavery petitions from constituents received renewed public attention when Senate Republican leadership "gagged" Elizabeth Warren of Massachusetts during debate over Donald Trump's nominee for attorney general (Chait 2017).

During the Twenty-Fourth (1835–37) and Twenty-Fifth Congresses (1837–38), South Carolinians John C. Calhoun in the Senate and Henry Pinckey and James Hammond in the House of Representatives spearheaded efforts to block abolitionists from submitting antislavery petitions. *The Congressional Globe* (1836, 239) reports that on March 9, 1836, after weeks of discussion, Calhoun launched into a lengthy tirade that seems to have completely alienated most of the Senate, including some senators representing slave states, and his proposal was rejected by a vote of 36 to 10. Calhoun's only solid support came from Mississippi, Louisiana, and South Carolina. Even Virginia, Georgia, Alabama, and Tennessee were divided.

Voting against Calhoun's "gag rule" did not imply support for antislavery petitions, only rejection of Calhoun's position. On March 10, 1836, the Senate voted 24 to 20 to table discussion of a petition from the Society of Friends of Lancaster, Pennsylvania, to abolish slavery in Washington, D.C. (*Congressional Globe* 1836, 242). Debate on the issue resumed on March 16, 1836, when Senator Daniel Webster of Massachusetts presented four new petitions calling for the abolition of slavery and the slave trade in Washington, D.C., that he wished referred to the Senate Committee for the District of Columbia. One of the petitions contained 2,425 signatures from "female inhabitants of the city of Boston" (ibid., 257–58). This motion was also tabled.

In the House of Representatives, where Mondays were "petition days," slavery's supporters were more successful at interfering with the right to petition. On February 1, 1836, Caleb Cushing of Massachusetts opened the session presenting a petition by "sundry citizens" from his home state on "the abolition of slavery and the slave trade in the District of Columbia." Hammond acknowledged the legal right to submit petitions, but demanded that (*continues on page 26*)

(*continued from page 25*)

the House refuse to receive this and similar abolitionist petitions because Congress had no constitutional right to abolish slavery in the District of Columbia. The Constitution, he argued, would never have been ratified by slave states if this power existed. He accused persons submitting these petitions of "pursuing a systematic plan of operations intended to subvert the institutions of the South" (*Register of Debates* 1836, 2447).

While New York's congressional delegation did not play a prominent role in "gag rule" debate that stretched from February into May, New York and New Yorkers were both the subject of ridicule, and a source of support, for the South Carolinians. In his initial statement, Hammond demanded to know from Northerners whether "[i]f a man in New York were to say of his neighbor what those papers say of the southern people, would he not be indicted as a slanderer?" (*Congressional Globe*, 24/1, 158). He then denounced "the whole gang of abolition orators and writers on both sides of the Atlantic," with specific reference to New Yorkers Arthur Tappan, Gerrit Smith, and William Jay, whom he denounced as a "most degenerate son" of John Jay for his abolitionist efforts including "the ultimate elevation of the black population to an equality with the white, in civil and religious privileges" (*Register of Debates* 1836, 2453; 2461).

The core of Hammond's testimony was a letter he purportedly received from an unnamed correspondent from "the western part of the State of New York." The writer denounced "The madness

which influences our northern people on the subject of slavery" and which is "well calculated to fill the stoutest with dismay." He feared that "[t]he spirit which followed the Utica and Peterboro' convention of abolitionists has totally changed the question from that of the emancipation of the slave to that of the continuance of the Union" (*Register of Debates* 1836, 2453).

According to Hammond and the anonymous author, "The North is now laboring to unite her people against you. The effort is immense and continual. The enclosed anti-slavery pamphlets and some 'Emancipators' were distributed at a Presbyterian prayer meeting in my neighborhood the other day, by the president of the anti-slavery society of this county, and were handed to me by the deacon of the church, through the hands of one of the men of my employ. The object is to unite the people in hatred of the South, by false representations of the condition of their slaves, and by charges of cruelty, immorality, and irreligion. I endeavor to convince my neighbors that these pamphlets are false in every particular, and that, if they join in the cry of abolition, they must partake of the enormous sin of bringing on a civil war, of destroying our union, and of causing a renewal of the horrors of St. Domingo."

On Thursday, February 4, Pinckney submitted a motion requiring that "all memorials which have been offered, or may hereafter be presented, to this House, praying for the abolition of slavery in the District of Columbia ... and every other paper or proposition that may be submitted in relation to that subject, be referred to a select committee, with instructions to report that Congress possesses no constitutional authority to interfere in any way with the institution of slavery in any of the States of this confederacy" (*Register of Debates* 1836, 2483). But it was not until May 26 that the House passed the Pinckney resolution establishing the "gag rule" and automatically tabling all antislavery petitions without granting them a hearing (*Congressional Globe* 24/1, 506). Similar resolutions were passed in succeeding congressional terms.

Eight years later, on December 3, 1844, John Quincy Adams of Massachusetts made a motion that the "25th standing rule," which had evolved from the initial Pinckney resolution, be rescinded (*Congressional Globe* 28/2, 7). Adams's resolution passed by a vote of 108 to 80. In 1844, New York State, with thirty-four representatives was the largest state delegation; it included twenty-four Democrats, descendants of the Jacksonians, and ten Whigs, a party that emerged from the anti-Jackson faction. None of this group had served in Congress when the initial "gag rule" was instituted in 1836.

While New York's Jacksonian Democrats overwhelmingly supported the gag rule in 1836, in a major shift, perhaps representing new thinking about the abolition of slavery on the part of the North or at least growing resentment toward Southern behavior in the House and Senate, eighteen New York State Democrats voted to rescind the "gag rule" and only two voted against the resolution. Eight Whigs voted Yea, none voted Nay, and two did not vote. This trend became even more pronounced two years later when the entire New York State delegation in the House of Representatives that was present and voting, members of the Democratic, Whig, and American parties, supported the Wilmot Proviso banning slavery in any new territory acquired from Mexico (*Congressional Globe* 29/1, 1218). However, while the ban was passed in the House, it was defeated in the Senate and never became law, one more example of legislative dysfunction in United States history.

2

RESISTANCE! RESISTANCE! RESISTANCE!

New York State's Radical Black Abolitionists and the Coming of the Civil War

ON JUNE 16, 1858, AT THE REPUBLICAN PARTY'S STATE CONVENTION IN SPRINGFIELD, Illinois, Abraham Lincoln delivered one of the most famous quotes in American history: "A house divided against itself cannot stand. I believe this government cannot endure, permanently half slave and half free" (Lincoln 1858). Lincoln's declaration became a major issue in his senatorial campaign against Stephen Douglas. In a series of debates, Douglas hammered away at Lincoln, demanding to know, "Why can it [the nation] not exist divided into free and slave States? Washington, Jefferson, Franklin, Madison, Hamilton, Jay, and the great men of that day made this government divided into free States and slave States, and left each State perfectly free to do as it pleased on the subject of slavery. Why can it not exist on the same principles on which our fathers made it?" (Douglas 1858). In his Freeport Doctrine, Douglas accepted the constitutionality of the Supreme Court's *Dred Scott* decision (1857) and argued that it was compatible with "Popular Sovereignty," which meant whites could decide on black rights and freedom on a local basis.

Given the events that followed, the intensification of sectional divisions, the election of Lincoln as president, and the Southern secession crisis, Lincoln's speech seems prescient and Stephan Douglas's question, "What makes division inevitable?" is rarely addressed. The failure to do so has had consequences. The assumption of inevitability, as well as the focus in scholarship on abolitionist ideology rather than practice, has minimized the historical role of black resistance, including significant activity in New York State, as an underlying cause of the American Civil War and a major force in the struggle for emancipation (Litwack 1961; Foner 1970; Blight 1989; Horton 1993; Rael 2002; Singer 2004; Rael 2008; Singer 2008). In her recent encyclopedic study *The Slaves' Cause: A History of Abolition*, Manisha Sinha persuasively argues that black resistance to slavery, not bourgeois white liberalism, was at the heart of the abolitionist movement (Sinha 2016, 2–8).

From independence through the mid-1850s, abolitionism in the United States was a fringe movement dominated by small, ideologically dogmatic factions similar to,

29

and even paralleling, the evangelical movement during the same period. Eric Foner, in *Free Soil, Free Labor, Free Men* (1970), argues that the greatest obstacle facing abolitionists was indifference in the North where the Whigs and Democrats successfully kept the issue of slavery out of the political mainstream. William Lloyd Garrison (1831) had emphasized the need for a "greater revolution in public sentiment ... in the free states" in his initial editorial in *The Liberator* (Kennedy 2015, 260). At their national conventions in 1852, both the Whig and Democratic parties approved platforms endorsing the Fugitive Slave Law of 1850 in an attempt to bring closure to the debate over the future of slavery, a decision that helped bring about the eclipse of the Whig Party (Campbell 1968, 77).

Because of their marginalization, a dearth of political activity, and because many white abolitionists were prodigious writers and speakers, historians have tended to focus on their ideological debates, principally between allies and opponents of William Lloyd Garrison over whether the Constitution was a pro-slavery document, legal and social equality for free blacks, the role of women in the abolitionist movement, and the legitimacy of participation in the political process. Black abolitionists, when discussed at all, are usually viewed as supporting members of the different factions, who shifted sides over issues of particular concern to them such as colonization in Africa or the Caribbean.

However, if we focus on action rather than ideas, especially resistance to enslavement and racism, blacks, both free and enslaved, played a much more pivotal role in the struggle to end slavery, a view I share with historian Ira Berlin (*The Long Emancipation*). Berlin and I believe it was black activism, much of which was centered in New York State, that moved the challenge to slavery from the margins to the center of political debate. Prominent in this struggle were William Wells Brown, Arthur Crummell, Frederick Douglass, Henry Highland Garnet, Jermain Lougen, James W. C. Pennington, David Ruggles, James McCune Smith, Sojourner Truth, Harriet Tubman, and Samuel Ringgold Ward, who in their defiance of slavery and racism played a major role in radicalizing the abolitionist movement, precipitating the secession crisis, and moving the nation to Civil War.

Black resistance to enslavement and racism came in many forms. After Toussaint Loverture and the successful slave rebellion in Haiti, every hint of rebellion, and there were more than two dozen actual uprisings in the first half of the nineteenth century in the American South and the West Indies, sent ripples of fear through plantation societies. As a result, calls for open rebellion against slavery by David Walker, Reverend Henry Highland Garnet of Troy, and John Brown (who had support from Gerrit Smith of Utica and Peterboro, Frederick Douglass, and Harriet Tubman) increased concern in the Cotton Kingdom that the free states and the national government would not intervene to protect the slave system (Oakes 1986).

New York State was a hotbed of radical and influential black abolitionism from the American Revolution to the American Civil War (Goodman 1998, 56). New York City and

freedom seeker

Brooklyn were home to David Ruggles, secretary and principal organizer of New York's Committee of Vigilance, who actively battled kidnappers and assisted freedom seekers including Frederick Douglass (Berlin 2015, 70; Hodges 2010). *Freedom's Journal*, the first African American newspaper in the United States, and Charles Ray's *The Colored American* were published in New York City. Both papers stressed the fight against slavery and racial discrimination and the colonization of American blacks in Africa.

turn away from recolon.

Local black ministers such as the Reverend Peter Williams and the Reverend Nathaniel Paul were influential in turning white abolitionists like William Lloyd Garrison against the recolonization of black Americans in Africa and toward radical ideas like racial equality. Paul, the first pastor of the Union Street Baptist Church in Albany, demanded that African Americans "enter the field with a fixed determination to live and die in the holy cause" of ending slavery (Sinha 2016, 195). He traveled in England with Garrison in the 1830s campaigning against colonization schemes (Ripley 1986, 52; Sinha 2016, 221).

Other black ministers such as the Reverend Theodore Wright of New York's First Colored Presbyterian Church challenged racism within the abolitionist movement itself. At the 1837 New York State Anti-Slavery Society convention in Utica, Wright demanded, "Abolitionists must annihilate in their own bosoms the cord of caste." For Wright, it was "an easy thing to ask about the vileness of slavery at the South, but to call the dark man a brother, heartily to embrace the doctrine advanced in the second article of the constitution, to treat all men according to their moral worth, to treat the man of color in all circumstances as a man and brother that is the test" (Aptheker 1973, 171–72).

Nearly one-third of Garrison's *Thoughts on African Colonization* (1832) consisted of reprints of speeches and essays written by African Americans expressing their opposition to colonialism and much of it came from New York. In an 1830 July Fourth speech, Peter Williams, Rector of St. Philip's A. M. E. Zion Church, declared, "We are NATIVES of this country, we ask only to be treated as well as FOREIGNERS. Not a few of our fathers suffered and bled to purchase its independence; we ask only to be treated as well as those who fought against it. We have toiled to cultivate it, and to raise it to its present prosperous condition; we ask only to share equal privileges with those who come from distant lands, to enjoy the fruits of our labor" (Garrison 1832, 66). Williams's position was forcefully reasserted at a January 1831 open meeting of New York's black community that declared, "We claim this country, the place of our birth, and not Africa, as our mother country, and all attempts to send us to Africa we consider as gratuitous and uncalled for" (ibid., 14). Williams later resigned as rector of St. Philip's Church in a dispute over his antislavery activism. In his letter of resignation he explained that his opposition to the American Colonization Society was because of its endorsement of the idea "that a colored man, however he may strive to make himself intelligent, virtuous and useful, can never enjoy the privileges of a citizen of the United States" (Sernett 1999, 214).

some of them have never been to Africa

Eric Foner, in *Gateway to Freedom* (2015, 63–90), describes how the New York Vigilance Committee for the Protection of People of Color, principally because of the efforts of David Ruggles as secretary, became the model for organized Northern black resistance to enslavement. Founded in 1835, its strongest membership base was in the black church, although it did rely on white abolitionists such as the New York City silk merchants Lewis and Arthur Tappan for funds.

In the first annual report of the New York Committee of Vigilance (1837), Ruggles argued for a "practical" abolitionism that monitored the arrival of fugitives from the South; the arrival and departure of vessels engaged in the slave trade and ships with enslaved Africans on board; the actions of slave agents and kidnappers; the arrest of accused fugitives, the abduction of free blacks; and the recovery of people kidnapped and detained in the South (14). The Vigilance Committee's activities also included lobbying legislative bodies to recognize the civil rights of black citizens and defend the rights of accused fugitives and organizing mass protests whenever there were legal proceedings involving captured freedom seekers and members of the local black community.

According to Ruggles, writing for the Vigilance Committee, "To effect a mighty revolution, such as the general of slavery, requires agents, and funds, and time, and influence, proportioned to the magnitude of the work; but while we long and labor for the accomplishment of this noble cause, let us not lose sight of the minor evils, which tend in the aggregate to make up that monstrous system of iniquity; let us in every case of oppression and wrong, inflicted on our brethren, prove our sincerity, by alleviating their sufferings, affording them protection, giving them counsel, and thus in our individual spheres of action prove ourselves practical abolitionists" (New York Committee of Vigilance 1837, 13).

While the Vigilance Committee lost most of its legal challenges, it did have some dramatic successes, including the freeing of William Dixon in 1837. Perhaps its most important function according to Ruggles was assisting freedom seekers in their escape from slavery. He claimed that in its first year of operation alone it prevented three hundred people from "being carried back into slavery" (ibid., 64). Among his other activities, Ruggles boarded ships when they arrived in New York harbor to search for escapees and "servants" who were being transported through New York by enslavers. Ruggles himself was arrested in 1838 and charged with "harboring a criminal and encouraging a slave to escape," but the case was never tried (ibid., 73).

On November 13, 1872, the *Brooklyn Eagle* (1872, 2) included a notice that "Louis Napoleon, colored, slightly famous in times past as an engineer of the Underground Railway, in the transportation of slaves, has reached 71." Foner (2015, 98–99) described Napoleon as one of the key figures in the New York Vigilance Committee during the 1830s, 1840s, and 1850s, although very little is known about his life. Napoleon was closely associated with white abolitionist Sydney Howard Gay and at times Gay employed him as a porter in the office of the *National Anti-Slavery Standard* in lower Manhattan. Like

Ruggles, Napoleon actively searched the waterfront for newly arrived freedom seekers and enslaved Africans being transported by enslavers through the port of New York.

In November 1852, Napoleon helped eight enslaved Africans, two woman and their six children, escape from the Lemmon family while they were traveling by boat from Virginia to Texas via New York. At a court proceeding, the women and their children were represented by future president of the United States Chester Arthur. The judge in the case ruled that since slavery did not exist in the State of New York, the previously enslaved Africans were now free (*New York Times* 1852, 6). In response to this decision, the *Savannah Morning News* accused New York courts of "robbery" and the Virginia state legislature passed a resolution to support further legal action by the Lemmons, however in 1857 and 1860 New York State appeals courts ruled against them (Foner 2015, 140–42).

Among the most prominent antislavery activist ministers in New York was the Reverend Henry Highland Garnet (Crummell 1882; Ofari 1972). Garnet escaped from enslavement with his family when he was eleven and eventually settled in New York City where he attended the African Free School on Mott Street. His classmates included Alexander Crummell, Samuel Ringgold Ward, and James McCune Smith, the first African American to earn a medical degree.

Garnet and Samuel Ringgold Ward became major proponents of the independent Negro Convention movement because white opponents of slavery rarely supported equal rights and full citizenship for black Americans. Ward, who led two predominately white congregations in upstate New York, a Presbyterian Church in South Butler and a Congregationalist church in Cortland, challenged white abolitionists who "have not so much regard for the rights of colored men as they think they have.... I know not how else to account for their strong and determined action in defence [*sic*] of their own rights, while now they are comparatively mute concerning ours" (Ripley 1991, 341).

In 1843, at a National Negro Convention in Buffalo, Henry Highland Garnet issued a call for slaves to revolt against their masters. His ideas, which were similar to those espoused by David Walker in his famous *Appeal* (1829), were considered dangerous even by many abolitionists. These included Frederick Douglass, at the time allied with Garrisonians who opposed violence and preferred using moral and economic arguments to challenge slavery (Johnson and Smith 1999, 384). Garnet's words bear repeating (Aptheker 1973, 226–33) because of their forcefulness, and because of the threat they posed—whether real or imagined—to the Southern slavocracy.

This is the spirit Garnet and black abolitionists brought to the abolitionist movement. But it was their actions that made the war inevitable—why the nation could not survive half slave and half free.

A major reason for the centrality of New York's black abolitionists in the struggle to end slavery was that the combination of shipping, rail transportation, work, proximity to Canada, and the Erie Canal made the twin cities of New York and Brooklyn a hub

*Wanted ex slaves
their ability to be civil,
created split*

HENRY HIGHLAND GARNET CALLS FOR RESISTANCE (1843)

QUESTION TO CONSIDER

Why did abolitionists, including Frederick Douglass,
shy away from Garnet's call for resistance?

Brethren, arise, arise! Strike for your lives and liberties. Now is the day and the hour. Let every slave throughout the land do this, and the days of slavery are numbered. You cannot be more oppressed than you have been, you cannot suffer greater cruelties than you have already. Rather die freemen than live to be slaves. Remember that you are four millions!

Let your motto be resistance! resistance! resistance! No oppressed people have ever secured their liberty without resistance. Trust in the living God. Labor for the peace of the human race, and remember that you are four millions.

of the Underground Railroad (Foner 2015). In *The Life and Times of Frederick Douglass* (1892/1962, 200–201), Douglass described traveling from Baltimore to Wilmington, Delaware, by train, from Wilmington to Philadelphia by steamboat, and finally from Philadelphia to New York City by train. After hiding at the home of David Ruggles in Manhattan and then meeting up with and marrying his fiancée, Douglass and his new wife traveled by steamer to Newport, Rhode Island, and stagecoach to New Bedford, Massachusetts (ibid., 204–205). In his comprehensive biography of Ruggles, historian Graham Hodges (2010, 132–33) argues that Ruggles was an early and important influence on the future abolitionist leader.

Many freedom seekers from Eastern border states initially made their way to Philadelphia where they were assisted by William Stills and the Pennsylvania Society for the Abolition of Slavery or through South Jersey where there was a network of Quaker Underground Railroad stationmasters (Still 2007). From Philadelphia and South Jersey they traveled to New York and Brooklyn by boat, coach, and train. Once in the twin cities, freedom seekers were hidden by abolitionists until the now free but still endangered blacks could be routed to relative safety in Massachusetts or up the Hudson River by boat or train to Troy and then either north toward Canada via Lake Champlain or west along the Erie Canal to Syracuse, Rochester, and Buffalo. The Erie and Lake Champlain Canals not only were the main routes to ultimate safety but the canal locks and ports provided work, and sometimes a place to settle, during the journey. Henry Highland Garnet's call for resistance carried such power because black abolitionists and stationmasters on the Underground Railroad in New York were in active defiance of slavery, slavecatchers, and Fugitive Slave laws.

"Black defiance"

BATTLING SLAVECATCHERS IN BUFFALO

One of the most dramatic examples of black defiance took place in Buffalo, New York, and was described by William Wells Brown in his memoir, *Narrative of William W. Brown, Fugitive Slave* (Brown 1847, 109–24; Katz 1995, 154–55). Brown was born on a plantation near Lexington, Kentucky, in 1814 and escaped from slavery in 1834. He eventually moved to New York State where he lectured for the Western New York Anti-Slavery Society. Brown also worked for nine years on a Lake Erie steamboat and as a conductor for the Underground Railroad. He later wrote about this 1836 battle between slavecatchers supported by local police and Buffalo's black community, which mobilized to prevent a kidnapping and reenslavement.

According to Brown's account, "The alarm was given just as the bells were ringing for church. I was in company with five or six others, when I heard that a brother slave with his family had been seized and dragged from his home during the night previous. We started on a run for the livery stable, where we found as many more of our own color trying to hire horses to go in search of the fugitives" (Brown 1847, 112).

The liberators cornered the kidnappers in a tavern, freed the captive and his family, and brought them to the Niagara River where there was a ferry to convey them to Canada. However, the rescue was only temporary. Brown described how the sheriff and his men surrounded his group. "The sheriff came forward, and read something purporting to be a 'Riot Act,' and at the same time called upon all good citizens to aid him in keeping the 'peace.' This was a trick of his, to get possession of the slaves. His men rushed upon us with their clubs and stones and a general fight ensued. Our company had surrounded the slaves, and had succeeded in keeping the sheriff and his men off. We fought, and at the same time kept pushing on towards the ferry.... After a hard-fought battle, of nearly two hours, we arrived at the ferry, the slaves still in our possession. Here another battle was to be fought, before the slaves could reach Canada. The boat was fastened at each end by a chain, and in the scuffle for the ascendancy, one party took charge of one end of the boat, while the other took the other end. The blacks were commanding the ferryman to carry them over, while the whites were commanding him not to. While each party was contending for power, the slaves were pushed on board, and the boat shoved from the wharf. Many of the blacks jumped on board of the boat, while the whites jumped on shore. And the swift current of the Niagara soon carried them off, amid the shouts of the blacks, and the oaths and imprecations of the whites. We on shore swung our hats and gave cheers, just as a reinforcement came to the whites. Seeing the odds entirely against us in numbers, and having gained the great victory, we gave up without resistance, and suffered ourselves to be arrested by the sheriff's posse." Members of the freedom posse were eventually placed on trial and "fined more or less from five to fifty dollars each." Brown concluded, "Thus ended one of the most fearful fights for human freedom that I ever witnessed" (Brown 1847, 118–23).

RESISTING THE FUGITIVE SLAVE LAW

This type of resistance to slavery became particularly disruptive after Congress approved the Compromise Act of 1850 that allowed California to enter the union as a free state. The South accepted a voting imbalance between free and slave states in the Senate as long as the North was willing to ensure compliance with a stringent Fugitive Slave law. Unlike the Fugitive Slave Act of 1793, which made enslavers and their agents solely responsible for the capture and return of freedom seekers who escaped from bondage, the 1850 act mandated heavy fines and jail sentences for anyone who assisted suspected runaways and actually required bystanders to participate in their apprehension. Defiance of this law by black abolitionists and white supporters was one of the major forces driving a wedge between the North and South and propelling the nation toward Civil War (Foner 2015; Campbell 1968; Dew 2001; Freehling 2007).

During debate in the United States Senate (Amherst College 2009), Senator John C. Calhoun of South Carolina, a former vice-president of the United States, threatened secession by Southern enslavers unless Northern "agitation" against slavery ceased. According to Calhoun, it was this agitation, not slavery, that threatened national unity (26–33). In an effort to appease the South, Senator Daniel Webster of Massachusetts defended the Compromise and the Fugitive Slave as necessary "for the preservation of the Union" and American "liberty," at least liberty for Whites (Amherst College 2009, 34–40). The most outspoken opponent of appeasement was Senator William Seward of Auburn, New York. Responding to Webster, Seward declared,

> [I]t is insisted that the admission of California shall be attended by a
> COMPROMISE of questions which have arisen out of SLAVERY! I AM OPPOSED
> TO ANY SUCH COMPROMISE, IN ANY AND ALL THE FORMS IN WHICH IT
> HAS BEEN PROPOSED.... Relying on the perversion of the Constitution,
> which makes slaves mere chattels, the slave states have applied to them
> the principles of the criminal law, and have held that he who aided the
> escape of his fellow-man from bondage was guilty of a larceny in stealing
> him.... We deem the principle of the law for the recapture of fugitives, as

thus expounded, therefore, unjust, unconstitutional, and immoral; and thus, while patriotism withholds its approbation, the consciences of our people condemn it.... We are not slaveholders. We cannot, in our judgment, be either true Christians or real freemen, if we impose on another a chain that we defy all human power to fasten on ourselves.... [T]he spirit of the people of the free states is set upon a spring that rises with the pressure put upon it. That spring, if pressed too hard, will give a recoil.... You will say that this implies violence. Not at all. It implies only peaceful, lawful, constitutional, customary action (ibid., 41–47).

While New York, unlike neighboring Connecticut, Massachusetts, Vermont, New Hampshire, Rhode Island, and Pennsylvania, never passed a formal personal liberty law designed to prevent local authorities from assisting in the recapture of freedom seekers, an 1840 law guaranteed that accused fugitives from slavery would have jury trials to establish their status. It also declared, "Every person who shall, without the authority of law, forcibly remove or attempt to remove from this state any fugitive from service or labor, or any person who is claimed as such fugitive, shall forfeit the sum of five hundred dollars to the party aggrieved, and shall be deemed guilty of the crime of kidnapping, and upon conviction of such offence, shall be punished by imprisonment in the state prison for a period not exceeding ten years" (Sinha 2016, 500; Edmonds 1869, 522). The 1842 Supreme Court decision *Prigg v. Pennsylvania* affirmed the constitutionality of the federal Fugitive Slave Act of 1793, but appeared to also accept the legitimacy of state sponsored noncompliance. However, the new Fugitive Slave law removed that legal maneuvering room for antislavery action (Foner 2015, 108–11).

In August 1850, just before the fugitive slave bill became national law, it was denounced by a convention of two thousand people, mostly blacks, held in Cazenovia, New York. Describing themselves as a "meeting of runaway slaves," they issued a "Letter to the American Slaves" pledging their support in the struggle to end slavery. The letter concluded, "Brethren, our last word to you is to bid you to be of good cheer, and not to despair of your deliverance.... Live! Live to escape from slavery! (Sinha 2016, 501; Aptheker 1973, 299). In Oswego, New York, black groups began to arm in self-defense; in response, the Rochester *Advertiser* warned local whites about the need to enforce the law (Campbell 1968, 63).

On September 28, 1850 (p. 2), the *Brooklyn Eagle* reported the first seizure (arrest) and processing (trial) under the new Fugitive Slave law in New York City. James Hamlet, a freedom seeker from enslavement in Baltimore, was apprehended by U.S. Marshals two years after his escape. Hamlet was identified in a quasi-legal proceeding by the son and son-in-law of the woman who claimed to be his "owner." A commissioner found in favor of the claimants and Hamlet was escorted south by a federal marshal, leaving behind his wife and children. Lewis Tappan, who had been active in organizing the defense of the *Amistad* captives, and members of the American and Foreign Anti-Slavery Society (AFASS) were furious with the federal government's legal complicity with slavery. The AFASS charged that Hamlet was denied a jury trial and the right of self-defense. Commissioners who decided the cases were only clerks, and were biased in favor of enslavers. They were awarded ten dollars for deciding in favor of the claimant but only five dollars if they ruled the accused was really a free man. The abolitionist organization issued a pamphlet promising assistance to free blacks and freedom seekers accused of being runaways. Meanwhile, Hamlet was immediately sold to a slave trader in Baltimore but was then ransomed when his Brooklyn neighbors raised $800 to purchase his freedom. Hamlet returned to New York City where he was greeted by an interracial crowd of about five hundred people who rallied against the Fugitive Slave Law (Tappan 1850).

Reverend Jermain Loguen, who was born enslaved in Tennessee in 1813 and escaped to the North and Canada as a young man in 1834, essentially declared war on the Fugitive Slave law in a speech delivered in Syracuse in October 1850. Loguen told a meeting presided over by the mayor of the city, "I don't respect this law—I don't fear it— I won't obey it! It outlaws me, and I outlaw it, and the men who attempt to enforce it on me. I place the governmental officials on the ground that they place me. I will not live a slave, and if force is employed to re-enslave me, I shall make preparations to meet the crisis as becomes a man" (Loguen 1859, 393–94).

The Cazenovia resolution and Loguen's fiery statement stand in sharp contrast to the response of most white Northerners. In New York City, at a meeting called by leaders of the business community, ten thousand people signed a petition supporting the Fugitive Slave law. The response among Northern whites in other states was similar. By the end of the summer of 1851, it appeared that white opposition to the Fugitive Slave law in the North had been quelled and prominent Southern spokesmen were claiming a great victory (Campbell 1968, 56–63, 115).

But black opponents of slavery were not willing to accept appeasement, and they pressed antislavery agitation. The first major tests of the Fugitive Slave law took place in Christiana, Pennsylvania, near the border with Delaware, and Syracuse, New York, in September and October 1851. At Christiana, free blacks forcefully prevented the capture of a freedom seeker and in an exchange of gunfire a Maryland enslaver, part of the group trying to recapture the freedom seeker, was killed. Thirty-six blacks and five whites, most of who were bystanders, were arrested and charged with treason for violating the Fugitive Slave law and rebelling against the government. Events in Christiania were heavily publicized in the national press, including the initial editions of *The New York Times*. Eventually, William Parker, the leader of the black resistance force, escaped to Canada with the assistance of Frederick Douglass. The other participants were found not guilty of treason and other charges against them were dropped (Katz 1974).

A month after the Christiana rebellion, Jermain Loguen and Samuel Ringgold Ward, led what has come to be called the "Jerry Rescue" in direct violation of the Fugitive Slave law (Loguen 1859; Singer 2004, 202). On October 1, 1851, federal marshals and local police arrested William "Jerry" Henry, suspected of being an escaped slave. *The New York Times* reported: "A colored man named W. Henry, who has resided in this city for some time past, was arrested this morning by U.S. Marshal Allen, as a fugitive slave. He is a cooper by trade, and was at work in his shop when he was arrested. The officer informed him that he was charged with some slight offence, and he allowed himself to be taken and handcuffed under that impression. He was taken before Commissioner Saline, and an examination gone into" (*New York Times* 1851a, 2).

During the afternoon, delegates from a convention of the antislavery Liberty Party made an unsuccessful effort to free "Jerry" and that evening a large crowd broke into the building where he was being held and freed him. William Henry was hidden for several days and then taken by wagon to Oswego, where he was able to cross Lake Ontario and enter Canada. Nineteen indictments were returned against the rescuers, including Jermain Loguen. The accused were bailed out by, among others, United States Senator William Seward. Legal proceedings dragged on for two years and Loguen eventually escaped to Canada. Ward, a runaway from enslavement who was also sought by authorities, fled the country and remained outside the United States, lecturing against slavery in Canada and Europe, for the rest of his life. Abolitionists succeeded in bringing deputy marshal Henry Allen up on criminal charges for his role in the kidnapping of William Henry, but Allen was acquitted by a jury that found that the Fugitive Slave law superseded local and state ordinances (*Syracuse Daily Journal* 1852, 98).

The Christiana rebellion followed by the Jerry Rescue in Syracuse helped convince Southerners that the North would never respect their "property rights." In response to Christiana, the *Daily Register* of Mobile, Alabama, declared, "The elements of discord have scarcely subsided into sullen calm, the grieved and injured Southern States have barely yielded to the importunities and assurances of their own patriotic citizens, that the hand of aggression would be stayed, and that the Compromise would be observed in good faith, when all this diabolical tragedy is enacted with all its vile and insulting circumstances" and an editorial in the Augusta, Georgia, *Constitutionalist* warned the South, "We have been fearing just such a result as this.... We have lost all our territory and got a Fugitive Slave Law, the recovery under which of our slaves, costs us more than they are worth, and the blood of our people besides" (Underground Railroad webpage, n.d.). According to the *Baltimore Sun*, "The law of the land" had been "wantonly and openly violated and the death of one, if not more of the best citizens of Maryland, has been the consequence" (Dickinson College House Divided webpage, n.d.). Following the Jerry Rescue the *New York Times* reported on similar Southern "indignation" (*New York Times* 1851b, 4).

Black abolitionists across New York State continued to challenge slavecatchers throughout the decade leading up to the Civil War. In March 1854, residents of Auburn, New York, aided in another "rescue" of an accused runaway (*Auburn Daily Advertiser* 1854). In Troy, at the juncture of the Hudson River and the start of the Erie Canal, Stephen and Harriet Myers operated a vital Underground Railroad safe house where they routed freedom seekers along the safest path to Canada. In Troy, Harriet Tubman was involved in a similar "intervention" that directly challenged the Fugitive Slave law (Bradford 1886, 124–27; Singer 2004, 204). In the spring of 1860 an accused fugitive from slavery named Charles Nalle was incarcerated in the local jail awaiting shipment south for reenslavement. Tubman, traveling through Troy, joined a crowd blocking the entrance.

As authorities tried to move Nalle, Tubman

> seized one officer and pulled him down, then another, and tore him away from the man; and keeping her arms about the slave, she cried to her friends: "Drag us out! Drag him to the river! Drown him! But don't let them have him!" They were knocked down together, and while down, she tore off her sunbonnet and tied it on the head of the fugitive. When he rose, only his head could be seen, and amid the surging mass of people the slave was no longer recognized.... Again and again they were knocked down, the poor slave utterly helpless, with his manacled wrists, streaming with blood. Harriet's outer clothes were torn from her, and even her stout shoes were pulled from her feet, yet she never relinquished her hold of the man, till she had dragged him to the river, where he was tumbled into a boat, Harriet following in a ferry-boat to the other side (Bradford 1886, 122).

Documentary evidence suggests that Frederick Douglass was also more radical than portrayed in history books (Schor 1979; Cohen 2008; Oakes 2008). Douglass broke with the Garrisonians in 1851 and shifted his support to political abolitionists affiliated with the Liberty Party who believed that the Constitution, because it did not actually endorse slavery, provided a possibility for opposing it (Sinha 2016, 492–95). He also appears moderate when compared to black abolitionists such as Henry Highland Garnet who espoused revolutionary action. However, frustration with racism and slavery did drive Douglass to militancy.

It was Frederick Douglass who sheltered William Parker, the leader of the Christiana resistance, after he escaped from authorities in Pennsylvania, and arranged his transit to Canada. In return, Parker gave Douglass the gun he used to kill the slave-catcher. In his memoir, Douglass wrote, "I could not look upon them as murderers. To me, they were heroic defenders of the just rights of man against manstealers and murders" (Douglass 1892/1962, 280–82).

At the 1852 convention of the Free Soil party, Douglass gave an impromptu speech where he argued, "The only way to make the Fugitive Slave Law a dead letter is to make half a dozen or more dead kidnappers. A half dozen more dead kidnappers carried down South would cool the ardor of Southern gentlemen, and keep their rapacity in check" (Chesebrough 1998, 42). Douglass later wrote that the Fugitive Slave law "must be wiped out, and nothing short of resistance on the part of the colored man can wipe it out. Every slavehunter who meets a bloody death in his infernal business is an argument in favor of the manhood of our race" (Litwack 1961, 251).

During the winter of 1857–58, Douglass gave refuge in his Rochester, New York, home to John Brown who was a fugitive because of his involvement in the "Bloody Kansas" insurrection. In his memoir, Douglass admitted that he participated in developing Brown's plan to foment a slave rebellion that eventually morphed into the unsuccessful attack on the federal arsenal at Harpers Ferry. Douglass broke with Brown because he believed that the decision to target Harpers Ferry would draw the rebels into a "perfect steel-trap … and escape would be impossible" (Douglass 1892/1962, 319). Douglass was indicted by the State of Virginia as a co-conspirator and was forced to flee the country until Southern secession made the warrant moot. Late in his career, perhaps radicalized again by disappointment with the abandonment of Reconstruction, Douglass praised Brown for beginning "the war that ended American slavery and made this a free Republic. Until this blow was struck, the prospect for freedom was dim, shadowy and uncertain" (Ruchames 1969, 298).

The actual number of freedom seekers prosecuted under the 1850 Fugitive Slave Act was actually quite small; only 332 were apprehended between 1850 and 1860. A much smaller number, thirty-four or approximately 10 percent, were either released by authorities or rescued by abolitionists. Of the total, fifteen of the escapes and four of the rescues or releases occurred in New York State (Campbell 1968, 199–207). Yet despite the small number of people involved, the rescues took on tremendous symbolic importance in the decade leading up to the Civil War.

During the 1850s, Southern politicians and newspapers largely ignored black resistance to the Fugitive Slave law and blamed Northern state governments and Northern representatives in the House and Senate for failures to adequately enforce it (Dew 2001; Freehling 2007, 272–73). In a typical condemnation, Stephen F. Hale, a commissioner from Alabama wrote the governor of Tennessee in December 1860 in an effort to enlist his support for secession. According to Hale,

> A majority of the Northern States, through their legislative enactments, have openly nullified it, and impose heavy fines and penalties upon all persons who aid in enforcing this law; and some of those States declare the Southern slave-holder, who goes within their jurisdiction to assert

his legal rights under the Constitution, guilty of a high crime, and affix imprisonment in the penitentiary as the penalty. The Federal officers who attempt to discharge their duties under the law, as well as the owner of the slave, are set upon by mobs, and are fortunate if they escape without serious injury to life or limb; and the State authorities, instead of aiding in the enforcement of this law, refuse the use of their jails, and by every means which unprincipled fanaticism can devise, give countenance to the mob, and aid the fugitive to escape. Thus, there are annually large amounts of property actually stolen away from the Southern States, harbored and protected in Northern States, and by their citizens (Dew 2001, 93).

The importance of resistance to the Fugitive Slave law as a cause of the Civil War can also be seen in the secession documents of South Carolina, Georgia, Mississippi, and Texas. Each of these states listed the Northern failure to enforce the Fugitive Slave law of 1850 as a principle reason for the collapse of the union. During debate in Georgia, Thomas Cobb, a leading proponent of secession declared, "Protection to the life, liberty and property of the citizen is the corner-stone and only end of Government in the American mind.... But protection—whence comes it to us? Dare you to follow your fugitive into a Northern State to arrest him? The assassin strikes you down, and no law avenges your blood; your property is stolen every day, and the very attempt to recover it subjects you to the insults of the North" (Freehling and Simpson 1992, 13).

Major impetus for Southern secession came from the state of South Carolina, whose leaders made clear that the preservation of slavery and belief in racial inequality were at the heart of the movement (Sinha 2011, 60–63; Takaki 1965). During the 1860 South Carolina gubernatorial campaign, Edward Bryan, who also championed reopening the transatlantic slave trade, declared, "Give us slavery or give us death!" John S. Preston, a South Carolina delegate to the 1860 Democratic Party national convention who walked out in protest over the nomination of Stephen Douglas for president, proclaimed, "Slavery is our King—Slavery is our Truth—Slavery is our Divine Right" (Sinha 2000; Sinha 2011, 60–63; Bass 2010).

Alexander Stephens of Georgia, vice president of the Confederate States of America, believed the Constitution of the Confederacy "put to rest forever all the agitating questions relating to our peculiar institutions—African slavery as it exists among us—the proper status of the negro in our form of civilization. This was the immediate cause of the late rupture and present revolution." He declared the Confederacy was "founded upon ... the great truth that the negro is not equal to the white man; that slavery, subordination to the superior race, is his natural and moral condition" (Bass 2010).

A major target of the pro-slavery South was Stephen Douglas for proposing the Freeport Doctrine, a policy of benign neglect that would have allowed Northern states to avoid enforcement of the *Dred Scott* decision and implementation of pro-slavery statutes

not willing to give proper cred

within their own borders. Even when the abolitionists were directly criticized, the focus was on white opponents of slavery because Southern ideologues preferred to portray blacks as passive and accommodating.

Unfortunately, too often histories of the events leading up to the Civil War end up supporting this Southern bias against black efficacy. Proponents of slavery could not admit that blacks were either willing or capable of organizing effective protest against slavery, because such an admission undermined their racist defense of the slave system.

The American Civil War and the resulting emancipation of enslaved Africans in the United States were not inevitable in 1858. A house divided against itself may well have stood for many more years, if not for the actions of black abolitionists, freeman, and escapees, who directly challenged the Compromise of 1850 and the Fugitive Slave law. Frederick Douglass recognized this when he wrote, "The thing which more than all else destroyed the fugitive slave law was the resistance made to it by the fugitives themselves" at Christiana and Syracuse (Douglass 1892/1962, 280–82). The crucial role of black abolitionists from New York State in precipitating change needs to be written back into history.

TEACHING NOTES

Teaching about Slavery on Long Island using Primary Source Documents

QUESTIONS TO CONSIDER

1. How representative are local events and individual accounts of the broader sweep of history?

2. How can historians determine the historical accuracy of individual accounts from the past?

Problems for historians and teachers trying to piece together the past from primary sources include the incompleteness of what paleontologists call the "fossil record" and the need to decide which documents are reliable, which ones may convey faulty memories, and which were possibly intended to intentionally confuse or mislead the public. One of my big arguments against the national Common Core Standards' focus on the close reading of text is that text, when devoid of context, provides an incomplete story that can be misleading. Students get a very different impression of events depending on which text or documents (continues on page 44)

Black movement important. what docs? what impression will be left?

(continued from page 43)

they analyze. Although the primary sources about slavery on Long Island are incomplete, we do have much data available to help us put the story together for students. The British, who were primarily interested in taxing the colonists, kept detailed census records for the three Long Island colonies, Kings, Queens, and Suffolk. In 1698, the total population of the three counties was 8,261, of whom 1,053 or 12.8 percent were enslaved Africans. By 1723, the population of the three counties had risen to 15,650, of whom 2,542 or 16.2 percent were enslaved Africans. In 1771, the last census before independence, the population of Kings County was 3,623, 32.1 percent of whom were enslaved Africans. The population of Queens County was 10,980, 20.4 percent of whom were enslaved Africans and the population of Suffolk County was 13,128, 11.1 percent of whom were enslaved Africans. The total number of enslaved Africans in the three counties at the time of the American Revolution was 4,850 (Moss 1993, 54).

The first United States census was conducted in 1790. It discloses, for instance, that the Martin family, formerly sugar planters in Antigua, lived at Rock Hall in what is today Lawrence in Nassau County. They owned seventeen enslaved Africans, making them the largest slaveholders in Queens County (Rava and Matthew 2013).

Public records, including wills, also give historians an idea of who owned enslaved Africans. The collected papers of the Lloyd Family of the Manor of Queens Village on Lloyd's Neck includes deeds of sale and letters describing slave life, work, and value (Lloyd 1927). In 1773,

an inventory was made of the property held by Mary Platt Tredwell, a wealthy woman who lived in Smithtown. The inventory included twenty-six enslaved Africans ranging in age from "new born" to sixty years old (Singer 2008, 14). Their total value was £853 or approximately $128,615 in today's money. The 1679 will of Nathaniel Sylvester from Shelter Island listed twenty enslaved Africans. In the will, he attempted to keep five couples together but gave several of their children to his own sons and daughters (Marcus 1988, 51).

One of the more interesting wills was that of Richard Smith of Smithtown, dated April 26, 1720 (Marcus 1988, 77), which includes the following provisos:

- ❧ I give unto my son Richard my young Negro boy called Stephen
- ❧ I give unto my son Nathaniel my Negro boy called John
- ❧ I give unto my wife Hannah the use of my two Negro men also a young Negro girl as long as she remains my widow
- ❧ My will is that after my wife's death or marriage that the use of the Negro girl shall descend to my eldest Daughter Sarah.
- ❧ I give unto my son Richard after ye marriage or decease of my wife my Negro man called Harry
- ❧ My will is that if my mulatto Dick continues villainous and stubborn then my overseers shall dispose of him and ye effects to be employed for the use of my wife and children.

My suspicion is that the mulatto Dick was villainous and stubborn because he was enslaved by his biological father or one of his relatives and was not pleased with being inherited or sold.

In 1775, colonists in the town of Hempstead prepared a roll of slaveholders as part of the preparation for resistance to British occupation. Enslavers on the list included prominent local residents, some of whom are still honored by town or street names (Funnell 1937).

Criminal actions also tell us something about slave life on Long Island during the colonial era. On July 22, 1706, Edward Lord Viscount Cornbury, the provincial governor, armed justices of the peace in Kings County on Long Island with the death penalty in order to deal with African maroons who, after freeing themselves, were striking fear among the local colonists (Wilder 2000, 16). On the evening of January 24, 1708, an enslaved black woman and an enslaved Native American sought revenge on their owner, William Hallet Jr., of New Town, Queens County. They killed Hallet, his pregnant wife, and their five children. Authorities suspected a broader rebellion and arrested the two conspirators and several other Africans. On February 2, 1708, the woman was burned to death and the man was suspended in chains beside a blade that cut his flesh as he moved. Two other Africans were also executed (Hodges 1999, 64).

There were at least 131 documented runaways on Long Island (Hodges and Brown 1994). On August 13, 1750, the *New York Gazette* published a runaway slave ad: "Runaway about four weeks ago, from Simon Cregier of the City of New York, a Negro wench named Phoebe aged about 45 years, middle sized, and formerly belonged to Dr. Cornelius Van Wyck at Great Neck; she is well known at that part of Long Island, and about Flushing; she had a note with her to look for a master, but has not returned again; her clothing is uncertain. Whoever takes up and secures said Negro wench, so that her Master may have her again, should have forty shillings reward and all reasonable charges paid by Simon Cregier." New Yorkers who listen to rush hour traffic reports are definitely familiar with the name Van Wyck (84).

As late as July 1822, the *Long Island Farmer* published: "Ranaway form the subscriber; on the sixth of May, a Black boy named DAVID APPLEBY, five feet five inches high, very black, and very large white teeth. All persons are warned against harboring or employing said boy, at the peril of the law. Whoever will secure said boy and return him to his master, or lodge him in any public Prison, shall receive the above reward, but no charges paid" (Singer 2001, 36).

Perhaps the best-known Long Island freedom seeker was Venture Smith, whose autobiography is a major source of information about slavery on Long Island. There are disputes over the reliability of sources such as slave narratives, which may have been ghostwritten and usually were published by abolitionist organizations and used in the antislavery crusade. However, sometimes historians find the same story told in different sources from radically different perspectives. When that happens, similarities in the accounts support the reliability of not just the overlapping stories, but of the rest of the narratives as well. This narrative confluence occurred in the case of Venture Smith of Long Island, where the historical record includes both his autobiographical history of his life and a runaway slave advertisement distributed by George Mumford, the man who claimed to own him (Singer 2008, 57–58). (*continues on page 46*)

(*continued from page 45*)

Smith published *Narrative of the Life and Adventures of Venture Smith* in 1796. The entire manuscript is available online from the University of North Carolina at Chapel Hill at its *Documenting the American South* website. The book recounts Smith's capture in Africa as a young boy, the trip across the Atlantic Ocean to Barbados, and his eventual arrival on Fisher's Island on the Long Island Sound between New York and Rhode Island. Smith describes being mistreated by his master's son, a foiled escape attempt, and finally being able to purchase his freedom and the freedom of his wife and children. The foiled escape attempt is one of those valuable accounts where we have primary source documents that present events from different perspectives (Singer 2007, 2–6).

According to Venture Smith, "My master owned a certain Irishman, named Heddy, who about that time formed a plan of secretly leaving his master. After he had long had this plan in meditation, he suggested it to me. At first I cast a deaf ear to it, and rebuked Heddy for harboring in his mind such a rash undertaking. But after he had persuaded and much enchanted me with the prospect of gaining my freedom by such a method, I at length agreed to accompany him. Heddy next inveigled two of his fellow-servants to accompany us. The place to which we designed to go was the Mississippi. We stole our master's boat, embarked, and then directed our course for the Mississippi River. We mutually confederated not to betray or desert one another on pain of death" (Smith 1896, 16–17).

The runaway slave advertisement published by his enslaver in *The New-York Gazette or, The Weekly Post-Boy* on April 1, 1754, verifies much of Venture Smith's story. According to the advertisement, "Run away from George Mumford of Fisher's-Island, the 27th Instant, four Men Servants, a white Man and Three Negroes, who hath taken a large two-mast Boat, with a square Stern, and a large white Pine Canoe; the Boat's Timbers are chiefly red Cedar. The White Man named Joseph Heday, says he is a Native of Newark, in the Jerseys, a short well set fellow of a rudy complection.... Venture had a Kersey dark colour'd Great Coat, three Kersey jackets, two pair of Breeches of the same, a new cloth colour'd Fly-Coat, with red shaloon lining, a green ratteen Jacket, almost new, a crimson birded stuff ditto, a pair of large Ozenbrigs Trowsers, a new felt hat, two pairs of shoes, one pair new, several pair of Stockings; he is a very tall fellow, 6 feet 2 inches high, thick, square shoulders, large bon'd, mark'd in the face, or scar'd with a knife in his own country" (Hodges and Brown 1994, 49–50).

The location where the events took place, the number of people who tried to escape to freedom, the name of the leader of the group, the use of the boat, and Venture's African origins are all confirmed by Mumford in the advertisement.

3

ABOLITION ON THE MARGINS

So far as I am personally concerned, I feel no interest
in any history of it that may be written. It is enough for me
that every yoke is broken and every bondman set free.
Yet there are lessons to be drawn from it
that cannot fail to be serviceable to posterity....
There are innumerable battles yet to be fought for the right,
many wrongs to be redressed, many evil customs abolished,
many usurpations overthrown, many deliverances wrought;
and those who shall hereafter go forth to defend the righteous cause,
no matter at what cost or with what disparity of numbers,
cannot fail to gain strength and inspiration from
an intelligent acquaintance with the means and methods
used in the Anti-Slavery movement.

—William Lloyd Garrison,
in a letter written March 17, 1873

IN HER GROUNDBREAKING BOOK *THE SLAVE'S CAUSE: A HISTORY OF ABOLITION* (2016), Manisha Sinha documents the radical nature of the American movement to end slavery as well as the crucial role played by both free blacks and enslaved Africans, especially black abolitionists based in New York. Sinha argues persuasively that "[s]lave resistance," especially slave rebellions, "not bourgeois liberalism, lay at the heart of the abolition movement" (Sinha 2016, 1). During the Civil War, black and white abolitionists continually pushed to expand the struggle to encompass not just an end to slavery, but emancipation combined with respect for the freedman's humanity and recognition of full citizenship rights. Sinha credits abolitionists for stimulating a wave of social movements and laying the basis for democracy in the contemporary United States (ibid., 586–91).

However, the nature of abolitionism and abolitionists in the United States and their role in ending slavery and precipitating the American Civil War continued to be debated even as the nation commemorated the 150th anniversary of the Emancipation Proclamation and the passage of the Thirteenth Amendment to the Constitution, formally ending slavery in the United States. In February 2015, *The New York Times* published an opinion essay by Jon Grinspan, curator of political history at the Smithsonian National Museum of American History, that claimed "abolitionism," a movement much "lauded" in the United States for ending slavery was in reality a "flop." Grinspan also asserted, "Abolitionism's surprise victory has misled generations about how change gets made" (Grinspan 2015, SR6).

Grinspan argued that Southern intransigence and "mistakes," not Northern abolitionists, brought on the Civil War and the end of slavery. He quoted a statement by Frederick Douglass to the affect that Northern abolitionists should "Thank God!— The slaveholders themselves have saved our cause from ruin" (Foner and Taylor 2000, 445). The quote is from the May 1861 edition of *Douglass' Monthly*. Unlike Grinspan, Douglass did not believe abolitionism was a failure. According to Douglass, the South had "exposed the throat of slavery to the keen knife of liberty, and have given a chance to all the righteous forces of the nation to deal a death-blow to the monster evil of the nineteenth century" (ibid.). The slaveholders had given Northern abolitionists the opportunity they had fought for during the previous three decades.

Grinspan concluded that the popular misconception that the abolitionist movement ended slavery has contributed to a mistaken belief in the United States that radical activism produces social change. Instead, he credits the "flexibility of the Northern moderates, those flip-floppers who voted against abolition before they voted for it," with ending "250 years of slavery." Grinspan's conclusions, the prominence they received in *The New York Times*, the American newspaper of record, and the volume of responses, underscore the ongoing significance of the debate over the role played by American abolitionists as their campaign moved from the political margins to successful fruition.

Sinha and Grinspan are certainly not the first historical commentators to view American abolitionists through their own political lens. Consensus school historian Bernard Bailyn, writing in 1971, considered the call for abolition of slavery during the early years of the new nation a potentially dangerous and certainly divisive "fanaticism" (Bailyn 1973, 29). In an early edition of *The American Pageant: A History of the Republic* (Bailey and Kennedy 1983), a history textbook first published in 1966 and designed for college survey courses, the authors, Thomas Bailey and David Kennedy, described abolitionist writing as "merciless nagging" (Bailey and Kennedy 1983, 342), their speeches as "tongue-lashings" (ibid., 341), compared agents on the Underground Railroad to "cattle thieves" (ibid., 350), and charged that a generation of New England historians descended from abolitionists had written American history with a pro-abolitionist, "anti-Southern

bias" (ibid., 327). William Lloyd Garrison and the "extreme Garrison wing of the abolition movement" were dismissed as a "lunatic fringe" (ibid., 340).

Left-wing historians similarly interpreted the campaign to abolish slavery in the
United States in ways that forwarded their political agenda. Herbert Aptheker, a communist historian with roots in the political struggles of the 1930s, subtitled a monograph
Abolitionism (Boston: Twayne 1989) "A Revolutionary Movement." Aptheker's thesis was
that abolitionists led a revolutionary movement to transform the United States that cul-
minated in the American Civil War. Unfortunately for both freedmen and for American
society as a whole, their revolutionary goals were betrayed during the Reconstruction
period when U.S. political and economic leaders surrendered to reconciliation and racism.

One of the things that mark social movements is that they lack both the ideological and political cohesion Bailyn and Aptheker tend to credit the abolitionist movement
with. They are more or less temporary coalitions of people with diverse and sometimes
conflicting interests rather than disciplined revolutionary parties with clear goals and
organizational discipline. In addition, no matter how militant some individuals may be,
for most movement participants they are fundamentally reformist in nature, seeking to
change society but not transform it. In my view, the reformist nature of the American abolitionist movement and its lack of cohesion are aspects that placed a greater importance
on the role of abolitionists, particularly black abolitionists, who pushed the coalition to
increased radicalism.

In recent years, historians and the Hollywood film industry have debated the role of
abolitionists in the end of American slavery. In 2011, historian Eric Foner was awarded the
Pulitzer Prize, the Bancroft Prize, and the Lincoln Prize for his book *The Fiery Trial: Abraham
Lincoln and American Slavery*, where he traced what he saw as "the evolution of Lincoln's
ideas and policies about slavery from his early life through his career in the Illinois legislature in the 1830s, his term in Congress in the 1840s, his emergence as a leader of the new
Republican party in the 1850s, and his presidency during the Civil War" (Foner 2010, xvi).

In 2012, Daniel Day Lewis starred as Abraham Lincoln in a movie directed by
Steven Spielberg that was loosely based on sections of *Team of Rivals: The Political Genius
of Abraham Lincoln*, by Doris Kearns Goodwin (2005), and focused on political infighting
that led up to the passage of the Thirteenth Amendment. In 2013, the Public Broadcasting
System (PBS) aired a three-part documentary specifically on the role played by individual abolitionists in the struggle to end slavery in the United States. Foner returned to the
role played by abolitionists in ending slavery in 2015 with the publication of *Gateway to
Freedom, The Hidden History of the Underground Railroad* (2015). In *Gateway to Freedom*,
Foner credited abolitionists with precipitating the Civil War and the end of slavery through
their role in promoting the Underground Railroad, challenging fugitive slave laws, and
driving the South into rebellion.

I have long been concerned with the efficacy of social movements and their ability to promote positive, progressive, change. I think Garrison was right that an examination of the antislavery or abolitionist movement provides both valuable "lessons" and "inspiration" for those engaged in redressing wrongs and the defense of a "righteous cause" (Garrison 1981, 271–72).

An examination of the pre–Civil War movement to end the enslavement of Africans in the United States not only provides important insights into the history of this country, but into the life cycle of social movements in general. During the course of approximately three decades between 1831 and 1863, abolitionists moved from marginalization in the North with sharp internal divisions over issues such as whether the United States Constitution was a pro-slavery or antislavery document to achieving their primary goal, the emancipation of enslaved Africans (Foner 2006, 28). As late as 1859, prominent Northerners such as the poet and newspaper editor William Cullen Bryant still believed that slavery could be contained in the South where it would gradually but inevitably become extinct. He argued:

> The great body of the northern people have no desire nor intention to interfere with slavery within its present limits, except by persuasion and argument. They are unalterably opposed to the spread of it, as the south ought to be, but they are willing to leave the extinction of it in the states to the certain influences of commerce, of good sense, of the sentiment of justice and truth, and the march of civilization (Brown 1971, 408).

However, in 1861, despite the vehemence of pro-slavery advocates, the unwillingness of prominent Northerners to challenge the institution, the South, and support for slavery at the highest levels of the local, state, and national governments, Union troops marched into battle singing "John Brown's Body" in a war that finally brought an end to slavery in the United States. But victory divided the abolitionist coalition. Once the goal of ending slavery in the United States was achieved with passage of the Thirteenth Amendment to the Constitution, the forces that opposed slavery fractured and substantive freedom for the former slaves was largely postponed for more than one hundred years (Foner 2006).

While I am convinced that abolitionist agitation against the Fugitive Slave Act and the Compromise of 1850 was a turning point in the history of the movement and the nation, among the questions I am still grappling with is why the movement and its cause, which received a tremendous boost from these actions, seemed to lessen in importance for much of the rest of the decade? If it were not for Harriet Beecher Stowe's *Uncle Tom's Cabin* (1852) and John Brown's actions in Bloody Kansas and at Harpers Ferry, the movement might have largely disappeared from public attention. It may be that in an era before mass media, instant communication, and rapid transportation it was just not possible to sustain the level of activity and public notice the movement produced in 1850 and 1851.

It may also be that an ebb-and-flow pattern, rather than a linear but gradual groundswell may be inherent to the nature of social movements. For example, the modern African American civil rights movements had major successes in the 1950s with the *Brown* decision, the Montgomery boycott, and the desegregation of Little Rock High School, but it was six years after Little Rock that public attention focused on events in Birmingham and the March on Washington (Branch 1988). Abolitionists labored to end slavery throughout the thirty-year period discussed here, but their impact was contingent on events in the broader world over which they had no control.

Also, for much of the 1850s decade, the Senate and the courts were the focus of attention as they sought a solution that would both preserve the union and protect slavery in the South. It was their inability to find a successful solution with Popular Sovereignty and the *Dred Scott* decision that led to the fracturing of the Democratic Party, the election of a Northern regional candidate as president in 1860, Southern secession, and the national crisis that thrust slavery into the forefront of national consciousness and led to emancipation. It was this national crisis that caused Northerners to rapidly turn against the South and slavery and ultimately created the possibility for abolition to move from marginalization to emancipation.

Charles Tilly is perhaps the preeminent student of social movements. In his research and writing, he focused on the history of what he called "contentious politics" in nineteenth and twentieth-century Europe, which included the earliest modern social movements. Tilly argued that the democratization processes accompanying the Industrial Revolution in England and the French Revolution in continental Europe promoted social movements because they legitimized the idea of citizenship rights and public participation in decision making (Tilly 1999, 257–58; 2004, 3–5, 330). In many ways, the abolitionist movement in the United States was a classic Tillyan social movement consisting of "multiple and changing actors" that mounted "a sustained challenge to power holders in the name of a population living under the jurisdiction of those power holders by means of repeated public displays of that population's worthiness, unity, numbers, and commitment" (Tilly 1999, 256–57).

In important ways the abolitionist movement was a narrow movement within the broader Free Soil movement that wanted to keep slavery out of the Western territories but did not oppose, or actively oppose, slavery in the South (Foner 1970; Kraditor 1969). Its dramatic shift from marginalization to a significant force in society is similar to other American social movements, such as the labor and women's suffrage movements, antiwar movements, the twentieth-century African American civil rights movement, and Protestant evangelicalism, that took on greater prominence as conditions within American society changed.

The fractiousness and the ideological rigidity of opponents of slavery, especially in the 1840s, was a product of frustration and isolation that led to the formation of ideologically purer organizations. Part of this was a result of relatively distinct strands that

coalesced into the abolitionist movement. Among whites, they included gradual abolitionists who opposed slavery but were willing to see it fade away into the historical dustbin;
covert, and sometimes overt, racists who were probably more concerned with colonizing
freed blacks out of the country than with emancipation itself; political abolitionists who
preferred to work against slavery through established government and electoral channels; religious Protestant evangelicals such as the Tappan brothers who were involved in
range of reform movements against what they perceived as sinful behavior but who also
held conservative views on the place of women in society and the movement; and moral-
ists like Garrison and his followers, who were much more focused on the evils of slavery
than other concerns and were also more accepting of an activist role for women in the
movement (Sinha 2016, 224–27). Black abolitionists could belong to any of these strands,
especially if they were willing to accept secondary roles. Some, like Frederick Douglass,
bridged factions or shifted alliances. At the 1851 meeting of the American Anti-Slavery
Society in Syracuse, New York, Douglass broke with the Garrisonians and announced
support for the Liberty Party's political campaign to end slavery, precipitating a nasty split
with Garrison that ended up with two of the nation's leading abolitionists not speaking
with each other for years (Sinha 2016, 492–95). However, black abolitionists were more
likely to be what David Ruggles called "practical abolitionists," less wedded to particular
ideologies, and more interested in activities designed to free enslaved Africans and protect
freedom seekers. For, as Ruggles argued, "mere words are nothing—action is everything"
(Harding 1981, 139).

Arthur Tappan and Lewis Tappan established the first Anti-Slavery Society in New
York City in 1831. A New England Anti-Slavery Society was formed a year later. The local
associations became a national organization, the American Anti-Slavery Society (AASS),
following an 1833 meeting in Philadelphia. By 1840, the AASS had 250,000 members,
two thousand semiautonomous local chapters, and sponsored over twenty publications.
Disagreements within the abolitionist movement included heated debates over whether
the Constitution was a pro-slavery document, gradualism versus immediate and unconditional emancipation, racial equality, women's rights and participation in the antislavery
movement, obeying "immoral" laws, and finally, violent resistance. A rival group, the
American and Foreign Anti-Slavery Society, broke off in 1839–40 over the involvement
of women in AASS campaigns as lecturers and as members of its executive committee
and the group's opposition to involvement in electoral politics. Members of the breakaway
organization drifted through political organizations including the Liberty Party (1840–48)
and the Free Soil Party (1848–1854), and eventually aligned with the Republican Party.
These political parties, as Liberty Party organizer Salomon Chase argued, were antislavery in principle. This meant they were opposed to what they saw as the disproportionate
influence of Southern slave power in the national government and to slavery's extension,

but did not necessarily support the abolition of slavery in the South (Thomas 1965, 1–5; Ferrell 2006, 48–52, 79; Foner 1970, 78–82).

Meanwhile, black abolitionists, who were demanding full citizenship rights as well as an end to slavery, organized through their own National Negro conventions between 1831 and 1864. Referring to the paternalism of white abolitionists, an 1839 editorial in New York City's *Colored American* declared, "As long as we let them think and act for us, as long as we will bow to their opinions, and acknowledge that their word is counsel, and their will is law; so long they will outwardly treat us as men, while in their hearts they still hold us as slaves" (Quarles 1969, 168–96; Litwack 1965, 144). An unsigned article in the June 27, 1840, *Colored American*, possibly written by Ruggles, declared,

> As long as we attend the Conventions called by our white friends we will be looked upon as playing second fiddle to them. They will always form the majority at such Conventions, and the sentiments and opinions thus promulgated will go forth as the sentiments and opinions of white men, but when we act then they will see that the worm is turning. . . . We should enter upon the work with the honest conviction that we are doing what no others can do for us, and what cannot be effected under any other circumstances (Harding 1981, 139).

Abolition's organizational successes during this period were the product of sustained campaigns such as antislavery petition drives, fund raising to support *Amistad* captives and freedom seekers facing deportation South to reenslavement, publications, mailings, and meetings. After decades of marginalized struggle, ineffective and often fractious, it finally succeeded in mobilizing broader support because of the failure of its opposition in both the North and South after 1850 to arrive at a politically acceptable compromise that would protect the institution of slavery in the South while preventing its expansion into the West. This failure and the political suspicion it generated in the different regions of the country created opportunities for abolitionists to challenge the legitimacy of slavery and thrust into the national spotlight black abolitionists such as Frederick Douglass, Henry Highland Garnet, and Jermain Loguen, whose existence as educated, articulate, literate human beings challenged the premises that chattel slavery rested upon.

There are several keys to understanding the forces that marginalized and sustained the abolitionist movement while it remained trapped on the periphery of national consciousness in the 1830s and 1840s. In the North, slavery was dismissed as a Southern institution and attention was focused on economic growth, westward expansion, and the assimilation of waves of new immigrant groups. Meanwhile, Northern bankers, merchants, and industrialists were busy profiting from the financing of Southern and Caribbean plantations, providing planters with tools, materials, and luxury products, the domestic slave trade and the illegal continuing transatlantic slave trade, and the sale of slave-produced commodities (Beckert 2015; Baptist 2014).

As an example of Northern business attitudes toward slavery, after the annual meeting of the American Anti-Slavery Society in New York City in May 1835, Reverend Samuel J. May was approached by someone he described as "a partner in one of the most prominent mercantile houses in the city." According to May, he was told:

> "[W]e are not such fools as not to know that slavery is a great evil, a great wrong. But it was consented to by the founders of our Republic. It was provided for in the Constitution of our Union. A great portion of the property of the Southerners is invested under its sanction; and the business of the North, as well as the South, has become adjusted to it. There are millions upon millions of dollars due from Southerners to the merchants and mechanics of this city alone, the payment of which would be jeopardized by any rupture between the North and the South. We cannot afford, sir, to let you and your associates succeed in your endeavor to overthrow slavery. It is not a matter of principle with us. It is a matter of business necessity. We cannot afford to let you succeed. And I have called you out to let you know, and to let your fellow-laborers know, that we do not mean to allow you to succeed. We mean, sir," said he, with increased emphasis, "we mean, sir, to put you Abolitionists down—by fair means if we can, by foul means if we must" (May 1869, 127–28).

The position of Northern business leaders on slavery changed little during the ensuing decades. In January 1861, New York City mayor Fernando Wood proposed that the city secede from the union along with the South to better maintain business ties (Singer 2008, 81). At the same time, delegations consisting of New York's business and financial leaders traveled to Washington, D.C., where they lobbied Congress for concessions to the South in order to avoid secession and possible civil war (Foner 1941, 248–49).

A major force sustaining the abolitionist movement was its rootedness in Protestant evangelicalism. In the eighteenth century, abolition was part of the dissenter, especially the Quaker, tradition (Ferrell 2006, 9–14). In the nineteenth century, Calvinist and Methodist congregations not only provided abolitionists with a Christian spiritual community, but these denominations also served as abolitionist communities whose members had faith in the eventual end of slavery. Milton Sernett in *North Star Country* (2002) describes the connections between religious revivalism in upstate New York's "Burned-over District" and antislavery sentiment during the 1820s and 1830s (Sernett 2002, 3–23). At the center of these movements was Charles Grandison Finney, a young lawyer turned Presbyterian minister, who traveled between frontier towns in the area. Finney preached a doctrine of free will, including the will to abandon the sinful practice of human slavery. According to one estimate, there were more than 1,300 revivals in upstate New York between 1825 and 1835 (ibid., 16). One of the practices that empowered Finney's campaigns was his permitting women to give public religious testimony in mixed gender meetings, an experience that contributed to the growth of the women's rights movement of the 1840s (ibid., 17).

While Finney was not active as an abolitionist, he inspired others who became leaders in the movement. In 1827, his followers founded the Oneida Academy on a farm west of Utica on the Erie Canal. In July 1832, students at the now called Oneida Institute organized New York State's first antislavery society (Sernett 2002, 28–29). Black abolitionist ministers Henry Highland Garnet and Alexander Crummell both attended Oneida (ibid., 70). Protestantism also provided a home and a way of making a living for other leading black abolitionists including Jermain Loguen of Syracuse and Samuel Ringgold Ward of Cortland.

The broader "abolitionist" movement was based on the Free Soil, Free Labor (FSFL) ideology described by Eric Foner (1970) that developed in the Liberty Party in the 1840s and became identified with the emerging Republican Party in the 1850s. While these were initially third parties engaged in electoral politics and were not classical Tillyan social movements, they were deeply involved in shaping the way Americans, especially in the North and West, viewed their country. In some ways their ideology was similar to the yeoman farmer tradition championed by Thomas Jefferson in the 1780s and Jacksonian democracy in the 1830s, but in this case the extension of slavery into the new western states and territories and the political power of the slave South were seen as anathema to liberty, prosperity, and social mobility for the white population of the nation.

The FSFL parties and the abolitionists appealed to overlapping constituencies; the FSFL parties were broad enough that they included antislavery activists such as William Seward of New York and accommodationists with slavery like the supporters of Abraham Lincoln who, in order to preserve the Union, could live with slavery in the South as long as the institution was not permitted to extend West. Eric Foner, the premier historian writing about the pre- and post–Civil War era argues that while Lincoln himself hated slavery, he "revered the Union and the Constitution and was willing to compromise with the South to preserve them. His speeches combined the moral fervor of the abolitionists with the respect for order and the Constitution of more conservative northerners" (Foner 2006, 31).

While some abolitionists functioned within the FSFL parties, others could not. Garrisonians rejected the Constitution as a pro-slavery document and political participation in the system as an accommodation to injustice. On July 4, 1844, Garrison publicly burned a copy of the U.S. Constitution, condemning it as a "Covenant with Death, an Agreement with Hell." Earlier, in an editorial in *The Liberator*, he wrote:

> There is much declamation about the sacredness of the compact which
> was formed between the free and slave states, on the adoption of the

Constitution.... We pronounce it the most bloody and heaven-daring arrangement ever made by men for the continuance and protection of a system of the most atrocious villainy ever exhibited on earth.... It was a compact formed at the sacrifice of the bodies and souls of millions of our race, for the sake of achieving a political object—an unblushing and monstrous coalition to do evil that good might come. Such a compact was, in the nature of things and according to the law of God, null and void from the beginning. No body of men ever had the right to guarantee the holding of human beings in bondage. Who or what were the framers of our government, that they should dare confirm and authorize such high-handed villainy—such flagrant robbery of the inalienable rights of man—such a glaring violation of all the precepts and injunctions of the gospel—such a savage war upon a sixth part of our whole population? ... They had no lawful power to bind themselves, or their posterity ... by such an unholy alliance. It was not valid then—it is not valid now.... If the Union can be preserved by treading upon the necks, spilling the blood, and destroying the souls of millions of your race, we say it is not worth a price like this, and that it is in the highest degree criminal for you to continue the present compact. Let the pillars thereof fall—let the superstructure crumble into dust—if it must be upheld by robbery and oppression (Garrison 1832, 52).

Other abolitionists were willing to participate in electoral politics but were incensed by the Republican Party's willingness to accept the continuation of slavery in the South. Gerrit Smith and William Goodell, leaders of the Liberty Party in New York State, refused to support any group that recognized the constitutionality of slavery anywhere in the United States (Foner 1970, 302). However, despite the fact that some of its most prominent adherents rejected the FSFL parties, the abolitionist movement benefited from this broader movement and ideological debate.

For much of the 1840s and 1850s, the abolitionist movement was a coalition internally divided over issues such as whether the United States Constitution was a pro-slavery document, immediate versus gradual emancipation, the possibility for recolonizing freed blacks in the Caribbean or Africa, broadening the movement to include women's rights and equal participation, and whether, once freed, blacks should receive full citizenship rights. Frederick Douglass argued that racism was "the greatest of all obstacles in the way of the anti-slavery cause" (Foner 2011, 122). In the 1840s, Horace Greeley, editor of the *New York Tribune* wrote that equal suffrage for blacks in New York State would fail if put to a popular referendum, because of white prejudice (Foner 1970, 262–63). In the 1850s, Democrats repeatedly charged that Republicans wanted to grant blacks full equality, which they did not, and even branded it the "Nigger Party" (ibid., 263). Some Republicans, especially in the West, answered these charges by declaring themselves the real "white man's party" (ibid., 265). At the outbreak of the Civil War only five New England states permitted blacks to vote in elections on the same basis as whites (Foner 2010, 94). Eric Foner argues in the Pulitzer Prize–winning *The Fiery Trial* (2010) that as a result of this intense racism, when Lincoln ran for president of the United States in 1860, he was careful not to identify the Republican Party with "Negro equality" (ibid., 133).

William Lloyd Garrison, who published *The Liberator* in Boston, Massachusetts, was the archetypal Tillyan political entrepreneur dedicating his life to the campaign to end slavery in the United States. I also include Gerrit Smith, the Tappan brothers, Frederick Douglass, and Henry Highland Garnet, all of New York, in this category. In the first issue of *The Liberator* (January 1831), Garrison included an address to the public where he explained:

> During my recent tour for the purpose of exciting the minds of the people by a series of discourses on the subject of slavery, every place that I visited gave fresh evidence of the fact, that a greater revolution in public sentiment was to be effected in the free states—*and particularly in New-England*—than at the south. I found contempt more bitter, opposition more active, detraction more relentless, prejudice more stubborn, and apathy more frozen, than among slave owners themselves (Fredrickson 1968, 22).

Although Garrison was prone to be vitriolic in his condemnation of a Northern audience he felt had rejected the antislavery cause, there is an element of truth in this statement; the abolitionist movement remained on the margins in the North for most of the three decades preceding the American Civil War. In July 1834, over the course of a week, white mobs attacked black and white abolitionists in New York City. The rioting followed two months of unsubstantiated rumors that the abolitionists were promoting interracial marriage. On July 4, an integrated group of abolitionists were driven out of the Chatham Street Chapel where they gathered to celebrate the seventh anniversary of the end of slavery in New York State. Later in the week, the home of Lewis Tappan, a prominent white abolitionist, was looted and burned. His brother Arthur Tappan's store on Pearl Street in lower Manhattan was stoned. Churches that were viewed as friendly to the abolitionist cause, and the homes of their ministers, were destroyed. In the Five Points district, approximately five hundred black residents were driven out of their homes, which were then sacked and burned (Burrows and Wallace 1999, 556–58).

Between 1834 and 1837, mobs of whites attacked black communities in Boston, Massachusetts, Cincinnati, Ohio, Hartford, Connecticut, Pittsburgh, Pennsylvania, and Utica, New York. They also attacked white abolitionists. Theodore Weld was stoned and severely injured by a mob in Troy, New York, that refused to permit him to speak in a local church (Sinha 2016, 228). The renowned American poet John Greenleaf Whittier was stoned in Concord, New Hampshire, when he tried to speak out against slavery. Garrison was dragged through the streets of Boston with a rope and threatened with lynching. In 1837, a white abolitionist was murdered in Alton, Illinois, while defending a printing press used to publish antislavery literature (Ferrell 2006, 54–58; Cook 1999, 128–66). Manisha Sinha's *The Slave's Cause* cites more than seventy incidents of anti-abolitionist violence in the North, including forty-six incidents between 1834 and 1837 alone (Sinha 2016, 232).

Many in the North blamed the abolitionists for their own troubles. In 1835, the *New York Commercial Advertiser* charged abolitionists with "having distracted churches, destroyed the peace of families and communities, embarrassed the literary and religious institutions, menaced the property and even the existence of the union, involved the officers of our government in dangerous perils, and created the most appalling apprehensions of a civil and servile war" (Ferrell 2006, 47).

Of course antislavery sentiments and abolitionists were not welcomed in the south either. In 1835, when the Tappan brothers organized to flood the South with antislavery literature, white mobs in Charleston, South Carolina, stole and burned the mailbags. A town in Louisiana offered a $50,000 reward for the capture of Arthur Tappan dead or alive and the mayor of Brooklyn, New York, at that time an independent city, had to arrange for evening patrols in Brooklyn Heights to protect Tappan and his home (Burrows and Wallace 1999, 559–60).

Support for the abolition of slavery among political leaders and the vast majority of white voters was not much greater when Senator Daniel Webster of Massachusetts endorsed the Compromise of 1850, which included provisions strengthening federal fugitive slave laws. It made it easier for slaveholders to claim that a black person living in a free state was an escaped slave. The law required Northerners to assist in the recovery of Africans who had escaped from slavery, denied fugitives the right to a jury trial, outlawed state personal liberty laws that blocked enforcement of earlier fugitive slave acts, and made it a federal or national responsibility to enforce the law. In a speech delivered on the seventh of March, 1850, Webster argued the South had "just foundation" for its grievances against the North.

> [T]here has been found at the North, among individuals and among legislators, a disinclination to perform fully their constitutional duties in regard to the return of persons bound to service who have escaped into the free States. In that respect, the South, in my judgment, is right, and the North is wrong. Every member of every Northern legislature is bound by oath, like every other officer in the country, to support the Constitution of the United States; and the article of the Constitution which says to these States that they shall deliver up fugitives from service is as binding in

honor and conscience as any other article.... [T]he North has been too careless of what I think the Constitution peremptorily and emphatically enjoins upon her as a duty (Webster 1914, 618).

Webster also dismissed "Abolition societies" directly, claiming, "I do not think them useful. I think their operations for the last twenty years have produced nothing good or valuable.... I do not mean to impute gross motives even to the leaders of these societies, but I am not blind to the consequences of their proceedings. I cannot but see what mischiefs their interference with the South has produced" (Webster 1914, 619). Webster later led in the prosecution of abolitionists accused of rescuing a freedom seeker in Boston (Holt 2003, 605).

Senator William Seward of New York, who denounced the Fugitive Slave Act and the Compromise of 1850, branded Webster a "traitor to the cause of freedom," but to no avail (Scarry 2001, 149). The Fugitive Slave Act passed the Senate by a vote of 27 Yes, 12 No, and 21 absent or not voting. It was approved in the House of Representatives by a vote of 109 to 75, with the New York State delegation voting overwhelmingly in the negative (Tappan 1850, 12–16).

While passage of the Fugitive Slave Act was a defeat for antislavery forces, it also gave direction to the abolitionist struggle to end slavery. From the writing of the Constitution in 1787 until 1850, the new nation survived because competing political factions, especially regional ones, were balanced in the national government. With the admission of Tennessee as a slave state in 1796 there was an equal number of "free" (or almost free) and slave states, which meant the North and South had equal representation in the United States Senate. However, with the admission of California as a free state without a paired slave state, the electoral balance was broken. The South hesitantly accepted this new reality, contingent on Northern promises to respect the sanctity of Southern slave property and federal enforcement of fugitive slave laws.

Organized defiance of fugitive slave laws gave black and white abolitionists the wedge they needed to separate the North and South and challenge slavery. Both armed struggle and civil resistance started immediately, at Christiana, Pennsylvania, in September and at Syracuse, New York, less than a month later (Katz 1974; Sernett 2002, 136–45).

TEACHING NOTES

Black Suffrage and the Demand for Full Citizenship Rights

QUESTIONS TO CONSIDER

1. Why did the goals of black and white opponents of slavery differ?

2. Do these differences in their goals help explain the failure to develop a more racially just society after the Civil War and continuing racial inequality in the United States today?

In December 1840, the New York *Colored American* published a declaration from the "New York State Convention of Colored Citizens, to the People of the State." It was signed by the convention president Austin Steward and secretaries Charles L. Reason, Henry Highland Garnet, and William H. Topp (Gellman and Quigley 2003, 236–48). In the declaration, black abolitionists denounced the 1821–22 New York State Constitution, which used property requirements to effectively bar black New Yorkers from voting and demanded the restoration of voting rights as acknowledgment of full and equal citizenship. As the result of a $250 property qualification applied only to African American men (neither white nor black women could vote at the time), in 1840, fewer than three hundred black men out of a statewide African American population of almost thirty thousand were eligible to vote (Gellman and Quigley 2003, 236; Berlin and Harris 2005, 142). Earlier, under an 1811 law, black men who could prove their status as free men had been granted the right to vote in New York State if they met the same property requirements as whites (Gellman and Quigley 2003, 65–66). However, as the number of free blacks and potential voters in the state increased, there was growing concern about their potential electoral influence. In 1821, New York City probably had the largest free black population of any municipality in the Western Hemisphere (ibid., 77).

At the 1821 convention, debate over black suffrage and citizenship was marked by open racism and deeply imbued with prejudice, especially among upstate delegates. Erastus Root of Delaware County compared the state's black population to alien residents, "who may hold property and be protected by the laws of your country ... but he is not allowed to vote (Clarke 1821, 99; Gellman and Quigley 2003, 115). He accused black residents of New York City of simply voting according to the wishes of their wealthy employers (Clarke 1821, 100; Gellman and Quigley 2003, 114). During debate, Samuel Young of Saratoga County argued, "The minds of the blacks are not competent to vote. They are too much degraded to estimate the value, or exercise with fidelity and discretion that important right. It would be unsafe in their hands. Their vote would be at the call of the richest purchaser" (Gellman and Quigley 2003, 125). He was supported by Peter R. Livingston of Rhinebeck in Dutchess County, who demanded, "after having thus provided for their emancipation, and welfare, it behooves" the white population of the state "to have regard to the safety of ourselves." He warned the convention that black voters would be "dangerous to your political institutions" and demanded that delegates "put not a weapon into their hands to destroy you." According to Livingston, "Look at that people, and ask your consciences if they are competent to vote.... Out of about fifty petitioners, more than twenty could not even write their names—and those petitioners

were doubtless of the most respectable of the colour. Such persons must always be subject to the influence of the designing; and when they approach the ballot boxes, they are too ignorant to know whether their vote is given to elevate another to office, or to hang themselves upon the gallows" (ibid., 136).

In the end, the 1821 convention approved nearly universal suffrage for white men but the high property threshold for blacks. The constitution was overwhelmingly approved by New York State voters in January 1822 by 74,732 to 41,402 (Gellman and Quigley 2003, 200). In 1846, the constitution was revised again, and once again New York voters rejected equal male suffrage, this time by a vote of 224,336 to 85,406 (Gellman and Quigley 2003, 259).

1821 New York State Constitution

QUESTION TO CONSIDER

Why would New York State establish different voting qualifications for black men?

Article II, Section 1. Every male citizen of the age of twenty-one years, who shall have been an inhabitant of this state one year preceding any election, and for the last six months a resident of the town or county where he may offer his vote; and shall have, within the next year preceding the election, paid a tax to the state or county, assessed upon his real or personal property; or shall by law

be exempted from taxation; or, being armed and equipped according to law, shall have performed, within that year, military duty in the militia of this state; or who shall be exempted from performing militia duty in consequence of being a fireman in any city, town, or village in this state; ... according to law, shall be entitled to vote in the town or ward where he actually (*continues on page 62*)

(*continued from page 61*)

resides, and not elsewhere, for all officers that now are, or hereafter may be, elective by the people; but no man of colour, unless he shall have been for three years a citizen of this state, and for one year next preceding any election, shall be seized and possessed of a freehold estate of the value of two hundred and fifty dollars, over and above all debts and incumbrances charged thereon; and shall have been actually rated, and paid a tax thereon, shall be entitled to vote at any such election. And no person of colour shall be subject to direct taxation unless he shall be seized and possessed of such real estate as aforesaid.

4

NARRATIVES OF SLAVERY AND ESCAPE

The Importance of Solomon Northup

DOCUMENTING THE AMERICAN SOUTH, A WEBSITE DEVELOPED BY THE UNIVERSITY OF North Carolina, has autobiographies and biographies of approximately two hundred freedom seekers or former slaves in a section titled "North American Slave Narratives." An introduction explains that the narratives were promoted, distributed, and often ghost-written by abolitionists to teach white readers in the North and in Europe "about both the realities of slavery as an institution and the humanity of black people as individuals deserving of full human rights." They were "[a]dvertised in the abolitionist press and sold at antislavery meetings throughout the English-speaking world." Although the stories by and about freedom seekers were dismissed as propaganda by pro-slavery forces, the most popular of the narratives were reprinted multiple times and sold thousands of copies.

While a number of formerly enslaved individuals described their memories of the Deep South, most of the people who successfully escaped from enslavement prior to the Civil War were from the Border States. Among the more prominent escapees whose accounts are included in the "Narratives" are Frederick Douglass, Josiah Henson, James Pennington, Harriet Tubman, Samuel Ringgold Ward, and Leonard Black who escaped from Maryland, Jermain Loguen, who was from Tennessee, and Henry Bibb and William Wells Brown, who were from Kentucky. Well-known freedom seekers from other Southern states such as Henry "Box" Brown who escaped from Richmond, Virginia, and Harriet Jacobs from Edenton, North Carolina, are atypical.

According to the guide that accompanies the "Narratives," "Many Southern blacks, slave and free, who had access to evangelical Christianity, embraced it eagerly, adapting it to fit past and present experience. Slave narratives document the gamut of their religious experience and practice." African Americans brought their religious faith with them into freedom and several prominent escapees became Christian ministers, including Loguen, Pennington, Ward, and Black, to support themselves as well as to promote their religious beliefs and challenge slavery.

In many ways, Leonard Black's 1847 memoir *The Life and Sufferings of Leonard Black, a Fugitive from Slavery* is typical of the accounts written or dictated by many of the people who escaped from slavery. It was a sixty-three page pamphlet published by Massachusetts abolitionists to promote both what they considered righteous Christianity and the antislavery cause. A preliminary note by A. M. Macy, a member of a prominent Nantucket, Massachusetts, family, explains, "The book was written substantially by Mr. Black himself, but, in consequence of his deficiency of education … it needed considerable correction to fit it for the press. This work was kindly performed, gratuitously, by a friend of the author, who was, however, very careful to preserve the narrative as nearly unchanged as possible" (Black 1847, 2). In the introduction, Black described the purpose of his memoir. "Born and reared in slavery, I was, of course, deprived of education; and believing that I can be of service to the public in the ministry, I have published this account of my life and sufferings, with the hope that I might realize a sufficient sum from its sale, to enable me to procure a greater degree of education, thereby increasing my usefulness as a preacher" (ibid., 3).

According to Black, he was born in Anne Arundel County, Maryland, about 1817 and spent his childhood in Baltimore. After escaping from slavery in 1837, he became an itinerant preacher and pastor in Portland, Maine, Boston, Massachusetts, and Brooklyn, New York. While a minister at the Concord Baptist Church of Christ in Brooklyn, Black was identified as a fugitive slave and in 1851 he was forced to go into hiding to avoid recapture. At that point, he disappears from the historical record.

Black argued that, according to scripture, "slave-holders are worse than the devil," and he called on Christians to "Resist the devil, and he will flee from you" (Black 1847, 19–20). He described his former master, who was a "professor of religion" and a leader of the Methodist Church" in Baltimore as a "backslider" and "wanderer from God" who was "as cold as though he had never been warmed by the vivifying power of the religion of Jesus Christ" (ibid., 7–8). Black believed that he was "awakened by the Holy Spirit of God, by its divine influence operating on my mind, and … brought to submit to the will of God" (ibid., 20–21). As a reward for his faith, he was delivered from bondage by God "with a strong hand and an outstretched arm, as he did Israel of old" (ibid., 5–6).

For Leonard Black, the promotion of righteous Christianity and opposition to chattel slavery were part of the same ministry. In the conclusion to his memoir, he denounced slavery because enslaved Africans "are kept in darkness, and are borne down under a cruel, cruel oppression! All human rights are denied them as citizens! They are not recognized as men! My old master frequently said, 'he did not believe a d—d nigger had any soul!' " Black charged that "God-defying white man, without semblance of right, with no pretence but might" had reduced enslaved Africans "to mere things, mere chattels, to be bought and sold like hogs and sheep!" (ibid., 50–53).

While Leonard Black's memoir contains repeated reference to the horrors of slavery—his mother and sister were sold to a new owner in New Orleans (Black 1847, 6), he was severely and unjustly beaten by his owner (ibid., 6–7), he was poorly clothed and fed (ibid., 8), and he was exposed to the elements (ibid., 9)—it barely discusses either work or the African slave community. For one master, Black gathered wood (ibid.); for another he minded the charcoal fire (ibid., 11). At one time, he was severely injured while tending a horse (ibid., 12). Other than his relationship with his brothers, Black does not discuss ties with other enslaved Africans or a broader black community. Even his embrace of Christianity seems to take place without the benefit of a connection to a congregation (ibid., 21).

The absence of work and community and the focus on religious salvation in most of the runaway slave narratives, as well as the fact that the events recounted took place in the Border States rather than on Deep South cotton plantations, is what made *Twelve Years a Slave*, Solomon Northup's account of his enslavement in Louisiana so important as an exposé of the slave regime and as a historical document. Ulrich Phillips, who, ironically, was the best-known post–Civil War apologist for the Southern slave regime, a historian who dismissed most slave narratives as "dubious," believed Northup's narrative had "a tone which engages confidence. Its pictures of plantation life and labor are of particular interest" (Phillips 1918, 445).

Frederick Douglass recognized the special nature of Northup's account in reviews published in *The Liberator* and *Frederick Douglass' Paper* (Eakin and Logsdon 1967, ix). Douglass wrote: "For thirty years a *man*, with all a man's hopes, fears and aspirations—with a wife and children to call him by the endearing names of husband and father—and with a home, humble it may be, but still a home ... then for twelve years a thing, a chattel personal, classified with mules and horses. ... It chills the blood to think that such are."

Northup's book was republished in Philadelphia after the Civil War. In an introduction, the editors explained that his narrative made it possible "to understand the exact status of such a people in all its bearings, we can pursue no better course than to live among them, to become one of them, to fall from a condition of freedom to one of bondage, and the outrage of manacles" (Eakin and Logsdon 1967, xxiii–xxiv).

Before discussing the importance of Solomon Northup's memoir and Northup's experience as a slave in Louisiana during the 1840s and early 1850s, I want to acknowledge David Fiske, a retired librarian and independent historian specializing in the Capital Region of New York State for carefully reconstructing Northup's life before and after his kidnapping and enslavement (Fiske, Brown, and Seligman 2013). In the introduction to the 1967 edition of *Twelve Years a Slave*, Sue Eakin and Joseph Logsdon write, "What finally became of Solomon Northup can only be conjectured" (Northup 1853, xxiii). Thanks to Fiske, that is no longer completely true.

Solomon Northup was a free black man and a citizen of New York State. He lived in Saratoga Springs with his wife and three children. Northup was a skilled carpenter and violinist and also worked on the Lake Champlain Canal and on construction of the Troy and Saratoga railroad. In 1841, Solomon Northup was kidnapped by slave traders while on a trip to Washington, D.C., and his freedom papers were stolen. He was transported to Louisiana where he was sold as a slave. In Louisiana, Northup worked on cotton and sugar plantations until he was able to smuggle a letter to his wife and friends in New York. Using a New York State law designed to protect free black citizens from being sold into slavery, they secured his freedom through the courts.

Northup was finally rescued after being enslaved for twelve years. When he returned to New York, abolitionists helped him publish his memoirs as part of their campaign to abolish slavery. Solomon Northup's account is especially important as a historical document because he was able to describe slavery from the point of view of a free man and a skilled worker. It is also unique because Northup was enslaved on plantations in the Deep South.

Northup returned home to his family in Glen Falls, in the Capital District of New York State, in January 1853. Within two weeks he was participating in abolitionist rallies in Troy and Albany alongside Frederick Douglass, Jermain Loguen, and Stephen Myers. The February 11, 1853, issue of *Frederick Douglass' Paper* described Northup as recounting his story of enslavement with "child-like simplicity" (Fiske, Brown, and Seligman 2013, 27). By March, newspapers noted that Northup was collaborating with David Wilson to write his memoir. Sue Eakin and Joseph Logsdon, who essentially rediscovered and republished Northup's narrative in 1967, believe that "the prose style of the narrative clearly belongs to Wilson" and is similar to other books he authored (Eakin and Logsdon 1967, xiv). However, in this case the book largely follows the account told by Northup when he was first interviewed by a *New York Daily Times* reporter in Washington, D.C., during his return from Louisiana to New York (*New York Daily Times* 1853b, 1).

A publication notice for the narrative appeared in the *New York Daily Times* on April 22, 1853, and Frederick Douglass printed excerpts from the document toward the end of the month. The book was widely and positively reviewed and by mid-August 1853 eleven thousand copies had been sold. Ultimately, nearly thirty thousand copies were sold before the outbreak of the Civil War (Eakin and Logsdon 1967, 30–31). Eakin and Logsdon believe the published version of Northup's story was one of the most profitable ventures of its kind (ibid., xv), with Northup personally earning an estimated $3,000 from book sales (ibid., xxii).

To promote his book as well as to earn a living, Northup spoke at abolitionist meetings and rallies in Vermont, New Hampshire, and Massachusetts and in a number of cities along the Erie Canal from Albany to Buffalo. An article in *Frederick Douglass' Paper* reported on a January 1854 lecture in Buffalo where Northup told his story in "plain and candid language" intermingled with "flashes of genuine wit." The audience was "completely enraptured" by Northup's performance. In April and May 1854 a dramatic version of Northup's story was presented in Syracuse. Another version of the play was later staged in Vermont and Massachusetts (Eakin and Logsdon 1967, 38–41).

Jim Burch, who operated the slave pen in Washington, D.C., was arrested for his role in the Northup kidnapping and for selling a free man into slavery. However the D.C. court ruled that testimony by a "colored man" was inadmissible at trial and a slave trader who sometimes worked with Burch testified that Burch was swindled by the kidnappers who sold him a free man that he believed was already enslaved. Burch even accused Solomon Northup of being part of the conspiracy to defraud him. As a result of his machinations and the racism embedded in the legal system, charges against Burch were dismissed and he was released (*New York Daily Times* 1853a, 8). Solomon Northup described the arrest and trial of Burch and his accusations against Northup in the final chapter of his narrative (Eakin and Logsdon 1967, 244–49). In reply to the accusations, Northup wrote: "There may be those who will affect to believe the statement of the slave-trader—those, in whose mind his allegations will weigh heavier than mine. I am a poor colored man— one of the down-trodden and degraded race, whose humble voice may not be heeded by the oppressor—but knowing the truth, and with full sense of my accountability, I do solemnly declare before men, and before God, that any charge or assertion, that I conspired directly or indirectly with any person or persons to sell myself . . . is utterly and absolutely false" (ibid., 249).

In July 1854, Alexander Merrill and Joseph Russell, Northup's actual kidnappers, were apprehended. Merrill was captured in Gloverville, New York, by a group that included Solomon Northup. Russell was arrested while working as a captain on an Erie Canal barge. They were both transported to Ballston Spa in Saratoga County for trial. Court proceedings were repeatedly postponed because of legal issues, including the question whether the kidnapping had taken place in New York State or Washington, D.C., and which locality had jurisdiction. Charges against Merrill and Russell were finally dropped in May 1857. Fiske speculates that the case against the kidnappers had grown cold and that a conviction of white men for illegally selling a free black man into slavery was less likely after the Supreme Court's *Dred Scott* decision in March 1857 (Fiske, Brown, and Seligman 2013, 43–52).

According to Fiske, Northup's last documented public appearance was in Ontario, Canada, around the end of August 1857 (Fiske, Brown, and Seligman 2013, 42). Fiske sorts out different possible explanations for Northup's "disappearance" and believes the most likely was that Northup became a conductor on the Lake Champlain route of the Underground Railroad guiding freedom seekers north through Vermont to Canada (ibid., 57). Northup's activities are mentioned in Wilbur Siebert's history of the Underground Railroad in Vermont (Siebert 1937, 99).

Northup's account of his experience of enslavement may be unique as a historical document. I find especially important his comments on defiance, freedom, religion, the slave community, and work. Page numbers in this section refer to the online version of the original manuscript available at *Documenting the American South* (Northup 1853).

In his narrative, Northup described numerous acts of defiance where he and others risked death as they struggled to maintain a semblance of humanity under inhuman circumstances. In the slave pen in Washington, Northup sustained a severe beating by slave trader Jim Burch because he refused to acknowledge he was a slave. Burch struck him repeatedly with a wooden paddle and a "cat-o'-ninetails" (Northup 1853, 43–46). While on the boat from Washington, D.C., to New Orleans, Northup encountered Arthur, another free black man who had been kidnapped and sold into slavery. As he was brought on board, Arthur "protested, in a loud voice, against the treatment he was receiving, and demanded to be released. His face was swollen, and covered with wounds and bruises, and, indeed, one side of it was a complete raw sore" (ibid., 66). Arthur was a resident of Norfolk, Virginia, who had been "attacked by a gang of persons in an unfrequented street. He fought until his strength failed him. Overpowered at last, he was gagged and bound with ropes, and beaten, until he became insensible." Arthur and Northup plotted a rebellion on the slave ship, resolving to "regain our liberty or lose our lives" (ibid., 71), but were stymied by an outbreak of smallpox.

In Louisiana, Northup was "purchased" from his initial "owner" by John Tibeats, a white itinerant carpenter who had a reputation as a heavy drinker. After they disagreed while working on a construction project, Tibeats ordered Northup to prepare himself for a beating. Northup refused to passively acquiesce, striking and disabling Tibeats. Because of this act of defiance, Northup was nearly hanged by Tibeats and a posse of his friends. His life was saved by the intervention of an agent for his previous "owner" (Northup 1853, 109–17). Tibeats later tried to murder Northup again. This time Northup fled into the swamps that surrounded the Louisiana plantations, where he was hopelessly lost and nearly died (ibid., 136–43).

On several occasions in the manuscript Northup described the desire of the enslaved Africans for freedom, specifically challenging the myth that blacks were content in their enslavement. While reporting on the tensions with Tibeats, he wrote: "Oh! how heavily the weight of slavery pressed upon me then. I must toil day after day, endure abuse and taunts and scoffs, sleep on the hard ground, live on the coarsest fare, and not only this, but live the slave of a blood-seeking wretch, of whom I must stand henceforth in continued fear and dread. Why had I not died in my young years—before God had given me children to love and live for? What unhappiness and suffering and sorrow it would have prevented. I sighed for liberty; but the bondman's chain was round me, and could not be shaken off. I could only gaze wistfully towards the North, and think of the thousands of miles that stretched between me and the soil of freedom, over which a *black freeman may not pass*" (Northup 1853, 125–26).

During a detailed account of the life of an enslaved woman named Patsey whom he met on the Epps plantation where they were picking cotton, Northup wrote: "It is a mistaken opinion that prevails in some quarters that the slave does not understand the term—does not comprehend the idea of freedom. Even on Bayou Boeuf, where I conceive slavery exists in its most abject and cruel form—where it exhibits features altogether unknown in more northern States—the most ignorant of them generally know full well its meaning. They understand the privileges and exemptions that belong to it—that it would bestow upon them the fruits of their own labors, and that it would secure to them the enjoyment of domestic happiness. They do not fail to observe the difference between their own condition and the meanest white man's, and to realize the injustice of the laws which place it in his power not only to appropriate the profits of their industry, but to subject them to unmerited and unprovoked punishment, without remedy, or the right to resist or to remonstrate" (Northup 1853, 259–60).

Northup believed, "It is not the fault of the slaveholder that he is cruel, so much as it is the fault of the system under which he lives. He cannot withstand the influence of habit and associations that surround him.... There may be humane masters, as there certainly are inhuman ones—there may be slaves well-clothed, well-fed, and happy, as there surely are those half-clad, half-starved and miserable; nevertheless, the institution that tolerates such wrong and inhumanity as I have witnessed, is a cruel, unjust, and barbarous one" (Northup 1853, 206). However, he also argued, "Let them know the heart of the poor slave—learn his secret thoughts—thoughts he dare not utter in the hearing of the white man; let them sit by him in the silent watches of the night—converse with him in trustful confidence, of 'life, liberty, and the pursuit of happiness,' and they will find that ninety-nine out of every hundred are intelligent enough to understand their situation, and to cherish in their bosoms the love of freedom, as passionately as themselves" (ibid., 207).

In a number of places in the text Northup, who considered himself a religious man, described what he saw as the religious hypocrisy of Southern whites. On the William Ford plantation, enslaved Africans "usually spent our Sabbaths at the opening, on which days our master would gather all his slaves about him, and read and expound the Scriptures. He sought to inculcate in our minds feelings of kindness towards each other, of dependence upon God—setting forth the rewards promised unto those who lead an upright and prayerful life. Seated in the doorway of his house, surrounded by his man-servants and his maid-servants, who looked earnestly into the good man's face, he spoke of the loving kindness of the Creator, and of the life that is to come. Often did the voice of prayer ascend from his lips to heaven, the only sound that broke the solitude of the place" (Northup 1853, 97). Ford's wife gave one of the other slaves a copy of the Bible and Northup would secretly read it to him. Other whites, learning about the gift, remarked "that a man like Ford, who allowed his slaves to have Bibles, was 'not fit to own a nigger' " (ibid., 98).

According to Northup, Ford's brother-in-law also read "the Bible to his slaves on the Sabbath, but in a somewhat different spirit" (Northup 1853, 127). He focused on passages that demanded servants obey their masters, particularly the twelfth chapter of Luke: "And that servant which knew his lord's will, and prepared not himself, neither did according to his will, shall be beaten with many stripes" (ibid., 128).

Northup's discussion of slave community on Louisiana plantations permeates the entire document and only a few examples are presented here. The narrative includes an extended discussion of the Christmas season and its importance to the slave community because it provided the "only respite from constant labor the slave has through the whole year" (Northup 1853, 213). It was also one of the few occasions when people were well fed or had the opportunity to visit or gather together with enslaved Africans from neighboring plantations. As a result, marriages were "frequently contracted during the holidays, if such an institution may be said to exist among them. The only ceremony required before entering into that 'holy estate,' is to obtain the consent of the respective owners. It is usually encouraged by the masters of female slaves. Either party can have as many husbands or wives as the owner will permit, and either is at liberty to discard the other at pleasure. The law in relation to divorce, or to bigamy, and so forth, is not applicable to property, of course" (ibid., 221).

I think Solomon Northup's most important contribution in the manuscript is the insight he brings to work in the South from his perspective as a skilled worker who had been a free man. There has been significant debate over the efficiency and profitability of slavery in the American South. Eugene Genovese, in *The Political Economy of Slavery*), argued, "The South's greatest economic weakness was the low productivity of its work force" (Genovese 1965, 26). He promoted a thesis developed by sociologist Max Weber that "slave economies normally manifest irrational tendencies that inhibit economic development and endanger social stability" (ibid., 16). An alternative perspective was advanced by Robert Fogel and Stanley Engerman in *Time on the Cross* (1974), a two-volume book based on quantitative studies. They argued that agricultural production on Southern plantations was both efficient and profitable.

While most enslaved Africans had little incentive to apply themselves as either problem solvers or productive workers, Northup invested in work as a way to maintain his sanity and humanity. From Northup's perspective, much of the work he observed or participated in was poorly organized, often undermined by disrespect for and brutal treatment of the work force. Northup's near-fatal dispute with Tibeats, recounted above, grew out of an argument over which nails to use on a project (Northup 1853, 109). While working for William Ford, Northup was placed in charge of transporting lumber from Ford's mill to construction sites. The lumber was usually shipped on wagons using muddy, nearly impassable roads. Northup supervised the dredging and unblocking of streams so the lumber could be moved more efficiently and economically by raft (ibid., 98).

Northup provided extended descriptions of cotton and sugar production on the plantation of Edward Epps, where he lived and worked for ten years before being freed, the deployment of slave labor, and the role of the driver in agricultural production. Extended excerpts are included in the Teaching Notes section at the end of this chapter.

Northup detailed the seasonal agricultural calendar for both cotton and sugar cane, taking readers through the pre-preparation of the soil, planting, maintenance, and harvesting the crops. He described working conditions, especially during harvest, when enslaved workers were beaten if they failed to maintain the expected pace of work (Northup 1853, 165–66). Because Northup was not particularly adept at cotton picking, Edward Epps often hired him out to work on neighboring "sugar plantations during the season of cane-cutting and sugar-making," tasks for which Northup and Epps believed he was better suited (ibid., 208). Northup often worked in the sugar-house, where the syrup from the cane was processed into refined white sugar (ibid., 211).

While on the Epps plantation, Northup was eventually made a "driver." Drivers were enslaved blacks who worked under the supervision of a white overseer. Their tasks included whipping members of their labor gang who failed to maintain an appropriate pace of work. Drivers wore whips around their necks and "if they fail to use them thoroughly, are whipped themselves" (Northup 1853, 225).

According to Eugene Genovese in *Roll, Jordan, Roll*, drivers were often leaders of the slave community who negotiated, when possible, better conditions with overseers and owners (Genovese 1974, 383–88). Northup explained that, as a driver, "[i]f Epps was present, I dared not show any lenity, not having the Christian fortitude of a certain well-known Uncle Tom sufficiently to brave his wrath, by refusing to perform the office. In that way, only, I escaped the immediate martyrdom he suffered, and, withal, saved my companions much suffering, as it proved in the end" (Northup 1853, 226). However, during his eight years as a driver, he "learned to handle the whip with marvelous dexterity and precision, throwing the lash within a hair's breadth of the back, the ear, the nose, without, however, touching either of them" (ibid., 226). When Epps was in the vicinity, Northup would "commence plying the lash vigorously, when, according to arrangement, they would squirm and screech as if in agony, although not one of them had in fact been even grazed" (ibid., 227).

While in Louisiana, Northup continually thought of the possibility of escape. His best hope, he believed, was to smuggle a letter home informing his family and friends where he was being held. This required acquiring paper, pen, and ink, as well as somehow getting to a post office and convincing white authorities to accept the letter, a series of nearly impossible tasks. After being betrayed by one white man whom he asked for assistance, Northup finally sent a letter to associates in New York with the help of a white Canadian carpenter who was working temporarily in the region. This started the process that eventually ended with Solomon Northup's freedom.

Northup's story is also important because of the way it brought Northern white public attention to the reality of the kidnapping of free black citizens of their states by slavecatchers often working in complicity with local officials. Northup's story was detailed on page of the *New York Daily Times* on January 20, 1853. Coverage took about half of the page and described events from Northup's kidnapping and enslavement in Washington, D.C., through his liberation in Louisiana and return to Washington, D.C., twelve years later to confront his kidnappers in court.

The kidnappings, which had inflamed black communities for decades and led to the formation of vigilance committees, now became an issue for whites. In a sense, it was the Northern version of resentment paralleling Southern anger over what they perceived as the willingness of Northerners to assist freedom seekers in escaping from slavery.

Eric Foner, in *Gateway to Freedom*, estimates that more than three hundred freedom seekers were captured and returned to slavery in the 1850s under the Fugitive Slave Act, including twelve from New York City (Foner 2015, 134). Garrison, in *The Liberator*, estimated the number of free blacks kidnapped and sold into slavery between 1831 and 1860 at one hundred (Wilson 1994, 97). However, between 1825 and 1827 alone, the mayor of Philadelphia unsuccessfully tried to rescue through legal channels approximately twenty-five kidnap victims, mostly children, taken to the expanding cotton regions in the Deep South (Baptist 2014, 190).

Carol Wilson, in *Freedom at Risk: The Kidnapping of Free Blacks in America, 1780–1865* (1994), documents seventy kidnap victims. David Fiske, who pieced together details of Solomon Northup's life after he had been freed, put together a collective biography of fifty-seven kidnap victims, including fifteen from New York (Fiske 2016). Taking into account overlap in the two lists, their total is 122 free black citizens from the North kidnapped and sold into slavery by slavecatchers.

Fiske provides mini-biographies of kidnapping victims based on careful examination of surviving documents. Basically, these are the stories of people who escaped enslavement one way or another. The stories of the misfortunate who were successfully kidnapped, sold, and enslaved are probably lost. Like Northup, George Anderson, George Armstrong, John Hight, and Sarah Taylor were born in New York, tricked with a job offer into leaving home, kidnapped, and finally freed via legal proceedings, although none had the extended time enslaved that Northup had to endure.

George Anderson (Fiske 2016, 52–55) was born about 1827 and as a child he and his family lived in New York City. In 1858, he was offered a job caring for circus horses in Pennsylvania but was brought instead to Richmond, Virginia, where his abductors sold him as a runaway slave from Missouri. Anderson continued to maintain that he was a free man, which aroused local suspicion. Local officials contacted the mayor of New York who verified his story. Anderson and Mason Thomas, one of the kidnappers, were eventually sent to New York City. Court proceedings confirmed that Anderson was a free man while Thomas was convicted and sent to prison.

George Armstrong (Fiske 2016, 55–56) was born free in Jefferson County, New York, in about 1837, near the Thousand Islands, the St. Lawrence River, and the Canadian border. In 1860, while living in Watertown, Armstrong was lured into going to Washington, D.C., to seek work, where his traveling companion tried to sell him into slavery. Armstrong, who was literate, was able to get a message home. His family arranged for legal representation and support from New York State governor Edwin Morgan. Armstrong was released after a court hearing and able to return to home.

John Hight and Daniel Prue (Fiske 2016, 85–89) lived near Geneva, New York. In 1857, they traveled with a white acquaintance named Napoleon Van Tuyl to Columbus, Ohio, with the promise of a job at a hotel. While traveling by train Prue overheard Van Tuyl plotting to sell them into slavery and escaped, but Hight was taken to Covington, Kentucky, and then Louisville to be sold. When New York authorities learned what happened Governor John King sent an agent to recover Hight and apprehend Van Tuyl, who served two years in prison.

In 1858, Sarah Taylor (Fiske 2016, 101–102), a fourteen-year-old who lived in Manhattan, was offered a job as a servant in Newark, New Jersey. She was taken to Washington, D.C., where her "employers," a man and a woman, attempted to sell her. The proprietor of the hotel where they were staying was suspicious and informed New York City authorities, who located Taylor and the kidnappers near Baltimore. Taylor was returned home and the couple was arrested, brought to New York City, and put on trial. The man was convicted and spent six months in jail. There is no record of what happened to the woman.

Other kidnapping cases developed less typically, each in its own way. David Tredwell (Fiske 2016, 107–108) was part of a group of black New Yorkers, some free and some enslaved, who were being illegally transported out of state in 1817 to be sold as slaves in the South. Members of the Hudson Valley Vigilance Committee stopped a boat holding them as prisoners near Poughkeepsie and had the crew arrested and the prisoners freed. Mary Underhill (ibid., 109–11) worked as a servant in New York City in 1819 when she was recruited for a higher-paying job. It turned out to be a trap, however the plot failed when the ship's captain who was supposed to carry Underhill into slavery reported the kidnappers to local authorities. In 1858 Isaac Moore (ibid., 94) was a free black teenager when he was grabbed off the streets of Manhattan and held aboard a ship in the harbor. After four days imprisonment, he was permitted to go on deck. Moore seized the opportunity to jump overboard and reported his kidnapping to the police, but the ship left port before the police could apprehend his kidnappers.

Other victims did not escape so easily. Hester Jane Carr (Fiske 2016, 60–61) was born in Virginia to free parents, probably in 1816. Carr moved to New York in 1835, where she worked in Manhattan as a servant. Carr later accepted a position as a free servant in Georgia, but while in transit there she was sold as a slave. Her former employer in New York verified her free status but Carr died before her legal case was resolved. Henry Dixon (ibid., 70–72) lived in Canada, upstate New York, Ohio, and England, but spent much of his youth in the Rochester area. In 1857, while traveling between Washington, D.C., and

Baltimore, Dixon was kidnapped and transported into slavery in Georgia. Dixon, who was literate, smuggled out a letter that eventually reached family members in Buffalo. New York State governor Myron Clark took up Dixon's case, but after that the story gets confusing. Dixon appears to have had a breakdown while enslaved and initially turned down the opportunity to return home. However, in 1859 his friends were able to purchase his freedom. Stephen Dickinson, Robert Garrison, and Isaac Wright (ibid., 67–70) were crewmen on a steamboat traveling from New York City to New Orleans. While in New Orleans, they were jailed, whipped, and charged with being fugitive slaves. Dickinson was repeatedly sold but finally got work on a ship and returned to New York City. Wright eventually escaped from enslavement in Tennessee with the aid of Joshua Coffin, a white abolitionist, but Garrison was not heard of again. Peter John Lee (ibid., 91–92), arrived in New York from Virginia in 1833, either escaping from slavery, or as he claimed, as a free man. Three years later Virginia authorities charged him with stealing a boat. He was arrested in Rye, New York, quickly put on a boat to Virginia, convicted there of theft, and enslaved. Lee later escaped and probably made his way to Canada.

TEACHING NOTES

Enslaved Labor in the American South

QUESTIONS TO CONSIDER

1. What do we learn about work on Southern plantations from Northup's narrative?

2. Does the involvement of abolitionists in retelling the stories of freedom seekers raise questions about their accuracy and value as historical documents?

3. How can historians confirm the accounts of enslavement told by freedom seekers like Solomon Northup?

Solomon Northup Describes Planting Cotton

The ground is prepared by throwing up beds or ridges, with the plough—back-furrowing, it is called. Oxen and mules, the latter almost exclusively, are used in ploughing. The women as frequently as the men perform this labor, feeding, currying, and taking care of their teams, and in all respects doing the field and stable work, precisely as do the ploughboys of the North.

The beds, or ridges, are six feet wide, that is, from water furrow to water furrow. A plough drawn by one mule is then run along the top of the ridge or center of the bed, making the drill, into which a girl usually drops the seed, which she carries in a bag hung round her neck. Behind her comes a mule and harrow, covering up the seed, so that two mules, three slaves, a plough and harrow, are employed in planting a row of cotton. This is done in the months of March and April.... When there are no cold rains, the cotton usually makes its appearance in a week. In the course of eight or ten days afterwards the first hoeing is commenced. This is performed in part, also, by the aid of the plough and mule. The plough passes as near as possible to the cotton on both sides, throwing the furrow from it. Slaves follow with their hoes, cutting up the grass and cotton, leaving hills two feet and a half apart. This is called scraping cotton. In two weeks more commences the second hoeing. This time the furrow is thrown towards

the cotton. Only one stalk, the largest, is now left standing in each hill. In another fortnight it is hoed the third time, throwing the furrow towards the cotton in the same manner as before, and killing all the grass between the rows. About the first of July, when it is a foot high or thereabouts, it is hoed the fourth and last time. Now the whole space between the rows is ploughed, leaving a deep water furrow in the center. During all these hoeings the overseer or driver follows the slaves on horseback with a whip, such as has been described. The fastest hoer takes the lead row. He is usually about a rod in advance of his companions. If one of them passes him, he is whipped. If one falls behind or is a moment idle, he is whipped. In fact, the lash is flying from morning until night, the whole day long. The hoeing season thus continues from April until July, a field having no sooner been finished once, than it is commenced again (Northup 1853, 163–65).

Treatment of New Enslaved Workers in the Cotton Fields

In the latter part of August begins the cotton picking season. At this time each slave is presented with a sack. A strap is fastened to it, which goes over the neck, holding the mouth of the sack breast high, while the bottom reaches nearly to the ground. Each one is also presented with a large basket that will hold about two barrels. This is to put the cotton in when the sack is filled. The baskets are carried to the field and placed at the beginning of the rows.

When a new hand, one unaccustomed to the business, is sent for the first time

into the field, he is whipped up smartly, and made for that day to pick as fast as he can possibly. At night it is weighed, so that his capability in cotton picking is known. He must bring in the same weight each night following. If it falls short, it is considered evidence that he has been laggard, and a greater or less number of lashes is the penalty.

An ordinary day's work is two hundred pounds. A slave who is accustomed to picking, is punished, if he or she brings in a less quantity than that. There is a great difference (continues on page 76)

(*continued from page 75*)

among them as regards this kind of labor. Some of them seem to have a natural knack, or quickness, which enables them to pick with great celerity [speed], and with both hands, while others, with whatever practice or industry, are utterly unable to come up to the ordinary standard. Such hands are taken from the cotton field and employed in other business (Northup1853, 165–66).

The Cotton Harvest

The cotton grows from five to seven feet high, each stalk having a great many branches, shooting out in all directions, and lapping each other above the water furrow.... Sometimes the slave picks down one side of a row, and back upon the other, but more usually, there is one on either side, gathering all that has blossomed, leaving the unopened boils for a succeeding picking. When the sack is filled, it is emptied into the basket and trodden down. It is necessary to be extremely careful the first time going through the field, in order not to break the branches off the stalks. The cotton will not bloom upon a broken branch. Epps never failed to inflict the severest chastisement on the unlucky servant who, either carelessly or unavoidably, was guilty in the least degree in this respect.

The hands are required to be in the cotton field as soon as it is light in the morning, and, with the exception of ten or fifteen minutes, which is given them at noon to swallow their allowance of cold bacon, they are not permitted to be a moment idle until it is too dark to see, and when the moon is full, they oftentimes labor till the middle of the night. They do not dare to stop even at dinner time, nor return to the quarters, however late it be, until the order to halt is given by the driver.

The day's work over in the field, the baskets are "toted," or in other words, carried to the gin-house, where the cotton is weighed. No matter how fatigued and weary he may be—no matter how much he longs for sleep and rest—a slave never approaches the gin-house with his basket of cotton but with fear. If it falls short in weight—if he has not performed the full task appointed him, he knows that he must suffer. And if he has exceeded it by ten or twenty pounds, in all probability his master will measure the next day's task accordingly (Northup 1853, 166–68).

Solomon Northup Explains Sugar Cane Production

The ground is prepared in beds, the same as it is prepared for the reception of the cotton seed, except it is ploughed deeper. Drills are made in the same manner. Planting commences in January, and continues until April. It is necessary to plant a sugar field only once in three years. Three crops are taken before the seed or plant is exhausted.

Three gangs are employed in the operation. One draws the cane from the rick, or stack, cutting the top and flags from the stalk, leaving only that part which is sound and healthy. Each joint of the cane has an eye, like the eye of a potato, which sends forth a sprout when buried in the soil. Another gang lays the cane in the drill, placing two stalks side by side in such manner that joints will occur once in four or six inches. The third gang follows with hoes, drawing earth upon the stalks, and covering them to the depth of three inches.

In four weeks, at the farthest, the sprouts appear above the ground, and from this time forward grow with great rapidity. A sugar field is hoed three times, the same as cotton, save that a greater quantity of earth is drawn to the roots. By the first of August hoeing is usually over. About the middle of September, whatever is required for seed is cut and tacked in ricks, as they are termed.

In October it is ready for the mill or sugar-house, and then the general cutting begins. The blade of a cane-knife is fifteen inches long, three inches wide in the middle, and tapering towards the point and handle. The blade is thin, and in order to be at all serviceable must be kept very sharp. Every third hand takes the lead of two others, one of whom is on each side of him.

The lead hand, in the first place, with a blow of his knife shears the flags from the stalk. He next cuts off the top down as far as it is green. He must be careful to sever all the green from the ripe part, inasmuch as the juice of the former sours the molasses, and renders it unsalable. Then he severs the stalk at the root, and lays it directly behind him. His right and left hand companions lay their stalks, when cut in the same manner, upon his. To every three hands there is a cart, which follows, and the stalks are thrown into it by the younger slaves, when it is drawn to the sugar-house and ground (Northup 1853, 209–10).

Northup Describes the Sugar-House

The mill is an immense brick building, standing on the shore of the bayou. Running out from the building is an open shed, at least an hundred feet in length and forty or fifty feet in width. The boiler in which the steam is generated is situated outside the main building; the machinery and engine rest on a brick pier, fifteen feet above the floor, within the body of the building. The machinery turns two great iron rollers, between two and three feet in diameter and six or eight feet in length. They are elevated above the brick pier, and roll in towards each other. An endless carrier, made of chain and wood, like leathern belts used in small mills, extends from the iron rollers out of the main building and through the entire length of the open shed. The carts in which the (*continues on page 78*)

(*continued from page 77*)

cane is brought from the field as fast as it is cut, are unloaded at the sides of the shed. All along the endless carrier are ranged slave children, whose business it is to place the cane upon it, when it is conveyed through the shed into the main building, where it falls between the rollers, is crushed, and drops upon another carrier that conveys it out of the main building in an opposite direction, depositing it in the top of a chimney upon a fire beneath, which consumes it. It is necessary to burn it in this manner, because otherwise it would soon fill the building, and more especially because it would soon sour and engender disease. The juice of the cane falls into a conductor underneath the iron rollers, and is carried into a reservoir. Pipes convey it from thence into five filterers, holding several hogsheads each. These filterers are filled with bone-black, a substance resembling pulverized charcoal. It is made of bones calcinated in close vessels, and is used for the purpose of decolorizing, by filtration, the cane juice before boiling. Through these five filterers it passes in succession, and then runs into a large reservoir underneath the ground floor, from whence it is carried up, by means of a steam pump, into a clarifier made of sheet iron, where it is heated by steam until it boils. From the first clarifier it is carried in pipes to a second and a third, and thence into close iron pans, through which tubes pass, filled with steam. While in a boiling state it flows through three pans in succession, and is then carried in other pipes down to the coolers on the ground floor. Coolers are wooden boxes with sieve bottoms made of the finest wire. As soon as the syrup passes into the coolers, and is met by the air, it grains, and the molasses at once escapes through the sieves into a cistern. It is then white or loaf sugar of the finest kind—clear, clean, and as white as snow. When cool, it is taken out, packed in hogsheads, and is ready for market. The molasses is then carried from the cistern into the upper story again, and by another process converted into brown sugar (Northup 1853, 211–13).

5

WE MAY NEVER KNOW
THE REAL HARRIET TUBMAN

IN APRIL 2016, UNITED STATES SECRETARY OF THE TREASURY JACOB LEW ANNOUNCED that Harriet Tubman would be featured on the front of new twenty dollar bills. The design is expected to be made public in 2020 and the new bills will go into circulation later in the decade (Calmes 2016, A1). Tubman was a New Yorker by choice, a self-liberated former slave, a religious evangelical, an Underground Railroad conductor, as well as a Civil War scout and nurse. However, we may never know who the real Harriet Tubman was. There is even debate over her signature achievement as a conductor on the Underground Railroad leading enslaved Africans to freedom in the North and Canada. The number of trips she made to the South is not well documented and estimates range between seven and nineteen, although fourteen is probably the more accurate figure. Similarly, there is disagreement about the number of people she rescued on these trips, from sixty to almost four hundred (Sernett 2007, 56–62). The highly regarded *The Black Abolitionist Papers* (Ripley 1992) credits Tubman with "at least nine [trips] during the 1850s to lead some 180 slaves to freedom" (v. 5, 222).

Tubman's star as a major historical actor has risen and fallen in the past 150 years. In 1994, the National Council for History's U.S. history standards included six references to Harriet Tubman but none for Paul Revere, Thomas Edison, Alexander Graham Bell, or the Wright brothers (Sernett 2007, 1). However, in 2006, when *The Atlantic* magazine asked a panel of ten eminent historians, including Joyce Appleby and Doris Kearns Goodwin, to identify the one hundred most influential figures in American history, Tubman did not make a list that included ten other women, four white abolitionists, and eight African Americans. On this list, Edison ranked as the ninth most influential American, the Wright brothers twenty-third, and Bell as the twenty-fourth (Douthat 2006).

One reason we may never know who the real Harriet Tubman was is because her life has been reconstructed based on limited historical evidence to make what are essentially political points. I find it is useful to compare her tale to accounts of the life of Malcolm X. There is Ossie Davis's noble black prince, the changeling portrayed by Alex

Haley in Malcolm's Autobiography, Spike Lee and Denzel Washington's much cooler and more composed movie version, and the Malcolm buried beneath a mountain of information in Manning Marable's encyclopedic biography (Ellis 2010, 28–29; Haley 1965; Lee 1992; Marable 2011). Similarly, Harriet Tubman has been depicted in messianic terms as the Moses of her people and the Black Joan of Arc, portrayed as the noble Queen of the Underground Railroad, described using military parlance as General Tubman, and presented as a much simpler and maternal Mother Tubman or Aunt Harriet (Sernett 2007, passim).

One of the most powerful iterations of Harriet Tubman is a painting by Jacob Lawrence, depicting a youthful-looking, strong, upright, and barefoot Harriet wearing a red blouse and white skirt while holding a pistol in her hand as she pushes and leads a band of fugitive slaves to freedom. Surviving photographs provide us with very different images of Tubman. One photograph—historian Kate Clifford Larson (2004) dates it to 1887 or 1888 but other accounts differ—shows her with a group of African Americans, three children, two adult males, and an elderly woman. Tubman, to the far left in the picture, is hunched over, her shoulders facing inward. She holds a washing bowl in front of her and wears a long simple dress and a round-brimmed hat. This is certainly not the ferocious heroine portrayed by Lawrence.

There also survive a posed headshot of Tubman and at least five full-length portraits, two standing, and three sitting, as well as a widely circulated woodcut from the first edition of the Bradford (1869) biography where Tubman is portrayed as a Civil War scout carrying a rifle. One of the full-length portraits shows Tubman dressed in plain but formal dress with a neck scarf; it probably was intended as publicity for books. The most intriguing photograph, c. 1895, shows Tubman wearing a headscarf and looking much more like a veteran of the antislavery campaigns and the Civil War. With so many possible variations, it is impossible to tell which image is the real Harriet; or maybe they all are?

Tubman has become a legendary figure in elementary school classrooms and in children's literature. Like Paul Bunyan, John Henry, Betsy Ross, and Davy Crockett, her life is deeply woven into the myths we tell school children about the history of American society. Tubman stands as the personification of the ability of people to persevere against difficulties and injustices. She is probably the subject of more children's books than any African American historical figure, except perhaps Martin Luther King Jr. (Sernett 2007, 22). The Brooklyn Public Library lists twenty-eight biographies of Tubman in its juvenile collection. At the same time, her story has been sanitized, blemishes have been removed, radicalism has been deemphasized, as in the stories of other prominent black rebels, such as Rosa Parks, Martin Luther King Jr., and Frederick Douglass, to make them more appropriate as American heroes.

Because she was illiterate—it was illegal to teach enslaved Africans to read and write in the South—and perhaps also because of a brain injury she suffered when struck in the head in her youth, Harriet Tubman was forced to rely on others to write her story. Her chief spokesperson was Sarah H. Bradford, a white women, who was a schoolteacher from Geneva, New York. The text of Bradford's biography of Tubman suggests she was in awe of her friend and neighbor's achievements, although some authors believe she was not closely related to Tubman and was recruited to write the book (Larson 2004, 242).

Tubman, after the Civil War, was repeatedly in financial difficulty, and Bradford and Tubman's supporters saw promotion of her story as a way for her to achieve security and repay her debts. Among other things, Bradford arranged for the costs of publication to be donated (Larson 2004, 248). In the introduction to the 1869 edition of her biography of Tubman (*Scenes in the Life of Harriet Tubman*), Bradford claimed her "single object" (Bradford 1869, i) in writing the book was to argue Tubman's case for a Civil War veteran's pension; however she also wanted to ensure Tubman's place in history (ibid., 1). The biography was revised, lengthened, and reissued in 1886 as *Harriet Tubman, The Moses of her People*.

Larson (2004, 266) argues that Bradford's revisions to the biography reflect changes in American culture and society from the post–Civil War era to the post-Reconstruction period. They may also reflect changes in Tubman's own life. In 1856, Tubman was "wanted" in the South because of her activities on the Underground Railroad, theft of human "property," and violation of the Fugitive Slave laws. In the 1860s she served in the Union army as a nurse, cook, scout, and spy. Little, however, is known about Tubman's life in the 1870s and 1880s and what we do know suggests a series of problems including charges that she was involved in a financial scandal, the deaths of close members of her family including her mother and husband, and between 1882 and 1884, the destruction by fire of her home (ibid., 257–61).

Later in life, Tubman became a noted local storyteller elaborating on her own exploits and reworking her legend (Sernett 2007, 12). In an 1890s interview, she supposedly welcomed the appellation *Moses of her people*, claiming, "I felt like Moses. De Lord tole me to do dis. I said, 'O Lord, I can't—don't ask me—take somebody else.' Den I could hear de Lord answer, 'It's you I want, Harriet Tubman'—jess as clar I heard him speak—an' den I'd go agen down South an' bring up my brudders and sisters" (Sernett 2007, 42).

Among other things, in the second edition Bradford muted criticism of slavery, wrote passages in dialect, and used racial stereotypes in her descriptions of African Americans. In the preface to the 1869 edition, Bradford had no problem claiming Tubman's achievements deserved equal mention with those of Joan of Arc and Florence Nightingale, and that she was providing a "plain and unvarnished account of some scenes and adventures in the life of a woman who, though one of earth's lowly ones, and of dark-hued skin, has shown an amount of heroism in her character rarely possessed by those of any station in life.... Well has she been called "*Moses*," for she has been a leader and deliverer unto hundreds of her people" (Bradford 1869, 1). However, in the preface to second edition,

Bradford felt compelled to justify calling Harriet "Moses" when she was a woman and had "succeeded in piloting only three or four hundred slaves from the land of bondage to the land of freedom" (3–4).

Larson (2004, 266–70) offers a well-documented criticism of Bradford's work, but it is likely that without Bradford, Harriet Tubman would have been forgotten. Among other things, it was Bradford who secured endorsements of the biographies and Harriet Tubman's accomplishments from noted abolitionists and politicians, including Frederick Douglass, Gerrit Smith, Wendell Phillips, and William Seward.

Tubman was barely mentioned in major contemporary accounts of the Underground Railroad, which suggests her current renown developed after the fact. In 1883, R. C. Smedley, a white physician, published *History of the Underground Railroad in Chester and the Neighboring counties of Pennsylvania*. This region of Pennsylvania is located southwest

WILLIAM STILL ON HARRIET TUBMAN

QUESTION TO CONSIDER

What image of Harriet Tubman emerges from Still's account?

Time and again she made successful visits to Maryland on the Underground Rail Road, and would be absent for weeks, at a time, running daily risks while making preparations for herself and passengers. Great fears were entertained for her safety, but she seemed wholly devoid of personal fear. The idea of being captured by slave-hunters or slave-holders, seemed never to enter her mind. She was apparently proof against all adversaries. While she thus manifested such utter personal indifference, she was much more watchful with regard to those she was piloting. Half of her time, she had the appearance of one asleep, and would actually sit down by the road-side and go fast asleep when on her errands of mercy through the South, yet, she would not suffer one of her party to whimper once, about "giving out and going back," however wearied they might be from hard travel day and night. She had a very short and pointed rule or law of her own, which implied death to any who talked of giving out and going back. Thus, in an emergency she would give all to understand that "times were very critical and therefore no foolishness would be indulged in on the road." That several who were rather weak-kneed and faint-hearted were greatly invigorated by Harriet's blunt and positive manner and threat of extreme measures, there could be no doubt" (Still 1872, 297).

of Philadelphia on the Delaware River and definitely was an area where Tubman operated as a conductor. In a book that is more than four hundred pages long, Smedley included only three paragraphs about a "colored woman named Harriet Tubman" who was "active in helping hundreds to escape" (Smedley 1883/1969, 250). However, he does suggest she merits comparison with Joan of Arc because of her bravery, success, and her belief that she was in constant communication with God (ibid., 251).

Unlike Smedley, William Still, who published his history of the Underground Railroad in 1872, had significant personal experience in the struggle to end slavery. Still was a free black and an Underground Railroad stationmaster in Philadelphia as well as a member of Pennsylvania Anti-Slavery Society and secretary and executive director of the area's General Vigilance Committee (Still 1872, v). His eight hundred page book *The Underground Rail Road, A Record of Facts, Authentic Narratives, Letters, etc., Narrating the Hardships Hair-breadth Escapes and Death Struggles of the Slaves in their efforts for Freedom, as related by themselves and others, or witnessed by the author; together with sketches of some of the largest stockholders, and most liberal aiders and advisers, of the road* primarily focused on Philadelphia. It is filled with anecdotes and biographical information about abolitionists and fugitive slaves, but Still only has brief mentions of Harriet Tubman, including one incident where "Moses" arrived in Philadelphia with six "passengers" (ibid., 297–98).

In 1898, Wilbur H. Siebert, a historian and professor at Ohio State University, published what was at the time a definitive history of the Underground Railroad, entitled *The Underground Railroad: From Slavery to Freedom*. Tubman is only discussed in a five-page (185–89) section of the 478-page book. Siebert interviewed Harriet Tubman in 1897 (Sernett 2007, 59); however, according to footnotes the information on Tubman is almost entirely drawn from the second edition of the Bradford book.

"Captain Harriet Tubman" is briefly mentioned in the unpublished notebooks of New York City abolitionist Sydney Howard Gay, editor of the *National Anti-Slavery Standard* from 1844 to 1858. Gay appears to have met Tubman in May 1856 when she brought a party of four escapees to New York from Philadelphia. Gay mentioned that up until that point Tubman had made six return trips to the Maryland Eastern Shore, principally to rescue family members and "lead them out of Egypt." Not to minimize her efforts, which placed her life and freedom in danger, Gay's notes suggest that Tubman played a small role on the Underground Railroad in a geographically specific area (Foner 2015, 191–94).

I think Frederick Douglass might have provided the best explanation for the difficulty in defining Harriet Tubman in a letter to Tubman and Bradford prior to publication of the first edition of the Bradford biography. Douglass wrote,

> The difference between us is very marked. Most that I have done and suffered in the service of our cause has been in public, and I have received much encouragement at every step of the way. You, on the other hand,

have labored in a private way. I have wrought in the day—you in the night. I have had the applause of the crowd and the satisfaction that comes of being approved by the multitude, while the most that you have done has been witnessed by a few trembling, scarred, and foot-sore bondmen and women, whom you have led out of the house of bondage, and whose heartfelt "God bless you" has been your only reward. The midnight sky and the silent stars have been the witnesses of your devotion to freedom and of your heroism. Excepting John Brown—of sacred memory— I know of no one who has willingly encountered more perils and hard-ships to serve our enslaved people than you have. Much that you have done would seem improbable to those who do not know you as I know you (Bradford 1869, 134–35).

While Douglass was a spokesperson for the abolitionist cause and a public figure, Tubman, by necessity, worked at night, in private, and with the most marginalized members of the community. In addition, Douglass suggests that her exploits on the Underground Railroad in defiance of Southern slavery's power and as a scout for the Union Army during the Civil War seemed "improbable" because she was a woman, someone of African ances-try, and a former slave. The racism and gender bias of the period forced commentators such as Bradford and Siebert to defend Tubman's personal credibility when recording her accomplishments. Even John Brown, who called her "General Tubman," felt compelled to describe Harriet in masculine terms, "He [Harriet] is the most of a man naturally; that I ever met with" (Clinton 2004, 129).

In the first decade of the twenty-first century there were a series of new Harriet Tubman biographies. By far the most intriguing is a book by Milton Sernett (2007), *Harriet Tubman: Myth, Memory, and History*, that is more a commentary on the interplay between history and public memory than it is an actual biography. Sernett wanted to understand why Tubman so strongly captured the American imagination in the recent past, and to do this, he had to sort out the "legend" from the "lady" (Sernett 2007, 3). The book is broadly chronological, with chapters on the original or core Tubman myth, the Underground Railroad, Tubman during the Civil War, her relationship with Sarah Bradford, life and death in Auburn, New York, and popularization and new myths. I agree with Sernett that nations and social movements need heroes like Tubman. The best heroes are dead ones who do not embarrass them by developing new ideas and or taking unpopular political stands.

Sernett's book draws on both recent and past efforts to understand Tubman. He praises a 1943 book by Earl Conrad, *Harriet Tubman*, which inaugurates modern Tubman scholarship, books by Kate Clifford Larson, *Bound for the Promised Land: Harriet Tubman, Portrait of an American Heroine*, and Jean Humez, *Harriet Tubman: The Life and the Life Stories*, and a series of articles by James McGowan. McGowan later co-authored a biog-raphy with William Kashatus, *Harriet Tubman: A Biography*.

I found the Larson book to be carefully documented with reproductions of a runaway slave advertisement calling for the recapture of Harriet Tubman, known at the time as Minty (Larson 2004, 79), and four runaway slaves she had helped liberate (ibid., 147). According to the 1849 runaway slave ad, Tubman was twenty-seven years old, "of a chestnut color, fine looking, and about 5 feet high." The reward was $50 if she was captured in Maryland and $100 if she had escaped to another state. Larson also debunked the legend that Southerners had placed an extraordinarily high bounty of between $12,000 and $40,000 on Harriet Tubman because of her role in the Underground Railroad. Larson could find no evidence to support claims made by Sarah Bradford (ibid., 344).

Other recent Tubman biographies include Catherine Clinton, *Harriet Tubman: The Road to Freedom*, and Beverly Lowry, *Harriet Tubman: Imagining a Life*. Lowry's book is the least academic of this group. Her subtitle and opening author's note are suggestive of the problems faced by Tubman biographers. She explicitly states that in this work she has "reimagined Tubman's life "as best as I could" (Lowry 2007, 1).

Sernett agrees with Frederick Douglass's assertion that Tubman's fame was initially hidden from the public because the risks involved as a conductor on the Underground Railroad required secrecy to ensure success and survival. While largely unknown to whites prior to publication of the Bradford biography, Tubman was already known in black communities as "Moses" because of her frequent visits to the South "always carrying away some of the oppressed" (Sernett 2007, 42).

The earliest independent documentary evidence of Harriet Tubman's activities is in a brief letter written in December 1854 by Thomas Garrett. The letter was published in William Still's history of the Underground Railroad (1871). Garrett was an Underground Railroad stationmaster in Wilmington, Delaware, on the escape route to Philadelphia. The letter was written to J. Miller McKim, the corresponding secretary of the Philadelphia Anti-Slavery Society. The tone of the letter and the commentary provided by Still make it clear that McKim and Still were both familiar with Tubman and her work. Garrett wrote: "We made arrangements last night, and sent away Harriet Tubman, with six men and one woman to Allen Agnew's, to forwarded [*sic*] across the country to the city. Harriet, and one of the men had worn their shoes off their feet, and I gave them two dollars to help fit them out" (305).

Tubman is also briefly mentioned in an 1856 book written by Benjamin Drew, who met Tubman in St. Catharines, Ontario, the previous year (Sernett 2007, 15). In 1863, Tubman was introduced to a broader Northern public in a front page feature article in a Boston abolitionist newspaper, *Commonwealth*. Written during the Civil War in defense of emancipation, this article presented Tubman in heroic terms (ibid., 46).

In a book published in 1874, William Wells Brown described Harriet Tubman as a frequent presence at abolitionist meetings in the decade prior to the Civil War (Sernett 2007, 47). From an article in *The Liberator*, we know that Harriet Tubman was a speaker at an antislavery rally in Framingham, Massachusetts, on July 4, 1859 (ibid., 48). Thomas

Wentworth Higginson, who later was a white officer in command of black troops during the Civil War, introduced Tubman at the Framingham rally. In a letter written in June 1859, he wrote: "I have known her for some time and mentioned her in speeches once or twice—the slaves call her Moses. She had a reward of twelve thousand dollars offered for her in Maryland and will probably be burned alive whenever she is caught, which she probably will be, first or last, as she is going again" (Higginson 1921, 81). Decades later, in a book describing his contemporaries, Higginson wrote that he considered Harriet Tubman one of the most eminent figures of the age, "a black woman, who, after escaping from slavery herself, had gone back secretly eight times into the jaws of death to bring out persons she had never seen" (Higginson 1899, 227), however, curiously, he did not mention her by name.

One of the more interesting debates about Tubman concerns the nature of her religiosity and reflects the beliefs and politics of Tubman's biographers. According to Sernett, Sarah Bradford tried to fit Tubman's belief that she personally experienced divine guidance and had an active, even mystical relationship with God into her own more traditional Protestant religious framework (Sernett 2007, 135–38). Earl Conrad, writing within a Marxist tradition in the 1940s, promoted Tubman as a working-class revolutionary hero. He attributed Tubman's visions to the physical injury she incurred in her youth, rather than to her religious beliefs (Wald 2005; Sernett 2007, 139–40). In the 1990s, James McGowan gives much greater credibility to the possibility that Tubman actually had psychic powers (McGowan and Kashatus 2011, 15). More recently, Jean Humez situated Tubman's spirituality, visions, dream language, and belief in charms, within a syncretic slave Christianity infused with African ritual and belief (Humez 2003, 138). While it may be true that Tubman believed she had some kind of supernatural powers because of a close connection with God, that is different from suggesting that these powers actually existed.

There are significant questions about Tubman's relationship to prominent abolitionists, particularly William Seward, John Brown, and Frederick Douglass. Seward was probably the most prominent political abolitionist in the United States during the 1850s. As a senator from New York State, he was an outspoken critic of the 1850 Fugitive Slave law and he was one of the leading candidates for the Republican Party's presidential nomination in 1860. Larson believes the connection between Tubman and Seward developed out of a previous contact Tubman had with Auburn, New York, abolitionist Martha Coffin Wright (Larson 2004, 155). Wright's sister, Lucretia Coffin Mott, was a supporter of Underground Railroad activities in the Philadelphia region where Tubman operated. Wright's husband was Seward's law partner. Originally, Seward and his wife Frances helped Tubman and the Underground Railroad, hiding fugitive slaves in their home. In 1858, Seward became Tubman's benefactor. In open violation of the Fugitive Slave Act and the 1857 *Dred Scott* decision, Seward sold property to Tubman on the outskirts of Auburn for use by her family (ibid., 163–66). He required only a minimal down payment and charged a low quarterly fee for the principal and interest. When Tubman, always pressed for money, was unable to cover her expenses, Seward paid her property taxes and insurance (ibid., 184). During the Civil War, Seward helped Tubman secure a position as a nurse in a hospital for wounded black Civil War veterans (ibid., 229–30). Later, he supported her effort to secure a military pension. When Seward died, much of Tubman's debt to his estate was forgiven (ibid., 255).

Yet, despite this long term and seemingly significant partnerships, Seward biographies and papers do not mention his relationship to or support of Tubman. All evidence for a connection between Seward and Tubman comes from Tubman biographers, primarily Franklin Sanborn's brief article about Tubman published in 1863 and Bradford's *Scenes in the Life of Harriet Tubman* (1869, 73, 80–81, 112). Other than these sources, Larson (2004, 164) cites only one reference to the mortgage arrangement she located in the Seward Papers at Harvard University. I suspect the relationship, which made it possible for Tubman to do her work, have some economic security, and fulfill family obligations, was much more important to Tubman, a formerly enslaved, nonliterate, impoverished, largely unknown, African American woman, than it was to Seward.

While Seward hardly acknowledged a relationship with Tubman, John Brown probably exaggerated his connection to her and radical black abolitionists in order to establish his credibility as he recruited for the Harpers Ferry raid. According to a letter written by Brown in April 1858 (Sanborn 1863, 452), he met with Tubman in Canada where he enlisted her support for the raid, asking her to recruit runaway slaves and free blacks for the enterprise (Sernett 2007, 209). From the enthusiasm expressed in his letter, Brown was clearly impressed with Tubman and believed her participation would ensure the success of his plan. In the Bradford biographies, Tubman claimed to have had a vision of Brown before she met him and that she did not fully understand the vision until after the events at Harpers Ferry (Larson 2004, 158–59; Bradford 1886, 118–19). In Earl Conrad's biography of Tubman, he claims that she was scheduled to participate in the raid but could not because of illness (Conrad 1943, 126).

I think it is telling that no one from among Harriet Tubman, Frederick Douglass, and Jermain Loguen, who introduced Tubman to Brown in St. Catharines (Lawson 2004, 159), participated in the Harpers Ferry raid. Douglass, who had a longer and deeper relationship with Brown than Tubman (Douglass 1892, 314–25), decided not to join Brown because he felt the venture could not succeed. We do not know why Tubman was not there, but I suspect she was never completely on board with Brown's plan. Harriet Tubman worked at night and alone, and whatever her feelings for Brown or the Harpers Ferry raid, she was unlikely to enlist in someone else's operation.

Frederick Douglass was a prolific writer and frequent orator, yet he leaves behind almost no suggestion of a relationship with Harriet Tubman besides the 1868 endorsement of the Bradford biography. He did not mention Tubman or a relationship with her in any of the editions of his memoir. *Frederick Douglass: Selected Speeches and Writings* (Foner and Taylor 1999) includes the 1868 letter and mentions a January 1858 letter from Douglass to the Ladies' Irish Anti-Slavery Association where he referred to an unnamed "coloured woman, who escaped from slavery eight years ago," who "has made several returns at great risk, and has brought out since obtaining her freedom fifty others from the house of bondage. She has been spending a short time with us since the holidays. She possesses great courage and shrewdness, and may yet render even more important service to the Cause" (ibid., 600–601). However, in this letter Douglass did not mention Tubman by name.

The Frederick Douglass Papers in the Library of Congress's manuscript division, contain more than seven thousand items relating to Douglass's life as "an escaped slave, abolitionist, editor, orator, and public servant. The papers span the years 1841 to 1964, with the bulk of the material from 1862 to 1895. The collection consists of correspondence, speeches and articles by Douglass and his contemporaries, a draft of his autobiography, financial and legal papers, scrapbooks, and miscellaneous items" (Library of Congress, n.d.). There is correspondence between Douglass and Susan B. Anthony, William Lloyd Garrison, Gerrit Smith, Horace Greeley, and Grover Cleveland, but there are no references in the collection to Harriet Tubman.

Larson believes that Frederick Douglass and Harriet Tubman may have met in 1851 when Tubman led a band of eleven fugitives through Rochester on the route to Canada (Larson 2004, 92–93). Douglass mentions the "occasion" in his memoirs, because it stood out for him as "the largest number I ever had at one time, and I had some difficulty in providing so many with food and shelter" (Douglass 1892/1962, 266). However, he did not identify Tubman as part of this group, place her in the group in his 1858 letter to the Irish Ladies, or refer to the incident in his endorsement of the Bradford biography.

Larson also speculates that Tubman and Douglass knew each other while enslaved on Maryland's Eastern Shore, however, she concedes that "little documentation exists that definitely points to any relationship between Douglass and Tubman prior to Tubman's own liberation" (Larson 2004, 94). This kind of speculation, which I feel weakens the Larson book, underscores how little we actually know about Tubman. The reality is that there is little documentation of a relationship between Douglass and Tubman at any point in their lives, despite the fact that they lived about sixty miles apart in upstate New York for many years. For me, the absence of documentation points to the absence of a significant relationship.

Harriet Tubman's role in the Nalle Rescue in Troy, New York, on April 28, 1860, is documented by independent sources, but the sources tell different stories. Not surprisingly, Sarah Bradford places Harriet Tubman at the center of the events (Bradford 1886, 119–24). In the Bradford biography, it is Tubman who rushes to the "office of the United States Commissioner" following the arrest of Charles Nalle, "scattering the tidings as she went" (ibid., 120). It is Harriet standing in the window of the office wearing a "sun-bon-net" who signals to the group gathering outside and sends boys to cry "fire" in an attempt to draw an even bigger crowd. It is Harriet who blocks the stairwell as the marshals try to move Nalle (ibid., 121) and who finally commands the crowd to drag Nalle to the river, even as the marshals open fire (ibid., 123).

Concerned that some readers would find this account "too wonderful for belief," Bradford sought independent confirmation from Martin Townsend, the lawyer for Charles Nalle. Townsend confirmed that Tubman had grabbed a manacled Nalle and held onto him during a half-hour's struggle and was severely beaten by police (Bradford 1886, 126–27). Townsend, according to Bradford, commended Tubman who "exposed herself to the fury of the sympathizers with slavery, without fear, and suffered their blows with-out flinching" (ibid., 127).

Three contemporary newspaper accounts, however, have Tubman playing a less prominent role in the Nalle rescue. Bradford reprinted an article from the April 28, 1860, (which she misdated) *Troy Whig* in her appendix (Bradford 1886, 143–49). In the *Whig* version, key leadership roles are played by William Henry, "a colored man, with whom Nalle boarded" (ibid., 145), and Nalle's attorney, Martin Townsend, neither of whom is mentioned by Bradford in the text of the biographies. It is Henry who whips up the crowd to intervene and help Nalle escape. Although the article describes blacks and women in the crowd, there is no one mentioned who might have been Harriet Tubman.

The *Troy Daily Times*, April 28, 1860, also cites Henry and Townsend for their efforts to free Nalle, and credits Henry for arranging for Nalle's legal counsel. This news-paper noted the presence of a "somewhat antiquated colored woman, who at a later period became an active spirit of the *melee*, and who was said to be in some way related to the prisoner. She was provided with a signal to prepare those on the outside for an attack, when the prisoner should be brought forth." Later in the article, readers learn, "The most conspicuous person opposed to the legal course, was the venerable colored woman, who exclaimed, 'Give us liberty or give us death!' and by vehement gesticulations urged the rescuers on."

The New York Times's coverage of "The Slave Rescue at Troy" (May 1, 1860, 8) was somewhat less comprehensive than that of either Troy newspaper. It did not mention Henry, Townsend, Tubman, or the "somewhat antiquated colored woman." The report in the *New York Tribune* (May 1, 1860, 3), "The Slave Rescue at Troy," based on an account published in *The Troy Arena*, also did not mention Harriet Tubman by name. Milton Sernett, in his review of both primary sources and secondary accounts of the Nalle Rescue, found it almost impossible to sort out what actually happened in Troy that day, partly because "Tubman was fond of retelling," and perhaps elaborating on, "the story of the Nalle rescue in her later years" (Sernett 2007, 84).

Based on my reading of the sources and the biographies, this is the Harriet Tubman whom I found:

- For whatever reason—illiteracy, suspicion of others born out of enslavement, serious injury incurred as a youth, or personality—Harriet Tubman was a lone wolf who operated by herself. I think this explains why she did not participate in Harpers Ferry. As a conductor on the Underground Railroad, Tubman worked on the margins of society, which means that she left behind few eyewitnesses in a position to speak about her exploits and a slender paper trail.

- In some ways, calling her the Black Moses robs Tubman of her militancy. The biblical Moses acted as God's agent when he led the Israelites out of bondage in Egypt, not as a freedom fighter. Tubman not only led people to freedom, but she was willing and able to fight, as she demonstrated in Troy. On the other hand, Tubman was not the gun-toting revolutionary celebrated by Jacob Lawrence and Earl Conrad. Survival on repeated trips into the slaveholding South meant she had to be more cautious and calculating than the Lawrence portrayal.

- I have no idea of the extent of Tubman's physical disability and its impact on her mental functioning. Clearly, she was sustained by her religious conviction and what she felt was a personal relationship with God, which was not uncommon in that era. While she identified as a Christian, it is almost certain that she did not practice what would have been considered traditional Christianity in the United States at that time.

- The repeated violation of the Fugitive Slave Act of 1850 by abolitionists in the decade before the Civil War provoked the South's virulent reaction to this perceived threat to the sanctity of slave property. It undermined the precarious balance between regions established by the United States Constitution and precipitated both the Civil War and emancipation. Tubman, as a conductor on the Underground Railroad, contributed to the conditions that produced the impending crisis. Perhaps Tubman's greatest achievement, however, was her involvement in the Nalle rescue, because unlike her efforts on the Underground Railroad, it was done in the light of day and brought publicity to the cause at a particularly crucial moment.

Milton Sernett (2007) argues that Harriet Tubman has come to represent and personalize the Underground Railroad, in much the same way that Anne Frank represents the European Holocaust and Martin Luther King Jr. and Rosa Parks are symbols of the African American civil rights movement. However, as in each of these cases, the events were much larger than the individual. No one living person, no matter how great, could ever be Sarah Bradford's "Harriet Tubman, Moses of her People."

HARRIET TUBMAN IN THE NEWSPAPERS

QUESTION TO CONSIDER

Do we learn more about the reporters or about
Harriet Tubman from these accounts?

These newspaper reports are among the few independent accounts of Harriet Tubman. The scarcity of these sources is a major reason her life and achievements are mythologized. In her 1860 Boston speech, Harriet Tubman claimed to have traveled into the South eight times and to have rescued fifty of her "kindred and friends." In the 1865 account, she is described as speaking "in the peculiar plantation dialect and at times were not intelligible to the white portion of her audience." What is remarkable about Tubman in both of these accounts is that she seems so unremarkable.

"The Colored Woman Moses Tubman"

The audience grew weary; a black woman appeared upon the stage, and in the frantic applause which greeted her HINTON noticed a gentle hint for him to say goodbye, which he immediately did, and his farewell bow seemed to please the audience more than anything he had said. The colored woman who was spoken of above is a noted individual, she having escaped from bondage herself, and returning eight times into the "dark and bloody ground," has brought off fifty of her kindred and friends. Her real name is not known, but she is called MOSES TUBMAN. MOSES is black as the ace of spades. Her hair rejoices in wavy braids. She wears on her back a gingham dress and around her neck two white handkerchiefs. A hard hair plug, on the top of her head, with four little curls is lovingly wed, while the turn of her nose and the cock of her eye, to all the world shows, that dat nigga's sly. MOSES, or NANCY, as she prefers being called, made a speech, or rather she talked for about half an hour, during which time she related her experience in the South, her running away, her various slave stealing expeditions, and her great love for JOHN BROWN, Rev. Mr. MAY, and her old massa. She is too smart, knows too much,—is being lionized too constantly, and will run against a trouble, some time, in the shape of a mortifying rebuff, which she won't understand, and from which her friends will be unable to extricate her. When she had said all she could say, and had repeated it in varied language half a dozen times, she yielded the floor to WM.L. GARRISON (*New York Times*, June 5, 1860).

"Mrs. Harriet Tubman, the Colored Nurse and Scout"

Mrs. Tubman is a colored lady, of 35 or 40 years of age; she appeared before those present with a wounded hand in a bandage, which wound she stated was caused by maltreatment received at the hands of a conductor on the Camden and Amboy railroad, on her trip from Philadelphia to New York a few days since. Her words were in the peculiar plantation dialect and at times were not intelligible to the white portion of her audience. There was nothing particularly impressive in her remarks: she was born, she said, in the eastern part of the State of Maryland, and wanted it to be distinctly understood that she was not educated, nor did she receive any "broughten up;" "she came up." Therefore, she concluded she was not fit to mix in political matters. John Brown was one of her particular friends. Her master was a good man, but she knew that God had directed her to perform other works in this world, and so she escaped from bondage. This was nearly 14 years ago, since then she has assisted hundreds to do the same. Her narration of her sickness, previous to her escape, was filled with negro phrases and elicited shouts of laughter from the congregation, the whites entering most heartily into it (*Brooklyn Eagle* 1865c, 2).

TEACHING NOTES

History Told in Children's Books

QUESTIONS TO CONSIDER

1. What standard of accuracy should be used to evaluate historical fiction intended for children?

2. How much should we question the historical "myths" that are part of the national heritage?

George Washington's Birthday Cake

A major means by which younger children are introduced to the past is through children's literature, which means it is important that picture books and early readers respect the historical record (Damico et al. 2010, 1–12). New York abolitionists recognized this, and in the 1830s Lewis Tappan published an illustrated children's magazine, *The Slave's Friend*. Pages from the 1837 volume are available online through the New York Public Library. Illustrations include an abolitionist meeting, neck braces or coffles, and enslaved Africans being beaten (Tappan 1837).

Yet, as John Bickford notes in a study of children' literature depicting the African American civil rights movement, "patterns of historical misrepresentation were ostensible, derived mostly from errors of omission, and varied in degree of flagrancy (Bickford 2015, 708). As a corrective, he encourages teachers on all levels to incorporate primary sources, including contemporary illustrations, in their lessons.

Andrea Libresco, as an editor of the National Council for the Social Studies' journal *Social Studies and the Young Learner* and in *Every Book is a Social Studies Book* (2011), which she co-authored, champions the idea that teachers can use any children's book to teach social studies in some way. While this is a useful approach to ensure that children learn at least a little social studies and history, some children's books are definitely better than others. This section discusses two books that through image and text mythologize the history of slavery and abolition and an author, Virginia Hamilton, whose fictional work deserves to be celebrated and widely used.

The publisher Scholastic Corporation evidently thought U.S. school children needed a new picture book to help them celebrate George Washington's birthday. Unfortunately *A Birthday Cake for George Washington* (2015), by Ramin Gameshram, also seemed to celebrate slavery in the United States and was recalled two weeks after release. (*continues on page 94*)

(*continued from page 93*)

Scholastic received "blowback" for this decision and was accused of "self-censorship" by the executive director of the National Coalition Against Censorship. The publisher responded that the book was recalled because it failed to meet company standards for representing "complex subject matter" (Stack 2016, B6).

A Birthday Cake for George Washington is narrated by a young enslaved African girl named Delia. Images show happy black people baking George Washington a birthday cake. One panel announces, "Hercules, a slave, takes great pride in baking the president's cake. But this year there is one problem—they are out of sugar." But evidently, a sugar shortage was not the only problem in the new nation.

According to the book's author, the story was intended to shed light on the "complex and varied nature of enslaved existence," including "enslaved people who had a better quality of life than others and 'close' relationships with those who enslaved them." Actually, George Washington's relationship to slavery was not that complex and illustrates how deeply embedded the slave system was in the United States.

Washington became a slaveholder at the age of eleven, when his father died. By the time George Washington died in 1799, the enslaved population on his Mount Vernon planation included 318 people, 123 of whom had been enslaved directly by Washington himself and the rest of whom were part of the estate of his wife's children from a previous marriage. Instead of freeing the people he claimed to own in his will, Washington transferred ownership to his wife. Some of these people were freed in 1801 (Thompson 1999).

During the American Revolution, George Washington refused to enlist enslaved Africans who wanted to secure their freedom by joining the Revolutionary army, and at the end of the war he sent a letter to British commanders demanding that they return formerly enslaved Africans who were freed when they escaped to British lines. Washington objected to British plans to evacuate formerly enslaved Africans as a violation of the provisional peace agreement and sought to find and reacquire people he claimed were his own property (Singer 2008, 50).

Slavery was illegal in Philadelphia while it was the national capital in the 1790s. Enslaved Africans brought to Pennsylvania would officially be free after six months residence in the state. To evade the law, George Washington rotated enslaved Africans back to his Virginia planation before they would have to be emancipated. Apparently, Hercules so "enjoyed" being enslaved by George Washington that he escaped to freedom. After Hercules escaped bondage, Washington wrote a letter to his personal secretary Tobias Lear, demanding that Lear assist in Hercules's recapture. In the letter, after discussing new carpets, furniture, pots, and pans, Washington requested that Lear contact a Mr. Kitt to make "all the enquiry he can after Hercules, and send him round in the Vessel if he can be discovered & apprehended" (Washington 1797).

Martha Washington's personal "servant" also escaped while the family was in Philadelphia. According to a runaway slave ad posted in the *Pennsylvania Gazette*, "Absconded from the household of the President of the United States, Oney Judge, a light mulatto girl, much freckled, with very black eyes and bushy black hair, she is of middle stature, slender, and delicately formed, about 20 years of age.... [I]t is probable she will attempt to pass for a free woman.... Ten dollars will be paid to any person who will bring her home, if taken in the city, or on board any vessel in the harbor;— and a reasonable additional sum if apprehended at, and brought from a greater distance" (Niven 1916).

Upon learning that Judge had escaped to New Hampshire, Washington wrote officials there demanding her return because it "would neither be politic or just to reward unfaithfulness." Judge was interviewed by abolitionists in 1845 and explained, "Whilst they were packing up to go to Virginia, I was packing to go, I didn't know where; for I knew that if I went back to Virginia, I should never get my liberty."

These stories about George Washington and slavery would have been an important history lesson for young students and an important corrective to the myth that United States founders were committed to freedom for all. I do not think recalling a misleading children's book portraying happy enslaved people in the Washington household amounted to self-censorship by Scholastic. Rather, it was recognition of a mistake in judgment.

Were Abraham Lincoln and Frederick Douglass Friends?

Nikki Giovanni, University Distinguished Professor at Virginia Tech, is a true artistic revolutionary who has introduced black literary themes to a broad audience. However, her children's picture book *Lincoln and Douglass, An American Friendship* (New York: Holt, 2008) was seriously flawed by historical inaccuracies. According to the book jacket, "In 1865, at the reception to celebrate his second inauguration as president of the United States, Abraham Lincoln kept an eye out for a special guest: Frederick Douglass. Although Lincoln was white and Douglass was black, although Lincoln was born free and Douglass had been born a slave, both were central figures in the American abolitionist movement. This is a glimpse into an unusual friendship between two great American leaders.... Lincoln and Douglass formed a strong bond over shared ideals and worked alongside each other for a common goal." Giovanni, in an author's note, says that she wrote the book to show that people are capable of acting out of respect, rather than just out of fear and because Lincoln and Douglass had a "friendship that helped shape the world."

The book opens at Lincoln's second inaugural ball. Mrs. Lincoln asks the president if something is wrong, and he tells her, "I am looking for my friend Frederick Douglass. (*continues on page 96*)

(continued from page 95)

I had asked him to come and bring his wife." Suddenly, Lincoln sees Douglass and exclaims, "Here comes my friend Douglass." The two men shake hands and the book shifts into the past and focuses on the parallels in their early lives as they struggle to learn to read and write and dream about the future. One panel shows Lincoln and Douglass meeting as young men when Lincoln was elected to Congress in 1846.

The idea for this children's book came from a passage in Douglass's autobiography, *Life and Times of Frederick Douglass Written by Himself*, which was initially published in 1892. While some of the errors in the children's book are minor, others are more serious and present a distorted image of the struggle to end slavery. Lincoln was not a central figure in the abolitionist movement and he was not a congressman when he ran for president. Douglass did not receive a special invitation to the inaugural reception (unlike today, it was open to everyone); Lincoln was not expecting Douglass to attend; and Douglass was not accompanied to the reception by his wife. Mary Todd Lincoln, who had a close working relationship with Congressman Charles Sumner, a leading abolitionist, was not a Southern sympathizer.

Lincoln and Douglass could not have met in Washington, D.C., in 1847, as suggested in the book. Douglass was in Europe at the start of that year and when he returned in April he settled in Rochester, New York. He never went to Washington, D.C., in that period because it was a slave city and Douglass was a former runaway. According to Douglass's autobiography, the first time he met Lincoln was when he lobbied the president to recruit black troops for the war effort and to pay, arm, and treat them in the same way as white soldiers. No date is provided in the Douglass memoir, but Douglass did not begin to recruit black troops until February 1863. This meeting probably did not take place until July 1863 (Douglass 1962, 347). Although Douglass was pleased that Lincoln finally decided to authorize the recruitment of African American soldiers and improve their conditions, he felt slighted that he never received the military commission he was promised by Secretary of War Edwin Stanton (ibid., 357).

Douglass's memoir also gives a very different account of the inaugural activities (ibid., 365). No "colored person" had ever attended a reception at the White House, but Douglass decided, although uninvited, that he would attend and congratulate Lincoln on his reelection and conduct of the war. Douglass was accompanied to the event by a local woman named Louise Tobias Dorsey. They were initially barred from entry, but once he was inside, Lincoln did shake his hand and call him "my friend Douglass." However the encounter was brief and they never had the private moment on the balcony pictured in the book (ibid., 366).

In print and in his speeches after the Civil War, Douglass was laudatory of Lincoln; however, he did not hesitate to describe things the way he saw them. In April 1876, Douglass spoke about Lincoln at the unveiling of The Freedmen's Monument in Memory of Abraham Lincoln at Lincoln Park, Washington, D.C.

He described Lincoln when elected as

> preeminently the white man's President, entirely devoted to the welfare of white men. He was ready and willing at any time during the first years of his administration to deny, postpone, and sacrifice the rights of humanity in the colored people to promote the welfare of the white people of this country. In all his education and feeling he was an American of the Americans. He came into the Presidential chair upon one principle alone, namely, opposition to the extension of slavery. His arguments in furtherance of this policy had their motive and mainspring in his patriotic devotion to the interests of his own race. To protect, defend, and perpetuate slavery in the states where it existed Abraham Lincoln was not less ready than any other President to draw the sword of the nation. He was ready to execute all the supposed guarantees of the United States Constitution in favor of the slave system anywhere inside the slave states. He was willing to pursue, recapture, and send back the fugitive slave to his master, and to suppress a slave rising for liberty.... We are at best only his step-children (Foner 1999, 615–18).

This is a very different Lincoln, and a very different Douglass, from the ones portrayed by Nikki Giovanni. This is the real Lincoln and Douglass, not a fairy tale version. Douglass was a radical opponent of slavery and injustice while Lincoln was committed to compromise, and they were not friends in any meaningful sense of the word.

The People Could Fly

Instead of fictionalizing history and mythologizing historic figures, Virginia Hamilton uses fiction to introduce children to the history of slavery and African American resistance. Hamilton's "The People Could Fly" is a traditional African American folktale that celebrates African origins and beliefs and the human desire for freedom. It is included in a collection of twenty-four stories written for middle-level students (Hamilton 1985) and retold in a picture book for younger children (Hamilton 2004). The book for older children introduces them to "Bruh Rabbit" stories and a series of tales about freedom seekers escaping from slavery. In "The People Could Fly," flying is a metaphor for freedom. Readers "learn" that before they were enslaved and brought to the Americas, African people had the ability to fly. Once enslaved, this ability was forgotten until an old man named Toby decided he must help a young woman named Sarah and her baby escape from the slaver's lash to freedom. Toby utters magic words that reawaken Sarah's lost ability, and she and her baby soar into the sky. Other enslaved Africans call on Toby to help them and he assists as many as he can to fly away to freedom, but eventually Toby must escape himself while others remain behind. The story ends with parents telling their (continues on page 98)

(*continued from page 97*)
their children the story of Toby and the people who could fly as part of an oral tradition implanting the desire for freedom. I have used this story by Virginia Hamilton in classrooms ranging from preschool to middle school. Students have acted out the tale in costumes and with puppets and then we have talked about the impact of slavery on people's lives and the fundamental desire of all human beings for freedom.

The website *Teaching for Change* recommends more than two dozen picture books for teaching about slavery and resistance as well as fiction and nonfiction books for middle-level and high school students. Another important source for children's book that discuss the African American experience is the National Council for Social Studies list of Carter G. Woodson Book Award winners and honorees. A NCSS committee chooses six books to honor every year, two each for elementary (P–6), middle-level (5–8), and secondary (7–12). 2016 award winners included *Passenger on the Pearl: The True Story of Emily Edmonson's Flight from Slavery*, by Winifred Conkling. The book tells the story of an attempted escape from enslavement in Virginia in 1848 and includes primary source documents.

8

NEW YORK'S GRAND EMANCIPATION
JUBILEE CELEBRATIONS

HISTORIANS CONTINUE TO DEBATE THE SIGNIFICANCE OF THE EMANCIPATION Proclamation issued by Abraham Lincoln on January 1, 1863, and its actual and immediate impact on slavery in the United States (Jones 2013, 452–57). Lincoln's secretary of state, William Seward, described is as a mere "puff of wind over an accomplished fact" and believed it actually set back the cause of freedom (Guelzo 2004, 222; Donald 2003, 164–65). However, Henry Ward Beecher, abolitionist and minister of the Plymouth Church in Brooklyn, argued that while the Emancipation Proclamation "may not free a single slave … it gives liberty a moral recognition" (Strausbaugh 2016, 243).

Contemporary newspaper articles and speeches make clear that for the majority of abolitionists and free and freed black people it had tremendous symbolic importance and was cause for a "grand emancipation jubilee." Frederick Douglass later summarized these feelings in his autobiography: "THE first of January, 1863, was a memorable day in the progress of American liberty and civilization. It was the turning-point in the conflict between freedom and slavery. A death-blow was given to the slaveholding rebellion" (Douglass 1892/1962, 351).

According to a report in *The New York Times* (1863, 8), on January 1, 1863, there was a "GRAND EMANCIPATION JUBILEE. A Night-watch of Freedom at Shiloh Church. Great Excitement and Rejoicing Among the Colored People Prayers, Speeches, Songs, Dirges and Shouts." On Wednesday night December 31, "In anticipation of the Emancipation Proclamation which the President is expected to issue today, the colored people of this City held a grand jubilee last night at Shiloh Presbyterian Church, corner of Prince and Marion streets." The church and Marion Street are long gone; the site, now a shopping district in the Soho neighborhood near the intersection of Prince and Mulberry, is unmarked.

The article continued, "By 9 o'clock in the evening the church was filled to overflowing, nearly one-third of the audience being white. Rev. Henry Highland Garnet, pastor of Shiloh Church presided, and among the speakers were Rev. S.C. Jocelyn, C.C. Leigh, Edward Gilbert, Junius C. Morell, and others." Garnet was a leading black abolitionist for more than two decades whose family had escaped from slavery when he was a child. Jocelyn, Leigh, Gilbert, and Morell were all prominent local white abolitionists.

The ceremonies opened at 10 o'clock with a "prayer from Rev. Danl. H. Vandewoort, colored. After this came a hymn, and the Chairman then introduced Rev. G.S. Jocelyn, who spoke of the progress of Emancipation throughout the world.... The most loyal people in this country he said were the blacks, and if the President's Emancipation Proclamation had been issued on the firing of the first gun at Fort Sumter the nation would have been saved the deluge of blood that had since flowed throughout the land." Jocelyn's comments were greeted with loud applause.

The next speaker, Charles C. Leigh, represented the New York–based National Freedman's Relief Association. Leigh "recounted the meritorious deeds of the black men in past ages, and exhorted his hearers to emulate their example, and show themselves worthy of the position among the races which they aspired to reach. Turning to the institution of Slavery in this country, he spoke in severe terms of the support it had received from a corrupt and hireling clergy, ... who make the Word of God speak in favor of that 'sum of all villainies,' American Slavery." Leigh's remarks were also greeted with "great applause."

Julius Morell, who was born in North Carolina, "recounted many of the barbarities of Slavery that had come under his observation when a boy, and said that the present rebellion would have broken out long ago had it not been for the much reviled Abolitionists. The black men of the South were long ago maturing plans of a general uprising, which would have deluged the South in blood, but about that time the anti-Slavery societies of the North sprung up, and, through their preaching and promises, the slaves were induced to keep quiet." Morell believed he saw "the finger of God in this delay. It was His design to chastise the nation for the great sin of Slavery ere the bond of the slave were broken. This was now being done by civil war, when almost every home throughout the land was filled with lamentation and mourning."

At five minutes to midnight, Reverend Garnet interrupted the speaker and announced that "the audience would unite in silent prayer.... A solemn dirge was then played on the organ. At the close of which the whole audience knelt for five minutes in silent prayer. At the expiration of that time the choir sang the hymn commencing, 'Blow, ye trumpets blow, the year of jubilee has come;' in which the audience joined."

> Blow ye the trumpet, blow
> The gladly solemn sound,
> Let all the nations know,
> To earth's remotest bound:
> The year of Jubilee has come,
> Returning ransomed sinners home,
> Returning ransomed sinners home.

Garnet "then read a dispatch from Washington, saying that President Lincoln would issue the Emancipation Proclamation at 12 o'clock M., to-day. This announcement was greeted with the most tumultuous cheers, which lasted some minutes." It was followed by "three cheers for Abraham Lincoln" and "three cheers for freedom." Other speakers followed, and the jubilee was kept up to a late hour in the evening, the audience singing 'Old John Brown' and other similar songs, shouting, praying and rejoicing."

That same evening, the black population of Brooklyn, which at the time was an independent city across the East River from New York City, gathered for a three-day celebration of freedom at the Bridge Street AME church (*Brooklyn Eagle* 1863a, 2). Its pastor, Reverend James Gloucester, presided. Speakers included prominent individuals such as African American author and abolitionist William Wells Brown and Theodore Tilton, a white abolitionist representing the nearby Plymouth Congregational Church, as well as a man the *Brooklyn Eagle* identified as a "contraband," or runaway slave. The platform at Bridge Street AME was decorated with American flags and a banner celebrating previous emancipation days in New York (1827) and the British West Indies (1834).

Jubilee celebrations continued for a number of days at different sites around the city. On Friday, January 2, there was celebration at New York's Abyssinian Baptist Church and a lot more cheering (Douglass 1863). That Sunday, January 4, Reverend Henry Ward Beecher addressed a jubilant gathering at Plymouth Congregational Church. Discussing the Civil War, Beecher told his congregation, "There is a tremendous conflict going on between desposition [*sic*. despotism (?)] and liberty—between the oppression of the common people and their enfranchisement. It is a conflict of two opposing forces for the government of the continent—the spirit of Christian liberty and democracy, and the spirit of aristocratic oppression" (*New York Times* 1863b, 8). However, "[a]t last the Government of the United States stands straight again." Beecher praised Lincoln's action: "The President of the United States can be accused of no rashness—no hot haste in bringing himself to the stand-point where we now behold him. After months of anxious thought, desiring that some other way might be left him to strike a lasting blow at this rebellion, he has decreed freedom to 3,000,000 of slaves." Beecher closed with a passage from the eighteenth chapter of Revelations describing the fall of Babylon. "So may Slavery perish, and all who uphold it."

The next day, Monday, January 5, the "'Sons of Freedom,' an association of colored people," sponsored a rally at the Cooper Institute in New York City where Abraham Lincoln had delivered a speech in 1860 that helped propel him to Republican Party nomination and the presidency. According to *The New York Times* (1863b, 8), "A living stream of people set swiftly toward the doors long before the hour appointed for commencing the exercises, and filling the body of the house with a rush, eddied into the lobbies, percolated into the aisles, dashed its spray upon the platform, and overflowed into the street."

The *Times* reported that three-fifths of the group assembled at the Cooper Institute were "colored people" and "the remainder were sympathizing whites. The sexes, too, seemed to be about equally represented, and a larger number of intelligent, respectable, joyous faces never stamped an audience as being above mediocrity. There was enthusiasm beyond measure, but no disorderly demonstration, the feeling of joy which animated the congregation seeming to be subdued by its very intensity rather than made exuberant by its earnestness." Speakers included "the venerable Lewis Tappan."

At the Cooper Institute rally the opening prayer was delivered by the Reverend John T. Raymond, a leading black abolitionist, in which he gave "gratitude to God" and blessed the President. The audience cheered and then "united in singing the 'New John Brown Song,' an 'Emancipation Hymn,' and other lyrics."

> John Brown's body lies a-mouldering in the grave; (3X)
> His soul's marching on!
> Glory, glory, hallelujah! Glory, glory, hallelujah!
> Glory, glory, hallelujah! his soul's marching on!

I am not positive about the "Emancipation Hymn" but I believe it refers to a song celebrating the end of slavery in the British West Indies. I found the lyrics in *The Anti-slavery Harp: A Collection of Songs for Anti-slavery Meetings* edited by William Wells Brown and originally published in 1848.

> Praise we the Lord! let songs resound
> To earth's remotest shore!
> Songs of thanksgiving, songs of praise—
> For we are slaves no more.

Frederick Douglass, in the February issue of his monthly newspaper, reported, "Rev. H.H. Garnet presided with dignity, reading the Proclamation, and making a most appropriate and eloquent address" that concluded with "three cheers for the President ... followed successively by cheers 'for our native land,' for the Stars and Stripes, for the Abolitionists, and for Horace Greeley" (Douglass 1863). The *Times* report concluded, "The demonstration was a fitting expression of the triumph of the American Union over African Slavery."

Douglass of Rochester, New York, was present at the Emancipation Proclamation ceremony at Tremont Temple Baptist Church in Boston. Douglass and William Lloyd Garrison had been driven out of the church by anti-abolitionist rioters in December 1860. In his memoir, Douglass described the scene at the Tremont Temple in great depth, as well as the anticipation and trepidation in the crowd at possible disappointment:

> I was in Boston, and its reception there may indicate the importance
> attached to it elsewhere. An immense assembly convened in Tremont

Temple to await the first flash of the electric wires announcing the "new departure." Two years of war, prosecuted in the interests of slavery, had made free speech possible in Boston, and we were now met together to receive and celebrate the first utterance of the long-hoped-for proclamation, *if* it came, and, if it did *not* come, to speak our minds freely; for, in view of the past, it was by no means certain that it would come. The occasion, therefore, was one of both hope and fear. Our ship was on the open sea, tossed by a terrible storm; wave after wave was passing over us, and every hour was fraught with increasing peril. Whether we should survive or perish depended in large measure upon the coming of this proclamation. At least so we felt. Although the conditions on which Mr. Lincoln had promised to withhold it had not been complied with, yet, from many considerations, there was room to doubt and fear. Mr. Lincoln was known to be a man of tender heart, and boundless patience: no man could tell to what length he might go, or might refrain from going, in the direction of peace and reconciliation. Hitherto, he had not shown himself a man of heroic measures, and, properly enough, this step belonged to that class. It must be the end of all compromises with slavery—a declaration that thereafter the war was to be conducted on a new principle, with a new aim. It would be a full and fair assertion that the government would neither trifle, or be trifled with, any longer. But would it come? (Douglass 1892/1962, 352).

Every moment of waiting chilled the hopes and fears of Douglass and the assembled crowd.

A line of messengers was established between the telegraph office and the platform of Tremont Temple, and the time was occupied with brief speeches from Hon. Thomas Russell of Plymouth, Miss Anna E. Dickinson (a lady of marvelous eloquence), Rev. Mr. Grimes, J. Sella Martin, William Wells Brown, and myself. But speaking or listening to speeches was not the thing for which the people had come together. The time for argument was passed. It was not logic, but the trump of jubilee, which everybody wanted to hear. We were waiting and listening as for a bolt from the sky, which should rend the fetters of four millions of slaves; we were watching, as it were, by the dim light of the stars, for the dawn of a new day; we were longing for the answer to the agonizing prayers of centuries. Remembering those in bonds as bound with them, we wanted to join in the shout for freedom, and in the anthem of the redeemed (Ibid., 353).

In this account, Douglass was at his rhetorical best.

> Eight, nine, ten o'clock came and went, and still no word. A visible shadow seemed falling on the expecting throng, which the confident utterances of the speakers sought in vain to dispel. At last, when patience was well-nigh exhausted, and suspense was becoming agony, a man (I think it was Judge Russell) with hasty step advanced through the crowd, and with a face fairly illumined with the news he bore, exclaimed in tones that thrilled all hearts, "It is coming! It is on the wires!!" The effect of this announcement was startling beyond description, and the scene was wild and grand. Joy and gladness exhausted all forms of expression, from shouts of praise to sobs and tears. My old friend Rue, a colored preacher, a man of wonderful vocal power, expressed the heartfelt emotion of the hour, when he led all voices in the anthem, "Sound the loud timbrel o'er Egypt's dark sea, Jehovah hath triumphed, his people are free" (Ibid., 353).

Later, the crowd moved to the Twelfth Baptist Church and remained there until almost dawn on January 2. Douglass described the scene as "one of the most affecting and thrilling occasions I ever witnessed, and a worthy celebration of the first step on the part of the nation in its departure from the thraldom of ages" (ibid., 354).

The festivities were truly national in scope, at least in areas loyal to the United States. In Rochester, New York, commemorative exercises of a "religious character" were held on the Sunday following the issuance of the decree. In Orange, New Jersey, private dwellings were lit up. In Chicago, "the colored people celebrated the gladsome New Year's Day with appropriate public festivities—feeling sure of the coming of the Proclamation, before it was issued." One hundred guns were fired in salute on the Boston Common, in Albany, New York, Pittsburgh, Pennsylvania, and San Francisco, California. At Beaufort, South Carolina, "a celebration of the negroes was held in a live-oak grove, Gen. Saxton, Chaplain French, Col. Higginson, Mrs. Frances D. Gage (The *Independent*'s correspondent,) and others, in addition to the colored people, took part in the exercises. A set of colors, the gift of Dr. Cheever's church of New York, was presented to the negro brigade. A barbeque followed, consisting of twelve roasted oxen. The health of the President was drunk in molasses and water by the humble people whom he so greatly blest" (Douglass 1863).

In Washington, D.C., the nation's capital, "a great flock of contraband—men, women and children assembled" at a hospital for wounded soldiers. "At seven in the evening, a bell-man, rang a bell, calling the people together for the reading of the Proclamation" and a "prayer was offered by an aged contraband." "We 'seech thee, O Lord! To 'member the Union army, support dem on de right and left to carry on by work. Go before dem like a burning lamp. 'Member de President, de sea sailors and land trabbelers; 'member me, de meanest of dem all. Write us a ticket, and give us free admission to heaven. Amen" (Douglass 1863).

TEACHING NOTES

Renaming Public Places

QUESTIONS TO CONSIDER

1. Does changing the names of places
and institutions deny the contributions
made by imperfect people?

2. Will changing the names of places and institutions
correct the historical record or hide past injustices
from public view?

In his pathbreaking book, *Ebony and Ivy* (2013), historian Craig Wilder documents the ties between early American universities and slavery in the United States. He documents a slave sale by a University of Pennsylvania trustee, slave ownership by the first president of Dartmouth College, as well as ties between faculty, students, and trustees at Harvard, Yale, King's College (Columbia), the College of New Jersey (Princeton), and the College of Rhode Island (Brown), with enslavement and the transatlantic slave trade.

A campaign to honor the struggle to end slavery in the United States is an excellent project to engage students as active citizens responding to racism and in shaping the future of the United States (Singer 2015). During the Fall 2015 semester, students at Princeton University in New Jersey were demanding the renaming of its Woodrow Wilson School of Public and International Affairs and the Wilson College residential complex. While president of the United States in the early twentieth century, Wilson, who admired the Ku Klux Klan, resegregated the United States postal service and other civil service positions (*New York Times* 2015, A30). At Harvard Law School, students demanded that the school's "official seal" be dropped because it contains the family crest of the largest slaveholder in colonial Massachusetts. Isaac Royall Jr., whose father was a Caribbean slave trader, donated land to the university in 1817 to establish the law school (Gershman 2015). In New York City, Mayor Bill de Blasio called on Yale University to rename the residential college where his son lives. The college is named after John C. Calhoun, a Yale alumnus who was a Southern slaveholder and a chief advocate for slavery. De Blasio also said he is willing to listen to "concerns" about the New York City locations named after slaveholders and slave traders (Durkin 2015, 2). After two years of debate, Yale University decided to rename the college after Grace Murray Hopper, an alumna who was a (*continues on page 106*)

(*continues from page 105*)

pioneering computer scientist and a rear admiral in the U.S. Navy (*Washington Post* 2017).

Renaming New York City locations would be a big task. Not only does the city have the George Washington Bridge, Washington Heights, and Washington Square Park, Madison Square Garden, Madison Avenue, Astor Place, Delancey Street, and Chambers Street, but it also has a number of high schools and high school campuses named after slave-holders and slave traders. They include Washington and Stuyvesant in Manhattan, Madison and Jefferson in Brooklyn, Morris, Monroe, and Walton in the Bronx, and Francis Lewis in Queens. There are streets named after Washington, Jefferson, Monroe, and Madison in Brooklyn and a major thoroughfare named after Francis Lewis in Queens, as well as parks and playgrounds named after slaveholders including Schenck Playground in Brooklyn and Van Cortlandt Park in the Bronx. John Mullaly Park in the West Bronx is named after a Tammany Hall politico who was arrested during the Civil War for inciting antiblack riots. Citi Field in Queens and the Barclay Center in Brooklyn are both named after banks that profited from the transatlantic slave trade and the sale of slave-produced commodities.

This is not just a New York City issue. Averill Park, a town just outside of Troy, is named after Horatio Averill, a lawyer and real estate developer who played a role in one of Troy's signature historical events, the Nalle Rescue. It was Averill who identified Charles Nalle as a runaway slave, notified the Hansbrough family of Culpeper County, Virginia, that claimed to own him, and arranged for his arrest (Christianson 2010, 89). New York City and State are both named after James, Duke of York, head of the British Royal African Company, one of the seventeenth century's largest slave-trading concerns.

Rather than renaming the entire city, I have a different proposal. New York should celebrate the struggle to end slavery and build monuments and name parks and schools to recognize people and events that helped create a more just society. I have two suggestions and a commission could certainly name many more. The Shiloh Presbyterian Church on the corner of Prince and Marion streets, where black and white abolitionists welcomed the Emancipation Proclamation, is long gone and the site, now a shopping district in SOHO near the intersection of Prince between Lafayette and Mulberry, is unmarked. There is a public library nearby that could be renamed and would be an ideal place for a plaque recognizing both the jubilee celebration and Reverend Henry Highland Garnet, pastor of Shiloh Church, and a leading abolitionist. All that remains of the original Bridge Street AME church is the front of the building that is now part of a student center for the Polytechnic campus of New York University. The plaza, however, is still there and is part of the Metro Tech complex. It would be great to name the plaza "Grand Emancipation Jubilee Plaza" and make it the site of an annual commemoration. Maybe Metro Tech or NYU could even donate space for a permanent public exhibit.

Yale to Change Calhoun College's Name
to Honor Grace Murray Hopper

Yale President Peter Salovey announced today that the university would rename Calhoun College, one of 12 undergraduate residential colleges, to honor one of Yale's most distinguished graduates, Grace Murray Hopper '30 M.A., '34 Ph.D., by renaming the college for her.

Salovey made the decision with the university's board of trustees—the Yale Corporation—at its most recent meeting. "The decision to change a college's name is not one we take lightly, but John C. Calhoun's legacy as a white supremacist and a national leader who passionately promoted slavery as a 'positive good' fundamentally conflicts with Yale's mission and values," Salovey said. "I have asked Jonathan Holloway, dean of Yale College, and Julia Adams, the head of Calhoun College, to determine when this change best can be put into effect."

This decision overrides Salovey's announcement in April of last year that the name of Calhoun College would remain. "At that time, as now, I was committed to confronting, not erasing, our history. I was concerned about inviting a series of name changes that would obscure Yale's past," said Salovey. "These concerns remain paramount, but we have since established an enduring set of principles that address them. The principles establish a strong presumption against renaming buildings, ensure respect for our past, and enable thoughtful review of any future requests for change" (*YaleNews*, February 11, 2017).

7

LINCOLN AT GETTYSBURG

Were All Men Created Equal?

HISTORIANS AND POLITICAL SCIENTISTS ACROSS THE IDEOLOGICAL SPECTRUM CONSIS-
tently rank Abraham Lincoln as the greatest American president (Lindgren, Calabresi, Leo, and Smith 2000; Rottinghaus and Vaughn 2015). His 1863 speech at the dedication of the Gettysburg battlefield cemetery is also considered one of the foremost speeches in United States history (National Constitution Center 2015). In New York State, sample Common Core–aligned lessons for high school students use the Gettysburg Address as an "exemplar" to illustrate close reading of text (NYSED 2012). However, Lincoln's contemporaries, even members of his own political party, were less praising of both his performance as president and this speech.

On November 18, 1863, the *New York Times*, a Republican unionist newspaper, ran a brief note announcing, "The National Cemetery at Gettysburg, where the honored dead in the great battle sleep their last sleep, will be solemnly dedicated on Thursday, the 19th instant" (*New York Times* 1863d). The notice mentioned that a number of state governors, including New York State governor Seymour, would attend, but did not mention President Lincoln or the main speaker, Edward Everett. The exact same notice was published in the November 18 issue of the Copperhead Democrat *Brooklyn Eagle* but neither notice referenced a source. The *New York Tribune* attributed it to the Associated Press (*New-York Tribune* 1863, 1).

Coverage in New York newspapers was much more extensive over the next three days, November 19, 20, and 21. On the 20th, the *Times* (1) reported on "a solemn and imposing event" with an "oration by Hon. Edward Everett" and speeches by President Lincoln, Mr. Seward, and Governor Seymour. "The line of march was taken up at 10 o'clock, and the procession marched through the principal streets to the Cemetery, where the military formed in line and saluted the President. At 11 the head of the procession arrived at the main stand. The President and members of the Cabinet, together with the chief military and civic dignitaries, took position on the stand. The President seated himself between Mr. SEWARD and Mr. EVERETT after a reception marked with the respect and perfect silence due to the solemnity of the occasion, every man in the immense gathering uncovering on his appearance." The *Times* estimated the crowd at fifteen thousand men, women, and children (*New York Times* 1863e, 1).

Abraham Lincoln spoke after the opening prayer, and the *Times* printed the text of his address without comment, although it did describe Everett's speech, which it also printed, as an example of "splendid oration." In the same edition, the *Times* printed Governor Seymour's speech, however the text of Secretary of State Seward's brief comments was not published until the next day. The *Tribune* published, without comment, the text of both Lincoln's and Everett's speeches, starting on the front page, on November 20. Later, in an unpublished speech, *Tribune* editor Horace Greely wrote, "I doubt that our national literature contains a finer gem than that little speech at the Gettysburg celebration, November 19, 1863 ... after the close of Mr. Everett's classic but frigid oration" (Benton 1891, 380).

The *Brooklyn Eagle*, not surprisingly, was critical of both Lincoln and Everett. On November 20, it announced that Lincoln's speech had "failed" to reunite the nation, while Everett "let slip a great opportunity" to add to his reputation as an orator and statesman (*Brooklyn Eagle* 1863b, 2).

On November 19, 1863, Abraham Lincoln delivered what he considered to be "a few appropriate remarks" at the dedication of a cemetery at the Gettysburg battlefield in Pennsylvania to a crowd of about fifteen thousand people (Willis 1992). President Lincoln spoke for less than three minutes. There are no photographs of the speech because Lincoln gave the address before the photographers were set up. The speech itself was less than three hundred words long; yet Pulitzer Prize–winning Civil War historian James M. McPherson has argued that the Gettysburg Address is the "foremost statement of freedom and democracy and the sacrifices required to achieve and defend them" (Boritt 2008). In a eulogy for the assassinated president in June 1865, Senator Charles Sumner of Massachusetts commented that Lincoln was mistaken about the importance of the speech. "The world noted at once what he said, and will never cease to remember it. The battle itself was less important than the speech" (Sumner 1865, 41).

Below is one of several versions of the Gettysburg Address handwritten by Abraham Lincoln. It is considered the definitive version and is etched into the walls of the Lincoln Memorial in Washington, D.C.

The "four score and seven years ago" at the opening of the speech refers to the signing of the Declaration of Independence in Philadelphia in 1776 by the nation's founders. The Declaration of Independence famously promised "that all men are created equal, that they are endowed by their Creator with certain unalienable Rights, that among these are Life, Liberty and the pursuit of Happiness."

It was a promise the founders either never intended to deliver on, or what is more likely, a promise based on the idea that some men, and certainly women, were not included in the category "men." Most likely their community of men consisted of only white, Christian, English-speaking, adult males who owned property.

But in 1863, eighty-seven years later, whom did Abraham Lincoln include in the promises laid out in the Gettysburg Address? Who were the people included in this government of the people, by the people, and for the people? Was Lincoln proposing a more inclusive concept of men that recognized the full humanity of blacks, non-Christians, and possibly even women, or was it the same limited notion of manhood endorsed by the signers of the initial proclamation of nationhood? Answering these questions requires that we examine Lincoln's words and actions both before and after the Gettysburg Address.

A first clue to what Lincoln believed comes from a series of debates conducted when Abraham Lincoln and Stephen Douglas were campaigning to be selected by the state

ABRAHAM LINCOLN'S GETTYSBURG ADDRESS

QUESTION TO CONSIDER

Whom does Lincoln include in his vision for a more democratic America?

Four score and seven years ago our fathers brought forth on this continent, a new nation, conceived in Liberty, and dedicated to the proposition that all men are created equal. Now we are engaged in a great civil war, testing whether that nation, or any nation so conceived and so dedicated, can long endure. We are met on a great battle-field of that war. We have come to dedicate a portion of that field, as a final resting place for those who here gave their lives that that nation might live. It is altogether fitting and proper that we should do this.

But, in a larger sense, we cannot dedicate—we cannot consecrate—we cannot hallow—this ground. The brave men, living and dead, who struggled here, have consecrated it, far above our poor power to add or detract. The world will little note, nor long remember what we say here, but it can never forget what they did here. It is for us the living, rather, to be dedicated here to the unfinished work which they who fought here have thus far so nobly advanced. It is rather for us to be here dedicated to the great task remaining before us—that from these honored dead we take increased devotion to that cause for which they gave the last full measure of devotion—that we here highly resolve that these dead shall not have died in vain—that this nation, under God, shall have a new birth of freedom—and that government of the people, by the people, for the people, shall not perish from the earth.

legislature of Illinois as a United States Senator. On September 18, 1858 at Charleston, Illinois, Lincoln told the assembled audience:

> I am not, nor ever have been, in favor of bringing about in any way the social and political equality of the white and black races, that I am not, nor ever have been, in favor of making voters or jurors of negroes, nor of qualifying them to hold office, nor to intermarry with white people; and I will say in addition to this that there is a physical difference between the white and black races which I believe will forever forbid the two races living together on terms of social and political equality.... I will add to this that I have never seen, to my knowledge, a man, woman, or child who was in favor of producing a perfect equality, social and political, between negroes and white men (Lincoln 1989, 732).

I think Lincoln is very clear in this statement that when he speaks of men, women, and children, he is referring to white men, women, and children. This was before Lincoln was elected president and before the outbreak of the Civil War, but Lincoln's speeches, writings, and actions after these events continued to reflect this point of view about race and equality. William Seward of New York, who fully expected to secure the 1860 Republican Party nomination for president, believed that Lincoln was nominated primarily because Seward's antislavery views were so well known that Lincoln, below the national radar, made the more viable candidate for election (Stahr 2012, 193).

In his first inaugural address, Lincoln expressed support for the Corwin Amendment to the United States Constitution that would have barred Congress from interfering with the domestic institutions of the states, including "persons held to labor or service" such as enslaved Africans (Foner 2010, 158). On August 22, 1862, in a letter to Horace Greeley, editor of the *New York Tribune* and a leading abolitionist who was pressing for the immediate emancipation of enslaved Africans, Lincoln wrote:

> I would save the Union. I would save it the shortest way under the Constitution. The sooner the national authority can be restored; the nearer the Union will be "the Union as it was." If there be those who would not save the Union, unless they could at the same time *save* slavery, I do not agree with them. If there be those who would not save the Union unless they could at the same time *destroy* slavery, I do not agree with them. My paramount object in this struggle *is* to save the Union, and is *not* either to save or to destroy slavery. If I could save the Union without freeing *any* slave I would do it, and if I could save it by freeing *all* the slaves I would do it; and if I could save it by freeing some and leaving others alone I would also do that. What I do about slavery, and the colored race, I do because I believe it helps to save the Union (Foner 2010, 228).

In this letter, which was written while the president and the cabinet were discussing the possibility of issuing an emancipation decree in some form, Abraham Lincoln makes clear that his objective is saving the union, not the future of enslaved Africans. I think he also makes two other very important points. His actions must be guided by the way he views the constitutional powers of the president, executive powers that he believes are severely limited by constitutional restraints and do not grant him the authority to unilaterally abolish slavery. His goal is also and always to restore "the Union as it was," as a federal system where Southern white state governments may determine the rights of the blacks who reside within their states.

African American abolitionist Frederick Douglass remained very skeptical about Lincoln's intensions and program, even after the president issued a preliminary emancipation in September 1862. In November 1862, Douglass wrote in the *Douglass' Monthly*:

> It would be absurd and ridiculous to expect that the conquered traitors will at once cordially cooperate with the Federal Government.... They have got to be taught that slavery which they have valued as a blessing has ever been their direct calamity and curse.—The work before us is nothing less than a radical revolution in all the modes of thought which have flourished under the blighting slave system.... It is not likely ... that at the outset, the Southern people will consent to an absolutely just and humane policy towards the newly emancipated black people so long enslaved and degraded.... [T]he work does not end with the abolition of slavery but only begins (Douglass 2000, 522).

Douglass had good reason to mistrust Lincoln. On December 1, 1862, one month before the scheduled issuing of an emancipation proclamation, Abraham Lincoln offered the Confederacy another chance to return to the union and preserve slavery for the foreseeable future. In his annual Message to Congress, Lincoln recommended a Constitutional Amendment, which if it had passed, would have been the Thirteenth Amendment to the Constitution (Lincoln 1862/1895, 136).

The amendment included the following provisions:

1. Every State wherein slavery now exists which shall abolish the same therein at any time or times before the 1st day of January, A. D. 1900, shall receive compensation from the United States....

2. All slaves who shall have enjoyed actual freedom by the chances of the war at any time before the end of the rebellion shall be forever free; but all owners of such who shall not have been disloyal shall be compensated for them....

3. Congress may appropriate money and otherwise provide for colonizing free colored persons with their own consent at any place or places without the United States....

In this message to Congress, Lincoln proposed gradual emancipation that would not be completed for another thirty-seven years, taking slavery in the United States into the twentieth century; compensation, not for the enslaved, but for the slaveholder; and the expulsion, supposedly voluntary but essentially a new "Trail of Tears," of formerly enslaved Africans to the Caribbean, Central America, and Africa.

No wonder Frederick Douglass remained apprehensive as the date for emancipation approached. He recognized that "the federal arm had been more than tolerant to that relict of barbarism. It had defended it inside the slave states; it had countermanded the emancipation policy of John C. Fremont in Missouri; it had returned slaves to their so-called owners; and had threatened that any attempt on the part of the slaves to gain their freedom by insurrection, or otherwise, would be put down with an iron hand; . . . it had surrounded the houses of slaveholders with bayonets for their protection"; and Secretary of State William Seward "had given notice to the world that 'however the war for the Union might terminate, no change would be made in the relation of master and slave' " (Douglass and McKivigan 2012, 274).

In his memoir, Douglass described his thoughts in the hours before the Emancipation Proclamation was finally issued.

> [A]lthough the conditions on which Mr. Lincoln had promised to withhold it had not been complied with, yet, from many considerations, there was room to doubt and fear. Mr. Lincoln was known to be a man of tender heart, and boundless patience: no man could tell to what length he might go, or might refrain from going, in the direction of peace and reconciliation. Hitherto, he had not shown himself a man of heroic measures, and, properly enough, this step belonged to that class. It must be the end of all compromises with slavery—a declaration that thereafter the war was to be conducted on a new principle, with a new aim. It would be a full and fair assertion that the government would neither trifle, or be trifled with, any longer. But would it come? (Douglass 1962, 352–53).

It was a symbolic but in practical terms a very limited decree. Slavery did not end in the border states that had remained loyal to the Union. The decree did emancipate the millions of enslaved Africans in the South because the rebelling territories did not accept federal jurisdiction. At best, a few thousand enslaved Africans on plantations on the Georgia and South Carolina coast in areas controlled by Union troops were actually freed on that day.

But symbolism is important. Frederick Douglass called "the first of January 1863 . . . a memorable day in the progress of American liberty and civilization. It was the turning point in the conflict between freedom and slavery. A death blow was then given to the slaveholding rebellion" (Douglass 1962, 351).

However, Douglass's suspicions about Lincoln's motives and actions once again proved to be legitimate. On December 8, 1863, less than a month after the Gettysburg Address, Abraham Lincoln offered full pardons to Confederates in a Proclamation of Amnesty and Reconstruction that has come to be known as the Ten Percent Plan.

> I, Abraham Lincoln, President of the United States, do proclaim, declare, and make known to all persons who have, directly or by implication, participated in the existing rebellion, except as hereinafter excepted, that a full pardon is hereby granted to them and each of them, with restoration of all rights of property, except as to slaves, and in property cases where rights of third parties shall have intervened, and upon the condition that every such person shall take and subscribe an oath, and thenceforward keep and maintain said oath inviolate.... And I do further proclaim, declare, and make known that whenever, in any of the States of Arkansas, Texas, Louisiana, Mississippi, Tennessee, Alabama, Georgia, Florida, South Carolina, and North Carolina, a number of persons, not less than one tenth in number of the votes cast in such state at the presidential election of the year of our Lord one thousand eight hundred and sixty, each having taken the oath aforesaid, and not having since violated it, and being a qualified voter by the election law of the state existing immediately before the so-called act of secession, and excluding all others, shall reestablish a state government which shall be republican, and in nowise contravening said oath, such shall be recognized as the true government of the state (Lincoln 1894, 443).

While Lincoln also stated that "while I remain in my present position I shall not attempt to retract or modify the emancipation proclamation; nor shall I return to slavery any person who is free by the terms of that proclamation" (ibid., 455), it is important to emphasize that self-rule in the South would be restored when 10 percent of the "qualified" voters according to "the election law of the state existing immediately before the so-called act of secession" pledged loyalty to the union. Since blacks could not vote in these states in 1860, this was not to be government of the people, by the people, for the people, as promised in the Gettysburg Address, but a return to white rule.

Lincoln's ambivalence about constitutional limitations on presidential authority, the "indispensable necessity" of ending slavery, and the rights of freed blacks in a reconstructed union continued as he prepared for his 1864 reelection campaign. On April 4, 1864, Lincoln wrote to Albert Hodges, editor of the Frankfort, Kentucky, *Commonwealth*. He declared:

> I am naturally anti-slavery. If slavery is not wrong, nothing is wrong. And yet I have never understood that the Presidency conferred upon me an

unrestricted right to act officially upon this judgment and feeling. It was in the oath I took that I would, to the best of my ability, preserve, pro- tect, and defend the Constitution of the United States.... I understood, too, that in ordinary civil administration this oath even forbade me to practically indulge my primary abstract judgment on the moral question of slavery.... When early in the war, Gen. Fremont attempted military emancipation [in Missouri], I forbade it, because I did not think it an indispensable necessity. When a little later, Gen. [Simon] Cameron, then Secretary of War, suggested the arming of the blacks, I objected, because I did not think it an indispensable necessity. When, still later, Gen. [David] Hunter attempted military emancipation [in Georgia, Florida, and South Carolina], I again forbade it, because I did not yet think the indispensable necessity had come (Urofsky 2000, 218).

On August 19, 1864, Lincoln made clear in a discussion with Joseph Mills and Alexander Randall of Wisconsin that has actions in issuing the Emancipation Proclamation were solely intended to support the war effort. According to Mills's diary: "[N]o human power can subdue this rebellion without using the Emancipation lever as I have done. Freedom has given us the control of 200 000 able bodied men, born & raised on southern soil.... My enemies condemn my emancipation policy. Let them prove by the history of this war, that we can restore the union without it" (Lincoln 2008, 507).

In his Second Inaugural Address on March 4, 1865, Abraham Lincoln offered one of the most quoted lines in American oratory when he promised, "With malice toward none; with charity for all; with firmness in the right, as God gives us to see the right, let us strive on to finish the work we are in; to bind up the nation's wounds; to care for him who shall have borne the battle, and for his widow, and his orphan—to do all which may achieve and cher- ish a just, and a lasting peace, among ourselves, and with all nations" (White 2002, 17–19).

But to whom was Abraham Lincoln offering "malice towards none and charity for all"? As I read Lincoln's Second Inaugural Address, I see a war-weary and politically cautious president who never believed in racial equality; who in April 1861 accepted the proposed Corwin Amendment to the Constitution that would have prevented the national government from interfering with slavery in the South; who in December 1862, less than a month before finally issuing the Emancipation Proclamation, offered the South gradual compensated emancipation that would have extended slavery in the United States into the twentieth century, and who in the actual document sharply limited the scope of eman- cipation so that very few enslaved Africans out of the millions in bondage were directly and immediately affected. This Lincoln expressed tentative support for voting rights for black veterans, but did not believe he had the authority to enforce the idea.

Lincoln may well have been expressing the sentiments of his Northern support- ers. The *Times* described the speech as calm, modest, and reserved. It conveyed "trust without presumption; confidence without carelessness, a readiness to meet duty in any shape; composure under every trial; courage that can dare to the utmost; a magnanimity that finds it easy to forgive" (*New York Times* 1865a). However, in the *Tribune*, Horace Greeley expressed disappointment with Lincoln for insufficiently appealing to the "Rebels for a cessation of hostilities." According to Greeley, "Now is the fittest time for putting forth manifestations of generosity, clemency, magnanimity, which however they may be spurned by the Rebel chiefs, are certain to exert a great and salutary influence among their duped, disgusted, despairing followers" (*Tribune* 1865a, 4). Both newspapers were hoping and preparing for inevitable victory and peace; neither commented on the future of the formerly enslaved.

The *Brooklyn Eagle* continued to have little positive to say about the president. An editorial described the speech's primary "merit" as its brevity. After blaming Lincoln for the Civil War, it declared his speech "so crude and irreverent that it would be discreditable to a dull boy attached to an unpretentious orphan academy." A big part of the *Eagle*'s upset with Lincoln was his references to God's will. According to the *Eagle* editorial, God had "suffered the establishment of negro slavery" and "it is not permitted to Mr. Lincoln or anybody else to fathom the purpose of the Almighty in giving the Negro into bondage." According to the *Eagle*, "Good men, who regretted the existence of African slavery upon this Continent, could not deny that the negro profited by it more than the white man did," by being saved from "barbarism" and brought to "Christian civilization" (*Brooklyn Eagle* 1865a, 2).

Discussion of the implications of Lincoln's Second Inaugural Address for the future of the country and questioning of his presidency essentially ended six weeks later with the president's assassination. Even the *Brooklyn Eagle* was prepared to honor Lincoln, declaring that "the dead President is mourned as no other man perhaps ever by his countrymen, because of the belief which is everywhere felt that in his last days Mr. Lincoln's thoughts were turned to conciliation and peace" (*Brooklyn Eagle* 1865b, 2).

In the *Tribune*, Greeley wrote:

> For our own part, it intensifies our regret, while it is nevertheless our abiding consolation, that the lamented Head of the Republic now sleeping in his bloody shroud was never provoked to the exhibition of one trace of hate or even wrath toward those against whom he was compelled to battle for the life of the nation. . . . The blow that struck down Abraham Lincoln bereft the Union's misguided and criminal assailants of the firmest and most powerful opponent of all avoidable severity, all not indispensable harshness, in suppressing their Rebellion. His very public utterance—the speech of Tuesday night prior to his assassination—was conceived in this spirit, and had no other purpose than to reconcile the North to the most gentle and magnanimous treatment of the discomfited insurgents. . . . For

nothing can be further from the truth than the current notion that Mr. Lincoln was a man easily deflected from his course. He was slow to reach conclusions; but, once attained, they were immovable. He was among the last to perceive that the struggle into which we have been plunged could only be fought to a successful issue by openly recognizing the fact that Slavery had challenged the Union to mortal encounter and that the gage must be taken up as it was thrown down; but, once convinced of that fact, he was convinced forever. There was not in all America one man more inflexible in his resolve that Slavery should die and the Union be restored than was Abraham Lincoln. And whoever imagines that he could have been duped, or cajoled, or wheedled, out of his purpose on this head, does gross injustice to his memory.... Had he lived a very few days longer, we believe he would have issued a Proclamation of Amnesty which would have dissolved all that remains of the Rebellion, leaving its leaders no choice but between flight and unconditional surrender (*Tribune* 1865b, 4).

Greeley was convinced of both Abraham Lincoln's opposition to slavery and his willingness to grant amnesty to the South. I suspect that if Lincoln had lived, presidential reconstruction would not have differed much from the program promoted by his successor Andrew Johnson, and it probably would have received more support because of Lincoln's political capital earned as a victorious war president. In this circumstance, the United States may never have seen the Fourteenth and Fifteenth Amendments defining African Americans as citizens entitled to vote.

In 1963, one hundred years after the Emancipation Proclamation, one hundred years after Gettysburg, and one hundred and eighty-seven years after the signing of the Declaration of Independence, Martin Luther King Jr. told a crowd of hundreds of thousands gathered at the Lincoln Memorial in Washington, D.C.:

[O]ne hundred years later, we must face the tragic fact that the Negro is still not free. One hundred years later, the life of the Negro is still sadly crippled by the manacles of segregation and the chains of discrimination. One hundred years later, the Negro lives on a lonely island of poverty in the midst of a vast ocean of material prosperity. One hundred years later, the Negro is still languishing in the corners of American society and finds himself an exile in his own land (Marable and Mullings 2009, 380).

With these words, Martin Luther King echoed a warning issued by Radical Republican congressman Thaddeus Stevens on December 18, 1865. "We have turned, or are about to turn, loose four million slaves without a hut to shelter them or a cent in their pockets. The infernal laws of slavery have prevented them from acquiring an education, understanding the common laws of contract, or of managing the ordinary business of life. This Congress is bound to provide for them until they can take care of themselves. If we do not furnish them with homesteads, and hedge them around with protective laws; if we leave them to the legislation of their late masters, we had better have left them in bondage. If we fail in this great duty now, when we have the power, we shall deserve and receive the execration of history and of all future ages" (Fleming 149).

Based on what he wrote, said, and did, based on what we know about his ideas and the ideas of the time, was Abraham Lincoln in the Gettysburg Address limiting democracy in the United States to government of white people, by white people, and for white people? One hundred fifty years after the Emancipation Proclamation and the Gettysburg Address, Americans still have to decide how responsible Abraham Lincoln's biases and indecision were for the failure to create a society where "all men are created equal."

TEACHING NOTES

The Puzzling Mr. Seward

QUESTIONS TO CONSIDER

1. How do we evaluate historical figures who inevitably have inconsistencies and blemishes?

2. In the struggle to end slavery, should we honor the firebrands or the pragmatists?

Heroes such as Abraham Lincoln are inevitably flawed, and under closer scrutiny many may not be that heroic at all. Another example is the puzzling William Seward of Auburn, New York. Seward delivered excellent speeches. At least three of his antislavery speeches are among the more memorable from the antebellum United States. Seward stirred Northern opponents of slavery and enflamed Southern resentment with his condemnation of the Compromise of 1850. On the floor of the Senate, he was among the most outspoken critics of the *Dred Scott* decision. In an 1857 speech in Rochester, New York, Seward invoked a harbinger of civil war when he branded slavery the cause of the "irrepressible conflict" dividing the nation.

Seward was born in 1801 in the village of Florida, New York, about sixty-five miles northwest of New York City. He graduated from Union College in Schenectady and then studied law in Goshen and New York City. In 1823, he moved to Auburn, at the northern end of the Finger Lakes where he entered the law office of Judge Elijah Miller. A year later, he married Miller's daughter, Frances Adeline Miller (Stahr 2012).

As a lawyer, Seward defended runaway slaves in court and he and Frances aided Harriet Tubman, helping her secure a farm in Auburn, and hid freedom seekers in their home. They also supported Frederick Douglass's *North Star* newspaper. During 1858 debate over the admission of Kansas to the union, Senator James A. Bayard of Delaware accused Seward of not only believing in an end to slavery but of supporting "amalgamation," or racial intermixing, and the "extinction of the white race in the southern country" (Bayard 1855, 36).

Seward was elected to the New York State Senate in 1830 and elected governor in 1838 and 1840. While governor, he supported the right of black men to vote on an equal basis with whites, a decidedly unpopular position at the time (Sinha 2016, 321). From 1849 until 1861, he served in the United States Senate. He was a leading candidate for the Republican Party's presidential nomination in 1860 but lost out to Abraham Lincoln. After Lincoln's election, Seward gave up his seat in the Senate to join the cabinet as secretary of state.

In his speeches, Seward comes across as a pretty fiery abolitionist. That, and his activities with the Underground Railroad, probably cost him the 1860 Republican presidential nomination. But in practice Seward was a much more pragmatic politician who was willing to compromise with the South over slavery. In *Team of Rivals*, Doris Kearns Goodwin argues that Seward was "by temperament fundamentally conciliatory, eager to use his charisma and good natured manner to unify the nation and find a peaceful solution to the crisis," a perfect fit for Lincoln's cabinet, a seeming abolitionist who really was not an abolitionist at all. Seward understood himself this way. While he was viewed in the South with "alarm and apprehension," he claimed, "This general impression only amuses me," and that he was really a gentle lion (Goodwin 2005, 192). In Washington, Seward was a gracious host and his dinner parties attracted Southern pro-slavery advocates such as Jefferson Davis of Mississippi and John Crittenden of Kentucky as well as abolitionist Charles Sumner and Charles Francis Adams of Massachusetts (ibid., 193).

Seward's willingness to compromise, even on an issue as divisive as slavery, is nowhere more evident than in the role he played with the 1861 "Corwin Amendment" to the Constitution. Seward endorsed the amendment and is believed to have helped draft it along with Congressman Thomas Corwin of Ohio (Stahr 2012, 245). The amendment, which was approved by both houses of Congress and sent to the states for ratification, would have denied "Congress power to abolish or interfere, within any State, with the domestic institutions thereof, including that of persons held to labor or service by the laws of said State."

In December 1860, Seward was also instrumental in negotiating the "Crittenden Compromise" that would have blocked slavery north of the Missouri Compromise line while protecting it in the South (Stahr 2012, 215–16). In January 1861, Seward offered the South concessions including repeal of Northern personal liberty laws, passage of the Corwin Amendment, and admission of New Mexico to the union as a slave state (Foner 2010, 148). Carl Schurz, a leading Wisconsin Republican, was so disturbed by this seeming about-face by Seward that he wrote, "The mighty is fallen. He bows before the slave power He has trodden the way of compromise and concession, and I do not see where he can take his stand on this back track.... We believed in him so firmly and were so affectionately attached to him. This is the time that tries men's souls, and many probably will be found wanting." Seward's wife Frances was also gravely disappointed in him, warning, "You are in danger of taking the path which led Daniel Webster to an unhonored grave.... Compromise based on the idea that the preservation of the Union is more important than the liberty of nearly 4,000,000 human beings cannot be right" (Goodwin 2005, 302–303). Both the Corwin Amendment and the "Crittenden Compromise" became moot with Southern secession and the Civil War.

NEW YORK SENATOR WILLIAM SEWARD BATTLES AGAINST SLAVERY

QUESTIONS TO CONSIDER

1. How did Seward view the position of the Constitution on slavery?

2. Why did Seward believe division over slavery represented an "irrepressible conflict"?

William Seward's "Higher Law" Speech to the United States Senate (1850)

[I]t is insisted that the admission of California shall be attended by a COMPROMISE of questions which have arisen out of SLAVERY! I AM OPPOSED TO ANY SUCH COMPROMISE, IN ANY AND ALL THE FORMS IN WHICH IT HAS BEEN PROPOSED; ... What am I to receive in this compromise? Freedom in California. It is well; it is a noble acquisition; it is worth a sacrifice. But what am I to give as an equivalent? A recognition of the claim to perpetuate slavery in the District of Columbia; forbearance toward more stringent laws concerning the arrest of persons suspected of being slaves found in the free states; forbearance from the proviso of freedom in the charters of new territories.... Relying on the perversion of the Constitution, which makes slaves mere chattels, the slave states have applied to them the principles of the criminal law, and have held that he who aided the escape of his fellow-man from bondage was guilty of a larceny in stealing him.... We deem the principle of the law for the recapture of fugitives ... unjust, unconstitutional, and immoral; and thus, while patriotism withholds its approbation, the consciences of our people condemn it....

There is another aspect of the principle of compromise which deserves consideration. It assumes that slavery, if not the only institution in a slave state, is at least a ruling institution, and that this characteristic is recognized by the Constitution. But slavery is only one of many institutions there. Freedom is equally an institution there. Slavery is only a temporary, accidental, partial, and incongruous one. Freedom, on the contrary, is a perpetual, organic, universal one, in harmony with the Constitution of the United States (Byrd 1995, 300).

William Seward Denounces the Slave System, Rochester, New York (1858)

The slave system is one of constant danger, distrust, suspicion, and watchfulness. It debases those whose toil alone can produce wealth and resources for defense to the lowest degree of which human nature is capable, to guard against mutiny and insurrection, and this wastes energies which otherwise might be employed in national development and aggrandizement.... In states where the slave system prevails, the masters directly or indirectly secure all political power and constitute a ruling aristocracy. In states where the free-labor system prevails, universal suffrage necessarily obtains and the state inevitably becomes sooner or later a republic or democracy.... The two systems are at once perceived to be incongruous— they are incompatible. They never have permanently existed together in one country, and they never can.... [T]hese antagonistic systems are continually coming into closer contact, and collision results.... They who think that it is accidental, unnecessary, the work of interested or fanatical agitators, and therefore ephemeral, mistake the case altogether. It is an irrepressible conflict between opposing and enduring forces, and it means that the United States must and will sooner or later, become either entirely a slave-holding nation, or entirely a free-labor nation.... You will tell me that these fears are extravagant and chimerical. I answer, they are so; but they are so only because the designs of the slaveholders must and can be defeated. But it is only the possibility of defeat that renders them so. They cannot be defeated by inactivity. There is no escape from them, compatible with non-resistance (Kleiser 1911, 331–44).

William Seward Denounces the Dred Scott *Decision and Admission of Kansas as a Slave State (1858)*

The war between the United States and Mexico, and the acquisition of the Mexican provinces of New Mexico and Upper California, the fruits of that war, were so immediately and directly consequences of the annexation of Texas, that all of those events, in fact, may be regarded as constituting one act of intervention in favor of slave labor and slave States.... No one had ever said or even thought that the law of freedom in this region [Louisiana Territory] could be repealed, impaired, or evaded. Its constitutionality had indeed been questioned at the time of its enactment; but this, (continues on page 124)

(*continued from page 123*)

with all other objections, had been surrendered as part of the compromise. It was regarded as bearing the sanction of the public faith, as it certainly had those of time and acquiescence. But the slaveholding people of Missouri looked across the border, into Kansas, and coveted the land.... The new President [Buchanan], under a show of moderation, masked a more effectual intervention than that of his predecessor [Pierce], in favor of slave labor and a slave State. Before coming into office, he approached or was approached by the Supreme Court of the United States. On their docket was, through some chance or design, an action which an obscure negro man in Missouri had brought for his freedom against his reputed master. The court had arrived at a conclusion ... he was not, in view of the Constitution, a citizen of the United States, and therefore could not implead the reputed master in the Federal Courts.... The court did not hesitate to please the incoming President, by seizing this extraneous and idle forensic discussion, and converting it into an occasion for pronouncing the opinion the Missouri prohibition was void; and that, by force of the Constitution, slavery existed, with all the elements of property in man over man, in all the Territories of the United States.... Every nation has always some ruling idea, which, however, changes with the several stages of its development. A ruling idea of the colonies on this continent, two hundred years ago, was, labor to subdue and reclaim nature. Then African slavery was seized and employed as an auxiliary, under seeming necessity. That idea has ceased forever.... [T]he expansion of territory to make slave States will only fail to be a great crime because it is impracticable.... Freedom is the common right, interest, and ultimate destiny, of all mankind (*Congressional Globe* March 3, 1858, 939–44).

8

THE NEW YORK PRESS, RACISM, AND
THE PRESIDENTIAL ELECTION OF 1864

> *I use the word* nigger *in this chapter. I do not use it lightly and I will only use it when quoting directly from newspaper articles from the era. I do not believe it is possible to convey the depth of racism in New York and Northern society in general during the Civil War era without using this inflammatory and defamatory term. This chapter was written with research assistance from Joseph Palaia.*

TODAY, MOST SCHOLARS AND THE GENERAL PUBLIC RANK ABRAHAM LINCOLN AS THE greatest American president of all time; however, during the spring and summer of 1864, as the Civil War dragged on and Union forces appeared to be stalled in the field, many leading Republicans considered him a political liability. Lincoln himself feared he would not be reelected. An examination of the events and debates leading up to Lincoln's eventual reelection exposes the depth of racial animosity in the North during the Civil War, animosity that contributed to the abandonment of formerly enslaved Africans by the federal government at the conclusion of the war and the years of Jim Crow segregation that followed it.

Excerpts and headlines from two *New York Times* articles suggest both the precariousness of Abraham Lincoln's political fortunes during the summer of 1864 as war news was reported in the press and the extent of Northern white racism. The endemic and casual racism expressed in newspaper coverage of the war and the presidential contest both threatened Lincoln's reelection effort and undermined the possibility of social and political equality for African Americans in the postwar era, while establishing the conditions for a permanently fractured nation divided along the "color line."

On June 18, 1864, *The New York Times* headlines mistakenly reported "Petersburg Captured," which would have left Richmond, the Confederate capital, indefensible and made the end of the Civil war imminent. The headlines also praised the "Distinguished Gallantry of the Black Legion." Unfortunately for Lincoln and the Republicans, the report was inaccurate. Petersburg did not fall, and during the summer of 1864 Union forces performed badly in the Virginia campaign, enduring approximately one hundred thousand casualties.

On August 2, 1864, *The New York Times* again headlined the battle over Petersburg. This time the *Times* reported a "Desperate Attempt to Carry the Enemy's Position" and the "Failure of the Attempt." It also unfairly blamed defeat on "The Colored Troops Charged With the Failure." The formerly enslaved Africans made up only one of the four Union divisions that participated in the battle and were the last division deployed in the assault. The *Times* article did mention that the black troops "received galling fire," "kept on advancing," "rallied" after an initial retreat, and "again pushed forward," but were unsuccessful, "the greater part of their officers being killed or wounded." According to the *Times*, casualties for the seven "Colored" units who participated in the battle included at least fifty-three officers killed or wounded and 1,400 men dead, wounded, or missing in action.

On August 19, there was a meeting in New York City attended by prominent local Republican leaders including Horace Greeley, editor of the *New York Tribune*, former New York City mayor George Opdyke, and journalist Park Godwin, and a committee was appointed to issue a call for a new party national convention and to request that Lincoln withdraw as a candidate for president. Thurlow Weed, an important Republican Party political insider from upstate New York and mentor to Secretary of State William Seward, is reported to have commented, "Lincoln is gone." Weed later wrote William Seward that he had personally told Lincoln that "re-election was an impossibility ... nobody here doubts it; nor do I see any body from other States who authorizes the slightest hope of success." Greeley, in a letter to Opdyke, wrote, "Mr. Lincoln is already beaten. He cannot be reelected. And we must have another ticket to save us from utter overthrow" (McPherson 1964, 281; Waugh 1997, 264–75).

On August 22, 1864, in response to disappointing battlefield and political developments, Henry Raymond, editor of *The New York Times*, wrote to Lincoln: "I feel compelled to drop you a line concerning the political condition of the country as it strikes me. I am in active correspondence with your staunchest friends in every state and from them all I hear but one report. The tide is setting strongly against us. Hon. E. B. Washburne writes that 'were an election to be held now in Illinois we should be beaten.' Mr. [Simon} Cameron writes that Pennsylvania is against us. Gov. [Oliver] Morton writes that nothing but the most strenuous efforts can carry Indiana. This state [meaning New York], according to the best information I can get, would go 50,000 against us to-morrow. And so of the rest. Nothing but the most resolute and decided action on the part of the government and its friends, can save the country from falling into hostile hands" (Lincoln 2008, 517–18n).

Evidently, Lincoln shared these pessimistic views because on August 23, 1864, he and his cabinet members signed a pledge to support his successor in the event of his likely defeat in the upcoming presidential election. "This morning, as for some days past, it seems exceedingly probable that this Administration will not be re-elected. Then it will be my duty to so cooperate with the President-elect as to save the union between the election and the inauguration; as he will have secured his election on such ground that he cannot possibly save it afterwards." The handwritten note, which is on file in the Library of Congress, is signed "A Lincoln" (Lincoln 1989, 624).

Lincoln's concerns about the possibility of reelection were well founded. On September 2, Theodore Tilton, an influential local abolitionist and editor of *The Independent* in New York City, wrote a letter to Republican governors, co-signed by Greely and Godwin, asking them whether they thought Lincoln should be replaced on the Republican/Unionist ticket by another candidate (McPherson 1964, 282).

The military and political situations, however, quickly changed again on September 3, when the Northern public learned that Union forces under command of General William T. Sherman had taken Atlanta, Georgia. On September 3, 1864, the front-page headlines of *The New York Times* reported: "Atlanta. Fall of the Rebels Stronghold" and "A Thunderbolt for Copperheads." Combined with the taking of Mobile, Alabama, by Union forces and news of increasing Union military success in the Shenandoah Valley campaign in Virginia, these events transformed the political climate, saved Lincoln's presidency, and ensured his reelection.

On September 6, 1864, Horace Greeley, who had been actively exploring alternatives to Lincoln as the Republican Party's presidential nominee, unequivocally endorsed Lincoln for reelection. Theodore Tilton, who just days before was soliciting supporters in an effort to dump Lincoln, wrote to John Nicolay, Lincoln's private secretary: "We are going to win the Presidential election. The divisions are going to be healed. I have never seen such a sudden lighting up of the public mind as since the late victory at Atlanta." Tilton's conclusion was confirmed by James T. Lewis, governor of Wisconsin. "In my judgment the interests of the Union party, the honor of the Nation and the good of Mankind, demand that Mr Lincoln should be sustained and re-elected" (Holzer 2014, 527–29; McPherson 1964, 282–83).

This reversal of political fortune, Lincoln's reelection, and then his assassination and martyrdom have hidden somewhat the breadth and depth of anti-Lincoln, antiwar, and antiblack sentiment in the North, particularly in New York State and New York City. In New York City during the Civil War the *World*, *Freeman's Journal*, *Daily News*, *Journal of Commerce*, and *Weekly Day-Book* were closely aligned with the antiwar, pro-Southern, antiblack "Peace Democrats." The *World* was considered the leading Copperhead newspaper in the United States and its pages were virulently racist. The *Daily News* was edited by Ben Wood, brother of Mozart Hall political boss, mayor, and congressional representative Fernando Wood, who had called on New York City to secede from the Union along with the South in January 1861 and was a leading opponent of the Thirteenth Amendment to the Constitution ending slavery in the United States. In 1864, the *News* was accused of receiving payments from Confederate agents to promote antiwar rallies in New York City, and it inflamed racial tension by claiming that racial mixing or miscegenation was the "doctrine and dogma" of the Republican Party. The editorial page of the *Weekly Day-Book*, which from October 1861 to October 1863 was known as *The Caucasian*, carried the banner "White Men Must Rule America" (Holzer 2014, 345–52; Wood 1968, 35).

Other Copperhead newspapers in New York City were also openly racist and in the months leading up to the July 1863 Draft Riots encouraged opposition to the war effort and defiance of the draft. John Mullaly, editor of the Roman Catholic Church's newspaper, *Metropolitan Record*, called for armed resistance. At a Union Square rally May 19, 1863, Mullaly declared the war to be "wicked, cruel and unnecessary, and carried on solely to benefit the negroes, and advised resistance to conscription if ever the attempt should be made to enforce the law." Following the July Draft riots, Mullaly was indicted for "inciting resistance to the draft." The arrest warrant specifically cited an article from the *Metropolitan Record*, "Five Hundred. Thousand More Victims to Abolitionism." Mullaly was also charged with counseling Governor Horatio Seymour to "forcibly to resist an enrollment ordered by competent authority in pursuance of said act of Congress" (*New York Times* 1863a; *New York Times* 1864e; George 1978: 112–32).

The *Herald*, with the largest circulation in the country, was virulently anti-Lincoln and free with its use of sensational and incendiary language. In June 1863, anti-war Democrats and the *Herald* supported a mass antiwar rally at Cooper Hall in New York City, where the war was denounced as a rich man's war that violated the Constitution and would lead to freed blacks flooding north and competing for white jobs (*New York Times* 1863b). Governor Seymour appeared to endorse mob rioting in a July 4, 1863, speech at the Academy of Music in New York City. Seymour chastised the administration for branding as traitors "we who differ, honestly, patriotically, sincerely, from them with regard to the line of duty." He declared "that the bloody, and treasonable, and revolutionary doctrine of public necessity can be proclaimed by a mob as well as by a Government" (Greeley 1866, 500).

The August 23, 1863, issue of the *Herald* predicted that the Republican Party would eventually nominate and unite behind Lincoln when it realized he was the person "predestined and foreordained by Providence to carry on the war, free the niggers, and give all of the faithful a share of the spoils" (Waugh 1997, 307). On October 7, 1863, the *Herald* described the Ohio gubernatorial election as a battle to decide "whether the copperheads or the niggerheads are more obnoxious to the great conservative body of the people" (Waugh 1997, 15).

During the lead-up to the 1864 presidential election, the New York City "Democratic" press continued to viciously attack Lincoln. On February 19, 1864, *Herald* editor James Gordon Bennett wrote that Lincoln "is a joke incarnated. His election was a very sorry joke. The idea that such a man as he should be President of such a country as this is a very ridiculous joke" (Waugh 1997, 140). The problem for Democrats was that Bennett was politically eclectic and not a reliable supporter of potential Democratic Party candidates, particularly George McClellan. In the January 29, 1864, issue of the *Herald*, Bennett started promoting Ulysses S. Grant as a candidate for president and in October, after McClellan and Lincoln were nominated, he proposed that the Electoral College ignore the balloting and select Grant (Waugh 1997, 122–23, 325).

The *Journal of Commerce*, whose founders in 1827 included abolitionist Arthur Tappan, was much more clearly aligned with the antiwar Democrats. Gerald Hallock, its publisher and editor, claimed to personally oppose slavery, but argued that the federal government lacked the constitutional authority to end it outside of the District of Columbia. He hoped to preserve the Union by compromising with the South and in December 1860 participated in a private meeting of prominent New York City Democrats, merchants, and bankers where they blamed the secession crisis on "sectional agitators of the North" and organized a "Committee to the South, to lay our views before their statesmen, and to express our sympathy for their wrongs, and to assure them of our continued cooperation and hopes of success in speedily procuring for them that equality which abstract justice, as well as the Constitution, guarantees to them and their institutions" (*New York Times* 1860c). In 1861, a U.S. grand jury indicted Hallock for disloyalty for publishing articles that sympathized with the Confederacy, including a list of antiwar Northern newspapers that were opposed to the "unholy war." The *Journal of Commerce*'s federal mail privileges were suspended until Hallock resigned as its editor (Jackson 1995, 627: Holzer 2014, 345–49).

In May 1864, the *Journal of Commerce*, the *World*, and the *Herald* reported that Abraham Lincoln, fearing that the war effort was going badly, had issued a proclamation calling for a national day of fasting and the immediate recruitment of four hundred thousand more soldiers. The *Herald* became suspicious of the story and dropped coverage. The proclamation turned out to be a fraud perpetrated by reporters from the *Brooklyn Eagle* who were later charged with trying to manipulate the gold market. The editors of the *Journal of Commerce* and *World*, who published stories without verification, were arrested, although later exonerated, and publication of the newspapers was temporarily suspended (Holzer 2014, 489–92).

Lincoln was also attacked during the summer of 1864 for his pocket veto of the Wade-Davis Reconstruction Bill that would have required the rebelling Southern states to reapply for admission to the union after adopting new state constitutions banning slavery. Lincoln argued that the bill would have "inflexibly committed" the country to a "single plan of restoration" and negated "free-state constitutions and governments, already adopted and installed in Arkansas and Louisiana." Greely published a response to Lincoln by Senator Benjamin Wade of Ohio and Representative Henry Davis of Maryland in the *Tribune* on August 5, 1864. They charged that a "more studied outrage on the legislative authority of the people has never been perpetrated" (Waugh 1997, 259).

On August 6, 1864, the *Herald* applauded the attack on Lincoln, arguing that the Wade-Davis manifesto had branded Lincoln for his "arrogance, ignorance, usurpation, knavery and a host of other deadly sins, including that of hostility to the rights of humanity and to the principles of republican government." *Herald* editor James Gordon Bennett called on Lincoln to step aside and predicated it would lead to a new national convention that could potentially produce a unity candidate (Waugh 1997, 261). Keeping up the clamor against Lincoln, on August 16, 1864, the *World* reprinted an article from the *Richmond Examiner* claiming, "The obscene ape of Illinois is about to be deposed" (Tagg 2009, 415). The pro-Lincoln *New York Times* on August 10, 1864, was compelled to respond to the attacks on Lincoln from both sides, arguing that he was unfairly caught in the middle: "One denounces Mr. Lincoln because he did not abolish Slavery soon enough—another because he assumed to touch it at all" (*New York Times* 1864d).

The 1864 presidential election provided the Democratic Party press in New York City, as well as pro- and anti-war Democrats, another opportunity to express their open, casual, and nasty racism. During the campaign, Republican Party loyalists such as the *New York Times* also succumbed to racial prejudice. A key figure during this period was David Goodman Croly, who started his career as a journalist at the *New York Evening Post*, moved to the *Herald*, and ultimately ended up at the *World*. While at the *World*, Croly teamed with another *World* staff member, George Wakeman, to anonymously produce one of the more avowedly racist attacks on Republicans and African Americans produced during the Civil War. They wrote and distributed a seventy-two-page pamphlet titled "Miscegenation: The Theory of the Blending of the Races, Applied to the White Man and the Negro." In the pamphlet, Croly and Wakeman charged it was a war of "amalgamation" that's goal was the "blending of the white and black," starting with the intermixing of Negroes and Irish. Many, including the editors of the *World*, argued the incendiary pamphlet was the work of abolitionists and represented their actual program, rather than an attempt to undermine abolition (Kaplan 1991, 47–100; Waugh 1997, 317–20).

In a series of articles during April and May 1864, *The New York Freeman's Journal & Catholic Register*, a "peace at any cost" Democratic Party newspaper closely aligned with congressman and former mayor Fernando Wood, claimed that the "beastly doctrine of the intermarriage of black men and white women" had been "encouraged by the President of the United States" and that "filthy black niggers" were mingling with "white people and even ladies everywhere, even at the President's levees" (Kaplan 1991, 71).

The editors of the *Times*, sucked in by the fraud, wrote, "We regret to learn from numerous sources that we are on the point of witnessing intermarriage on a grand scale between the whites and blacks of this Republic. It has, as most of our readers are aware, been long held by logicians of the Democratic school, that once you admit the right of a negro to the possession of his own person, and the receipt of his own wages, you are bound either to marry his sister, or give your daughter in marriage to his son. The formula into which this argument has always been thrown was this: If all blacks are fit to be free every white man is bound to marry a black: 'Niggers' are blacks: Therefore every white man is bound to marry a 'nigger'" (*New York Times* 1864a). In the editorial, the *Times* blamed Horace Greely and the *Tribune* for contributing to the racial amalgamation movement.

A week later, on March 26, 1864, the editors of the *Times* wrote: "We have no hesitation in saying that if we had at the outset conceived it possible that hostility to Slavery would ever have led to wholesale intermarriage with negroes, or of all marriageable Republicans and their sisters, that party should never have received any countenance or support from this journal. We owe it to ourselves and posterity to say that the odious matrimonial arrangements, into which so many of those whose opinions on certain great questions of public policy we have hitherto shared, have taken us wholly by surprise" (*New York Times* 1864b).

However, by March 30, 1864, the *Times* realized it was a victim of a hoax. "Trusting entirely, as we stated at the time, to the assertions of the Copperhead press, we have made mention of sundry movements alleged to be in process for the more wide-spread diffusion of the new political gospel of Miscegenation.... [T]he Copperhead newspapers have been spreading false reports, which is scarcely conceivable." However, not only did the paper not apologize for its racism, but it complained, "The Copperheads are responsible for this state of things. They have aroused the whole colored community, by their highly-colored pictures of the connubial fate that awaits them at Republican hands, to a state of intense excitement" (*New York Times* 1864c).

The *Brooklyn Eagle*, published in what was at that time the independent city of Brooklyn, was among the most reliable "Peace" Democrat newspapers and among the most racist in the greater metropolitan area. The *Brooklyn Eagle* began publication in October 1841 and continued to publish until March 1955. At the outbreak of the Civil War it had the highest circulation of any evening daily newspaper in the United States. Walt Whitman was its editor from 1845 until 1848, and until 1853, when it became avowedly pro-Democrat, pro-slavery, and antiblack, it had generally praised the antislavery movement. However, the *Eagle* was so vehement in its opposition to the war, blaming the North for driving the South out of the union, that in August 1861 it was investigated by a federal grand jury. While no indictments were issued, the *Eagle* temporarily lost the right to use the postal service for delivery (Brooklyn Public Library, nd; Holzer 2014, 345).

During the nineteenth century, racism permeated the pages of the *Eagle*. A search for the word *nigger* on the Brooklyn Public Library website for the years between 1841 and 1860 yielded 526 hits; between 1861 and 1880, 705 hits; and between 1881 and 1902, 858 hits. A search for the words *darky* or *darkies* for the years between 1841 and 1860 yielded 83 hits; between 1861 and 1880, 400 hits; and between 1881 and 1902, another 829 hits. Miscegenation, a term first coined in 1864, yielded 91 hits between 1861 and 1880.

On September 19, 1864, as the 1864 presidential campaign picked up steam, the *Eagle* published an account of a "Democratic Mass Meeting at Montague Hall," across from Brooklyn City Hall. One of the principal speakers was John G. Schumaker, district attorney for Kings County from 1856 to 1859, corporation counsel for the city of Brooklyn from 1862 to 1864, a delegate to the Democratic National Convention in 1864, and member of the United States House of Representatives from Brooklyn from 1869–71 and 1873–77. In this speech, which was repeatedly interrupted with cheers from the audience, Schumaker represented the views, openly racist, of both Brooklyn Democrats and the *Eagle* regarding the 1864 presidential election:

> Mr. Lincoln had not the choice of a majority of the people of the United States, but the democratic party was divided between candidates, and it was defeated; and it was owing to that fact that Mr. Lincoln was able to disgrace the country and to drag our glorious stars and stripes through the dust. Years ago this fanatical party of which he is the fit representative, commenced their career by stealing the servant of Henry Clay, in New York, and they have continued stealing niggers ever since, until now they are stealing them wholesale. He presented a revolutionary platform, under which it was only a matter of time to determine when the negroes of the South should be all free and the white men of the North all slaves. Mr. Lincoln was elected upon that platform (*Brooklyn Eagle* 1864, 2).

In Brooklyn, as in New York City, the Democratic Party was divided into competing factions. Martin Kalbfleisch, mayor of Brooklyn from 1862 to 1864 and from 1867 to 1871, while a "Peace" Democrat, appears to have been a member of a political faction that the *Eagle* did not support, and his activities were rarely reported on in its pages. Between his terms as mayor, Kalbfleisch served in the House of Representatives where he joined with Fernando Wood of New York City in opposing the Thirteenth Amendment to the United States Constitution. While Kalbfleisch was ignored by the *Eagle*, his political machinations were covered by the rival Republican newspaper, the Brooklyn *Daily Tribune* and occasionally the *New York Times* (*New York Times* 1873, 5; *Brooklyn Eagle* 1873, 4).

In August 1863, the *New York Times* reported on a rally organized by the Brooklyn and King's County Democratic Party where Kalbfleisch was the featured speaker and drew heavy applause from the assembly. Kalbfleisch demanded that the war be immediately "terminated" (*New York Times* 1863c, 1). According to the article, "If the war was for restoring the Union, the Government would have the support of every Democrat in the country, and he hoped the party now administering the Government would become convinced of the necessity of presenting an unbroken front to the enemy. Let them show to the country that the war was waged to restore the Union, and it would not be long before the Stars and Stripes would again wave over every inch of territory in the country."

At another point in the speech, Kalbfleisch was interrupted from the floor by a shout he mistook for "Niggordom." Kalbfleisch replied, "If the gentleman has anything to say let him say it in a mannerly way. If the gentleman had rather embrace a nigger baby than a white one, let him say so."

Racism so distorted the editorial judgment of the Democratic Party press that it led to what can only be described as political fantasy. In the 1864 election, three states, Ohio, Indiana, and Pennsylvania, cast ballots on October 11, four weeks before the rest of the nation, and all three states were carried by Lincoln and the Union Party (*New York Times* 1864g, 1). Manton Marble of the *World*, however, continued to insist that Lincoln and the Republican/Unionist would be defeated in November. On October 13, Marble predicted, "General McClellan will be honestly elected President on the 8th of November next." The editor of the *Journal of Commerce* anticipated a close election but also proclaimed a McClellan victory (Waugh 2009, 338).

Despite the positive war news in the fall of 1864, Lincoln and the Republicans narrowly carried New York State in the presidential election, by a margin of less than 1 percent. It was Lincoln's narrowest margin of victory in any Northern state and was probably attributable to the seventy thousand absentee ballots cast by Union soldiers. Nearly four of five soldiers who voted supported Lincoln over McClellan, including 70 percent of the Army of the Potomac that was formerly under McClellan's command (Waugh 2009, 353; Burroughs and Wallace 1999, 903).

Lincoln performed particularly poorly in New York State's urban areas, where there were large numbers of newly registered immigrant voters. In New York City, Lincoln received less than one-third of the votes; he trailed Democratic candidate George McClellan by 73,716 to 36,687. McClellan also outpolled Lincoln in Kings County (Brooklyn), Albany County, and Erie County (Buffalo). The only major city Lincoln carried in New York State was Rochester (*New York Times* 1864h, 1).

In 1911, Sidney Brummer published a Columbia University doctoral dissertation detailing political factionalism in the two major parties in New York State during the Civil War years. According to Brummer, while there were pro-war and antiwar "peace" Democrats, many of the divisions within the party were rooted in struggles over machine control of patronage in the urban areas. The battle between the Tammany Hall of William Tweed and the Mozart Hall of Fernando Wood in New York City was among the most prominent and divisive. Similarly, Republicans were not only divided between Unionists and more radical supporters of abolition and rights for emancipated African Americans, but also between factions competing for lucrative federal contracts and appointments, especially control over the Treasury office and customhouse in New York City (Brummer 1911, 439–40).

After losing the gubernatorial election in 1858 and the presidential and New York City mayoralty balloting in 1861, the Democratic Party was in ascendancy again in New

York City and State in 1862. Antiwar Democrats swept every ward in New York City elections, Democratic Party candidate Horatio Seymour was elected governor, and former New York City mayor Fernando Wood was elected to Congress. The Society for the Diffusion of Political Knowledge, based in New York City, began to organize to defeat Lincoln in 1864 and replace him with George McClellan, former General of the Army of the Potomac and General-in-Chief of the Union Army. The leadership of the society included banker and Democratic Party operative August Belmont, inventor, educator, and nativist Samuel F. B. Morse, New Jersey Governor Joel Parker, Seymour, and Samuel Tilden, a corporate lawyer who would become governor of New York and a Democratic Party presidential candidate. The society independently published antiwar and anti-emancipation material, including openly racist pamphlets. One pamphlet presented the pro-Southern "Bible View of Slavery" and another, written by Morse, claimed to be an "ethical" defense of slavery. The society also contributed financial support to the Copperhead newspaper, the *New York World* (Tise 1990, 257; Hopkins 1863, 117–32).

In retrospect, given the hatred and racism of the antiwar Copperhead Democrats and the hesitancy and racism of both the pro-war Democrats and Unionist Republicans that were exhibited in New York City and State, it is amazing that slavery in the United States ended at all. Emancipation was a tribute to the doggedness of abolitionists, black and white, the need for black manpower for the North to win the war, and major miscalculations by Southern secessionists who mistakenly exaggerated Northern opposition to slavery and support for black rights.

TEACHING NOTES

The Miscegenation Hoax

The term *miscegenation* was first used in an anonymous pamphlet distributed in New York City in 1863. The seventy-two-page pamphlet claimed that the goal of Abraham Lincoln and the Republican Party was the "interbreeding" of "White" and African Americans in the United States. Many people thought the pamphlet, *Miscegenation: The Theory of the Blending of the Races, Applied to the American White Man and Negro*, was written by abolitionists who supported the idea. In February 17, 1864, Democratic congressman Samuel Cox of Ohio (1857–1865) denounced the pamphlet in a speech delivered to the House of Representatives. He claimed it represented the social philosophy of the Republican Party. Cox later represented New York City in Congress (1869–1889). The actual authors of the pamphlet were an editor and reporter from the *New York World*, a pro–Democratic Party newspaper. They wrote it to use stir up racist attitudes among white voters as part of the newspaper's opposition to Abraham Lincoln's reelection campaign. The pamphlet is accessible online at https://archive.org/details/miscegenationthe00crol.

Miscegenation: The Theory of the Blending of the Races,
Applied to the American White Man and Negro (1863)

QUESTION TO CONSIDER

In the 1960s, the Ku Klux Klan denounced the civil rights movement for trying to create a "mongrel race" in the United States. Why have interracial relationships, including interracial marriage, been such a hot-button issue in this country?

"The miscegenetic or mixed races are much superior, mentally, physically, and morally to those pure or unmixed," the author proclaimed. Furthermore, he argued, the strength of the American nation stemmed "not from its Anglo-Saxon progenitors, but from all the different nationalities.... All that is needed to make us the finest race on earth is to engraft upon our stock the negro element" (Croly 1864, 11).... It is idle to maintain that this present war is not a war for the negro.... It is a war, if you please, of amalgamation ... a war looking, as its final fruit, to the blending of the white and black.... Let the war go on ... until church, and state, and society recognize not only the propriety but the necessity of the fusion of the white and black—in short, until the great truth shall be declared in our public documents and announced in the messages of our Presidents, that it is desirable the white man should marry the black woman and the white woman the black man (18–19) .... [T]he solution of the negro problem will not have been reached in this country until public opinion sanctions a union of the two races ... that in the millenial [*sic*] future, the most perfect and highest type of manhood will not be white or black but brown, or colored, and that whoever helps to unite the various races of man, helps to make the human family the sooner realize its great destiny (Croly 1864, 64–65).

Congressman Samuel Cox (Ohio) Denounces
Miscegenation, Abolitionists, and Republicans

QUESTION TO CONSIDER

A statue honoring Samuel Cox is located in New York City's Tompkins Square Park. The plaque does not mention his racism or support for slavery. What should be done with this statue?

[W]e are warned to look the great fact in the face that millions unfit for freedom are yet to become free.... No effort on the part of the Democracy to achieve a peace through conciliation will now be listened to.... The war with its revolution goes on, and slavery as a political if not as a social institution may fall under its crushing car. It may be that all of the four million *(continues on page 136)*

(continued from page 135)

slaves will be thrown, like the one hundred thousand already freed, upon the frigid charities of the world. But, sir, if slavery be doomed too, alas! Is the slave.... The irrepressible conflict is not between slavery and freedom, but between black and white; and as De Tocqueville prophesized, the black will perish. Do gentlemen on the other side rely upon the new system, called by the transcendental abolitionists, "Miscegenation," to save the black? This is but another name for amalgamation; but it will not save the negro.... Theodore Tilton, the editor of the Independent (a paper publishing the laws of the United States by authority;) holds that hereafter the "negro will lose his typical blackness and be formal clad in white men's skins." But, sir, no system so repugnant to the nature of our race ... can save the negro.... I do not believe that the doctrine of miscegenation, or the amalgamation of the white and black, now strenuously urged by the abolition leaders, will save the negro. It will destroy him utterly. The physiologist will tell the gentleman that the mulatto does not live; he does not recreate his kind; he is a monster. Such hybrid races, by a law of Providence, scarcely survive beyond one generation (*The Congressional Globe*, February 19, 1864, 709–10).

Social Equality for the Negro

QUESTION TO CONSIDER

Why was racism such a powerful force at the time and
why has it continued to play a role in American society?

However reprehensible the new doctrine of "miscegenation" may appear to some of our Republican friends, it is certain that their party is making the way clear for the experiment. In the Senate, yesterday, the word "white" in the section of the bill defining the qualification of voters in the new territory of Montana, was stricken out. The negro is placed upon a level with the white man there. A few of the Republican Senators broke loose from their party moorings, but the word was stricken out by a vote of 22 to 17.... In our State Senate an attempt is being made to go a step further by admitting on terms of equality white and colored children in our public schools. If we can make the little folks familiar in their youth, they will fraternize more readily when they grow up, and the "unreasonable prejudice" which stands in the way of raising "the more perfect race" may be removed. The effect of the law proposed at Albany will be to destroy the usefulness of our public school system. The more wealthy class will not suffer their children to associate with negroes, and our public schools will be left to the children of those who will have to barter their self-respect to secure their children an education. Our common schools would very soon become "poor schools" and from a pride, however false, would be avoided (*Brooklyn Eagle*, April 1, 1864).

ABOLITION

From Marginalization to Emancipation

IN THE 1980S, AS A HIGH SCHOOL SOCIAL STUDIES TEACHER, I USED *THE AMERICAN Pageant 7th edition*, by Thomas A. Bailey and David M. Kennedy, as the assigned text in the advanced placement United States History class. Bailey and Kennedy were known at the time as consensus historians; their text focuses on broad areas of agreement and continuing growth and development in American history. Points of conflict and tension were minimized in their analysis of the past, and injustices were presented as unfortunate aberrations from the main democratic thrust of U.S. history. Demands for radical change were dismissed as extremist, unnecessary, and disruptive. For example, in the chapter "The South and the Slave Controversy," Bailey and Kennedy argued that the U.S. Civil War would have been avoidable if extremists on both sides, but especially among the Northern abolitionists, had not undermined compromises and plunged the nation into catastrophic war.

I find the Bailey-Kennedy position remarkably similar to explanations for the crisis offered by Southern proponents of secession, who blamed Northern disregard for constitutional principles for the impending civil war. For example, in November 1860, just after the election of Abraham Lincoln, the *New Orleans Daily Crescent* ran an editorial "The Constitution—The Union—The Law" favoring preservation of the union, but not a "Union to be maintained at the sacrifice of a violated Constitution, by a persistent refusal to obey the mandates of the Supreme Court, and by a general nullification of the laws of Congress, by the majority section, to oppress and outrage the minority portion of the confederacy." The problem, according to the *Daily Crescent*, was the "Abolition or Black Republican party of the North" with a "history of repeated injuries and usurpations, all having in direct object the establishment of absolute tyranny over the slaveholding States." Northern abolitionists were to blame for the crisis because "[t]hey have robbed us of our property, they have murdered our citizens while endeavoring to reclaim that property by lawful means, they have set at naught the decrees of the Supreme Court, they have invaded our states and killed our citizens, they have declared their unalterable determination to exclude us altogether from the Territories, they have nullified the laws of Congress, and finally they have capped the mighty pyramid of unfraternal enormities by electing Abraham Lincoln to the Chief Magistracy, on a platform and by a system which indicates nothing but the subjugation of the South and the complete ruin of her social, political, and industrial institutions" (*New Orleans Daily Crescent* 1860).

The *Daily Crescent* insisted, as did other Southerner newspapers, that "[t]he Constitution of the country recognizes slaves as property; the laws of Congress recognize slaves a property; the decisions of the Supreme Court recognize slaves as property; and the constitution, the laws and the courts declare that runaway slaves shall be restored to their owners." They were especially incensed because nine Northern states—Maine, Vermont, Massachusetts, Connecticut, Pennsylvania, Indiana, Michigan, Wisconsin, and Iowa—had passed laws criminalizing Southerners who attempted to regain slave property in clear violation of the Constitution and these states had not been penalized. The New York State legislature had debated a measure negating the Fugitive Slave Law in 1858, but it had not been passed (*New York Times* 1859a, 4).

According to Bailey and Kennedy, white southerners were "Slaves of the Slave System" who would have eventually accepted calls by "reasonable" abolitionists for the gradual elimination of slavery. Unfortunately for the United States, "Garrisonian Militants" shattered "the atmosphere of moderation" by provoking violence until "The South Lashes Back." Garrison himself was dismissed as "the emotionally high-strung son of a drunken father." The historians concluded, "Abolitionist extremists no doubt hastened the freeing of the slave by a number of years. But emancipation came at the price of a civil conflict that tore apart the social and economic fabric of the South" (Bailey and Kennedy 2008, 386). Additionally, as a result of the Civil War, "bewildered blacks were caught in the middle.... Emotionalism on both sides thus slammed the door on any fair adjustment" (ibid., 344).

But it is hard to see how abolitionist "extremists" could have had so much sway when so many powerful and influential Northerners were arrayed against them. Senator Stephen Douglas, who had just lost the election to Lincoln, tried to forestall the crisis in December 1860 by proposing a "bill amending the Fugitive Slave law of 1850, so as to provide more effectually for the recovery of 'persons held to service escaping from one State to another.'" *The New York Times* endorsed his plan, believing that "it cannot fail to pave the way for action on the part of the Northern States, which may give the Union men of the South a better basis for their efforts to preserve the Union than they have at present." The *Times* also endorsed compensation for slaveholders who lost property when fugitives were aided through unconstitutional means (*New York Times* 1860b, 4).

Southern Unionists and prominent Northern politicians and business leaders continued to seek a negotiated settlement with the South up until the inauguration of

Lincoln at the end of March 1861 and the attack on Fort Sumter on April 12. In January, Virginia issued a call for a conference where representatives from "slaveholding or non-slaveholding" states could make an "earnest effort to adjust the present unhappy controversies" (Dummond 1931, 242). More than 130 delegates from twenty-one states participated in a Washington peace conference that extended for most of the month of February. They included representatives of the New York City elite who had been working for reconciliation between the North and South for the better part of three years. William Dodge, who represented New York City merchants, told the body:

> I speak to you now as a business man, as a merchant of New York, the commercial metropolis of the nation. I am no politician. I have no interest except such as is common to the people. But let me assure you that even I can scarcely realize, much less describe the stagnation which has now settled upon the business and commerce of that great city, caused solely by the unsettled and uncertain conditions of the questions which we are endeavoring to arrange and settle here.... All alike, employers and employed, with all dependent upon them, are looking anxiously and I wish I could say hopefully, to the Congress of the United States, or to this conference, as the only sources from which help may come.... I am not here to argue or discuss constitutional questions. That duty belongs to gentlemen of the legal profession. I have lived under the Constitution. I venerate it and its authors as highly as any man here. But I do not venerate it so highly as to induce me to witness the destruction of the Government rather than see the Constitution amended or improved. I regret that the gentlemen composing the committee did not approach these questions more in the manner of merchants or commercial men.... We would have left open as few questions as possible. Those we would have arranged by mutual concessions. Mr. President, I speak as a merchant. I have a deep and abiding interest in my country and sorrow as I witness the dangers by which it is surrounded. But I am here for peace (Chittenden 1864, 192).

A majority report of the Washington peace conference proposed a constitutional amendment incorporating most of the principles embedded in the compromises of 1820 and 1850 with the addition of compensation for escaped slaves. Unfortunately for Unionists, but fortunately for enslaved blacks, there was no realistic hope of the compromise actually being approved as a constitutional amendment by the House of Representatives and the Senate (Dummond 1931, 250).

I think the two key reasons why compromise was no longer possible were the South's belief that the North, provoked by the abolitionist movement, and especially black abolitionists, would not respect slave property and enforce the fugitive slave laws and the

Supreme Court's *Dred Scott* decision, and Southern fear, which Eric Foner believed bordered on the hysterical, of abolitionist-inspired slave rebellions. The South viewed John Brown's attack on the federal arsenal at Harpers Ferry, which never had any chance of succeeding, as part of a chain of slave rebellions that included Toussaint Louverture in Haiti, Denmark Vesey in Charleston, Gabriel Prosser and Nat Turner in Virginia, and Sam Sharpe in Jamaica (Foner 2006, 32). However, there was some legitimacy to the Southern fears. Frederick Douglass, who was indicted in Virginia as a co-conspirator with Brown, and John Brown initially hoped to build a guerrilla army of fugitive slaves and free blacks in the Appalachian Mountains that would raid plantations and encourage a constant stream of runaways and rebellions (Douglass 1962, 314–16).

It was the Southern reaction, rather than the actual attack on Harpers Ferry, that reenergized the Abolitionist movement and once again thrust it into the national spotlight. Soon after the attack, the Northern press and prominent abolitionists distanced the movement and the North from Brown. The *Albany Evening Journal* accused the Democratic press of suggesting that " 'Old Brown's' insane invasion was countenanced by leading Republicans" (*Albany Evening Journal* 1859). William Cullen Bryant, editor of the *New York Evening Post*, dismissed John Brown's "crazy attempt to excite the slaves of Virginia to revolt" (Brown 1971, 407). The *New York Times* reported on a petition being circulated around the city "expressing sympathy with the men of the South in the present crisis, and their abhorrence of the motives and acts of John Brown and his followers" (*New York Times* 1859b, 4).

The Reverend Henry Ward Beecher, pastor of the Plymouth Congregational Church in Brooklyn, New York, and a prominent abolitionist, declared: "We have no right to treat the citizens of the South with acrimony and bitterness because they are involved in a system of wrong doing.... The preaching of discontent among the bondsmen of our land is not the way to help them.... No relief will be carried to the slaves or to the South as a body by any individual or organized plans to carry them off or to incite them to abscond.... We must maintain sympathy and kindness toward the South.... You should care for both the master and the slave.... You ought to set your face against and discountenance anything like an insurrectionary spirit" (Beecher and Scoville 1888, 303).

However, the rush to judgment followed by the execution of Brown transformed him into a martyr embraced by abolitionists. Wendell Phillips, who gave a eulogy at Brown's funeral in North Elba, New York, declared: "I feel honored to stand under such a roof. Hereafter you will tell children standing at your knees, 'I saw John Brown buried,— I sat under his roof'.... God make us all worthier of him whose dust we lay among these hills he loved. Here he girded himself and went forth to battle. Fuller success than his heart ever dreamed God granted him. He sleeps in the blessings of the crushed and the poor, and men believe more firmly in virtue, now that such a man has lived. Standing here, let us thank God for a firmer faith and fuller hope" (Ruchames 1969, 266–69).

Six months later, Henry David Thoreau also spoke in North Elba. According to Thoreau: "John Brown's career for the last six weeks of his life was meteorlike, flashing through the darkness in which we live. I know of nothing so miraculous in our history.... Years were not required for a revolution of public opinion; days, nay hours, produced marked changes in this case. Fifty who were ready to say, on going into our meeting in honor of him in Concord, that he ought to be hung, would not say it when they came out. They heard his words read; they saw the earnest faces of the congregation; and perhaps they joined at last in singing the hymn in his praise" (Ruchames 1969, 272–77).

Even the moderate Bryant was outraged by the execution of Brown. He wrote: "It is not the usual course of justice to hurry men in this way to the gallows" (Brown 1971, 408).

In 1881, speaking at Harpers Ferry, Frederick Douglass asked, "Did John Brown draw his sword against slavery and thereby lose his life in vain?" His response to his own question captured the impact of Brown on the abolitionist movement and the abolitionist movement on the nation. John Brown

> began the war that ended American slavery and made this a free Republic. Until this blow was struck, the prospect for freedom was dim, shadowy and uncertain. The irrepressible conflict was one of words, votes and compromises. When John Brown stretched forth his arm the sky was cleared. The time for compromises was gone—the armed hosts of freedom stood face to face over the chasm of a broken Union—and the clash of arms was at hand. The South staked all upon getting possession of the Federal Government, and failing to do that, drew the sword of rebellion and thus made her own, and not Brown's, the lost cause of the century (Ruchames 1969, 298–99).

Based on the things I have written in this book, I add five supportive points to this statement by Frederick Douglass.

1. Industrial change in the North, coupled with territorial expansion and geographic barriers to plantation slavery in the West, ended political balance between the North and South producing a constitutional crisis and conditions where abolitionists could more effectively challenge slavery.
2. Abolitionists labored with determination and frustration to end slavery throughout the thirty-year period discussed in this book, but their impact was contingent on events in the broader world over which they had no control. In the end Southern panic and Civil War produced the conditions to end slavery in the United States.
3. It was resistance to the fugitive slave laws by the abolitionists, especially African American abolitionists, during the 1850s that put the Slave South on edge and set the stage for John Brown.

4. It was Southern fear of blacks and a possible slave revolution, heightened to the point of hysteria by Brown's essentially ineffective actions, that precipitated secession, the Civil War, and ultimately moved the abolition of slavery from marginalization to emancipation.

5. Slavery in the American South was unlikely to wither away on its own. It was central to the economy of the South, not marginal as it was in the North during the earlier era of emancipation. Unlike in the British Caribbean where there were relatively few whites and compensated emancipation ended African enslavement without war, white populations deeply imbued with racism in the American South were not going to peacefully accept a voluntary end to slavery.

TEACHING NOTES

Local History: "Brooklyn's In The House"

QUESTIONS TO CONSIDER

1. How valid are historical generalizations based on local events?

2. How can the local histories of different communities be used to teach about major historical developments?

Local histories illuminate broader historical developments. They also show how events in one locale influence the decisions made by people in other communities, such as Syracuse abolitionists responding to the kidnapping of James Hamlet of Brooklyn in September 1850 by preparing for what would become the "Jerry Rescue" a year later.

"Brooklyn's In The House," on the contemporary rap scene, is the title of a hip-hop release by Cut Master D.C. In efforts to bring the story of slavery in the United States and the struggles to end it to a broader public, the office of the District Attorney of Kings County (i.e., Brooklyn) released a fifty-five-minute long movie in 2011 on *Slavery and the Law*. It documented the creation of a mural by Brooklyn teenagers who were learning about the legal status of enslaved Africans in Colonial America and the new nation and its impact on the post–Civil War era and the contemporary world. I was involved in the production as an on-camera commentator, a consulting historian, and in writing a curriculum guide for secondary school classes.

The Brooklyn Historical Society in Brooklyn Heights, the Weeksville Heritage Center in Bedford-Stuyvesant, and the Irondale Ensemble Project in Fort Greene teamed up to rediscover and present to the public the story of Brooklyn's role in the struggle to abolish slavery in the United States, with permanent exhibitions as part of the project *In Pursuit Of Freedom*. Their goal is also to restore Brooklyn to the forefront of the continuing campaign for social justice in the United States.

Their plan includes twenty highly visible historical markers placed at different sites in the borough. I am also lobbying to rename the plaza in front of the former Bridge Street African Wesleyan Methodist Episcopal Church, now the admissions building for the Polytechnic Institute of New York University, at the Metro Tech Center in Downtown Brooklyn. It was the site of an Emancipation Proclamation day grand jubilee and should be renamed Emancipation Proclamation Plaza.

At the time of the American Revolution, about one-third of the population of Kings County were enslaved Africans, but their contributions to clearing the forests, dredging the harbors, and building the infrastructure of Brooklyn has largely been erased from history. The former African cemetery in the Kings County town of New Lots is now a playground between Schenck, New Lots, and Livonia Avenues and Barbey Street under the IRT #3 line.

Ironically, the park is named for one of the largest slaveholder families in the area. According to the 1820 census, as New York State approached the 1827 date set for full emancipation, Tunis Schenck, who owned the farm, still owned seven enslaved Africans. A plaque in Schenck Park commemorates the family's contributions to the history of Brooklyn: "The family first lived in Brooklyn in colonial times," it was "descended from Johannes Schenck of Holland," and "members of the family served in political office over several generations." The plaque mentions that the "park was the site of Public School 72, which was abandoned in 1944," but it does not mention the enslaved Africans who lived there and built the early farms, roads, and homes of Brooklyn.

We know about the abandoned African cemetery because of an interview published in the *Brooklyn Eagle* on September 19, 1886. It included reminisces of local farmer Stephen Vanderveer. According to Vanderveer, "In those days there were as many Negroes as whites in this neighborhood. The latter were buried in front by the roadside and the former away back near the swamp. . . . In 1841 we saw the necessity of having a new burying ground, as the black people were overcrowding us in the old one. Therefore we purchased the ground alongside the church and removed a great many of the dead from across the road. I have not taken up all my people yet, but I expect to do so before long." Eventually, the white dead where relocated to the new cemetery across New Lots Avenue beside the Dutch Reformed Church. Blacks were left behind and their plots were built over.

The Bridge Street African Wesleyan Methodist Episcopal Church has a long, rich history as part of the struggle to end slavery and achieve equal rights for African Americans in New York and the nation. (*continues on page 144*)

(continued from page 143)

It is designated as a New York City historical landmark and there is a barely visible unofficial marker outside the building placed by a local development group. The building is now named for a Polytechnic alumnus who paid for its restoration, and passers-by have no idea of its original purpose or history.

Bridge Street Church was incorporated in 1818 when black parishioners split off from the First Methodist Episcopal Church of Brooklyn because of the racial bias of the church's leadership. From 1854 to 1938 the congregation held services at 309 Bridge Street (now 311) in a majestic brick building with two large columns. It was built in 1846–47 and was originally the First Free Congregational Church of Brooklyn. Since 1938, the Bridge Street Church is located at 277 Stuyvesant Avenue in the Bedford-Stuyvesant neighborhood of Brooklyn. Among the achievements of the Bridge Street Church was starting an African Free School in Brooklyn. Its trustees were also instrumental in the establishment of the Weeksville community, an important refuge for local blacks, especially during the 1863 New York Draft Riots.

From December 31, 1862, to January 2, 1863, Bridge Street Church hosted a three-day "celebration of freedom" when the finalized Emancipation Proclamation was signed and put into effect. The program included speeches by African American historian and activist William Wells Brown and a white abolitionist, Theodore Tilton. Tilton was a newspaper editor affiliated with Reverend Henry Ward Beecher and Brooklyn's Plymouth Congregational Church. A month later, Frederick Douglass spoke at the Bridge Street Church and launched a campaign to recruit black soldiers for the Union army. In 1865, Harriet Tubman was a featured speaker at the church discussing her experiences on the UGRR and in the Union Army as a scout and nurse.

10

"THE EXECRATION OF HISTORY"

New York's Opposition to Congressional Reconstruction

EXECRATION IS A WORD RARELY USED TODAY. I HAD TO LOOK IT UP TO BE SURE OF ITS meaning. *Merriam-Webster's* defines it as the "act of cursing or denouncing," that is, the curse itself as well as the thing being cursed (www.merriam-webster.com/dictionary/execration). When Congressman Thaddeus Stevens of Pennsylvania warned his colleagues in the House of Representatives that failure to ensure racial equality in the post–Civil War era would condemn them to the "execration of history," he meant they and the nation would be cursed for all time (*Congressional Globe* 39/1 1865, 72).

Stevens, chair of the House Ways and Means Committee and champion of black citizenship rights, was probably the most radical of the Radical Republicans in the House of Representatives during Reconstruction. In a memoir on Washington, D.C., during the Civil War years, Noah Brooks described Thaddeus Stevens as the "oldest and the ablest man in congressional life … never tender-hearted, winning, or conciliatory. He was argumentative, sardonic, and grim" (Brooks 1896, 225–26). Stevens was among the most "acrid of Lincoln's critics" when congressional radicals feared the president would compromise with the South on the future of slavery toward the end of the war (ibid., 232).

Eric Foner, in *Reconstruction: America's Unfinished Revolution, 1863–1877*, called Stevens the preeminent leader of the Radicals in the House of Representatives and a "master of Congressional infighting, parliamentary tactics, and blunt speaking" (Foner 1988, 229). In *Team of Rivals*, Doris Kearns Goodwin was more critical of Stevens whom she saw as uncompromising when he skewered William Seward in 1861 (Goodwin 2005, 368) and Abraham Lincoln in 1865 (ibid., 694) for what he suspected was backtracking in their opposition to slavery.

On December 18, 1865, Stevens challenged the fundamental premise of Lincoln's Reconstruction Plan and the platform of New York Democrats, based on the expectation that somehow the South could simply return to the United States and the nation could be restored "as it was." Stevens claimed, "Nobody, I believe, pretends that with their old constitutions and frames of government they can be permitted to claim their old rights under the Constitution. They have torn their constitutional States into atoms, and built on their foundations fabrics of a totally different character. Dead men cannot raise themselves. Dead States cannot restore their existence as it was." But the reality was that New York Democrats did believe this could, and should, be done.

While Stevens argued the South must enter the Union "as new states or remain as conquered provinces" and that "Congress must create States and declare when they are entitled to be represented," his Democratic Party opponents wanted the South restored to the union as if they had never rebelled (Strausbaugh 2016, 344–48).

Stevens also wanted quick action to ensure the political rights and economic viability of formerly enslaved Southern blacks. According to Stevens,

> We have turned, or are about to turn, loose four million slaves without a hut to shelter them or a cent in their pockets. The infernal laws of slavery have prevented them from acquiring an education, understanding the common laws of contract, or of managing the ordinary business of life. This Congress is bound to provide for them until they can take care of themselves. If we do not furnish them with homesteads, and hedge them around with protective laws; if we leave them to the legislation of their late masters, we had better have left them in bondage. If we fail in this great duty now, when we have the power, we shall deserve and receive the execration of history and of all future ages (*Congressional Globe* 39/1 1865, 72).

This was another position New York's political leadership would not accept. Even the *New York Times*, a unionist Republican newspaper, admonished Stevens for his "extreme views," especially his insistence that "no State should ever be admitted from, the South until negro suffrage has been conceded, and that every freedman should have a homestead secured to him from the confiscated land of the rebels" (*New York Times* 1865b, 4).

A year later, Thaddeus Stevens continued his battle against Andrew Johnson's presidential Reconstruction initiatives. On January 3, 1867, he declared, "Unless the rebel States, before admission, should be made republican in spirit, and placed, under the guardianship of loyal men, all our blood and treasure will have been spent in vain." At the core of his proposal was ensuring voting rights for the formerly enslaved.

> [T]hey form the great mass of loyal men. Possibly with their aid loyal governments may be established in most of those States. Without it all are sure to be ruled by traitors; and loyal men, black and white, will be oppressed, exiled, or murdered.... The white Union men are in a great

minority in each of those States. With them the blacks would act in a body; and it is believed that in each of said States, except one, the two united would form a majority, control the States, and protect themselves.... If impartial suffrage is excluded in the rebel States then every one of them is sure to send a solid rebel representative delegation to Congress, and cast a solid rebel electoral vote. They, with their kindred Copperheads of the North, would always elect the President and control Congress.... For these, among other reasons, I am for negro suffrage in every rebel State. If it be just, it should not be denied; if it be necessary, it should be adopted; if it be a punishment to traitors, they deserve it (*Congressional Globe* 39/2 1867, 251–52).

As a followup to debate over black suffrage, Stevens introduced a bill, H.R. 29, at the start of the 40th Congress for the confiscation of all public lands held by Confederate states and the seizure of rebel estates and their redistribution to "the slaves who have been liberated by the operations of the war" with "to each male person who is the head of a family, forty acres; to each adult male, whether the head of a family or not, forty acres; to each widow who is the head of a family, forty acres" (*Congressional Globe* 40/1 1867, 59, 203).

An examination of the proceedings of the House of Representatives in the *Congressional Globe* shows that during the post–Civil War Reconstruction period Thaddeus Stevens's greatest adversaries and the most outspoken opponents of congressional or Radical Reconstruction were members of the New York State Democratic Party congressional delegation led by Fernando Wood, John Winthrop Chanler, and James Brooks and allies such as Albany's John V. L. Pruyn and Martin Kalbfleisch of Brooklyn. While frequently divided into warring and shifting political factions on their home turfs, New York Democrats were more or less a unified and vitriolic opposition in the House to Radical Reconstruction and justice for the formerly enslaved (Myers 1917, 200–203).

At a massive Union Square preelection rally in September 1864, New York City Democrats approved resolutions declaring that "the only just purposes of the present war are the restoration of the Union of the States, and the authority of the Constitution" and opposition to the Republican Party's "impracticable attempt to raise the black man to the political and social level of the white" (*New York Times* 1864, 8). As Congressman Martin Kalbfleisch of Brooklyn reminded the House of Representatives in January 1865, "The platform upon which those us of from New York representing Democratic constituencies stood when we were elected was, 'the Constitution as it is and the Union as it was'" (*Congressional Globe* 38/2 1865, 529).

Fernando Wood (1812–1881) is the best-known and documented member of the antiwar New York City Copperhead Democrats. He was first elected to Congress as a Democrat in 1840 (Dodge and Koed 2005, 2194). After being defeated in a bid for reelection he was appointed to a patronage position as an agent for the state department in the Port of New York by Democratic Party administrations. In the 1850s he shifted his attention to local politics. He was defeated in an initial mayoral bid in 1850, but was elected mayor of New York City in 1854. Wood was defeated for reelection in 1858, broke with Tammany Hall to establish his own political club called Mozart Hall, and was elected mayor again in 1860. Wood was elected to Congress in 1862, was defeated in 1864, and elected again in 1866, when his political faction rejoined Tammany. This time, Wood served in Congress from March 1867 until his death in February 1881. As mayor, in January 1861 Wood suggested that New York City secede from the union along with the South to maintain their business ties. In a speech to the city Common Council, Wood argued that the "dissolution of the Federal Union is inevitable" and proposed, "New York should endeavor to preserve a continuance of uninterrupted intercourse with every section," and to do this it should secede from the union itself and become "a free City." He concluded, "When disunion has become a fixed and certain fact, why may not New York disrupt the bands which bind her to a corrupt and venal master. New York, as a *Free City*, may shed the only light and hope for a future reconstruction of our once blessed Confederacy" (Mushkat 1990; *New York Times* 1861, 2). Later, in Congress Wood fought against the Thirteenth Amendment formally ending slavery in the United States, because an end to slavery would make it impossible for Southern planters to repay their debts to New York City merchants. Wood was censured by the House in January 1868 for calling its Reconstruction proposals "a bill without a title, a child without a name and probably without a father, a monstrosity, a measure the most infamous of the many infamous acts of this infamous Congress" (*Congressional Globe* 40/2 1868, 542).

John Winthrop Chanler was one of the more prolific spokesmen for the New York City antiwar Democrats in Congress. Relatively little is known about his life except that he was born in South Carolina, graduated from Columbia College, studied law in Germany, married into the Astor family, served in the state legislature, and represented New York State in the House of Representatives as a Democrat from March 1863 to March 1869 (Dodge and Koed 2005, 807; Bernstein 1990, 146). House minutes published in the *Congressional Globe* suggest that Chanler had a record of sarcastic responses and racist opposition to even moderate Reconstruction goals. Chanler was censured by the House of Representatives on May 14, 1866, for calling congressional Reconstruction "wicked and revolutionary" and House members who voted to overturn presidential vetoes "malignant and mischievous" (*Congressional Globe* 39/1 1866, 2574–75).

James Brooks (1810–1873), editor of the *New York Daily Express*, was elected to Congress from New York City as a Whig in 1848 and 1850 (Dodge and Koed 2005, 714). During the 1850s he migrated from the Whigs to the Democrats, and he supported James Buchanan for president in 1856 and Stephen Douglas in 1860. In 1861, he actively urged that the Southern states be permitted to leave the union. Brooks was elected to Congress as a Democrat in 1862, was narrowly defeated in a contested election in 1864, and then reelected in 1866. He actually held his seat from March 4, 1865, to April 7, 1866, while the results of the 1864 contest were being adjudicated. Brooks led Democratic Party opposition to the impeachment of Andrew Johnson and was rewarded for his loyalty with an appointment as a government director of the Union Pacific Railroad.

John V. S. L. Pruyn (1811–1877) was a member of one of Albany's oldest and most prominent families. A lawyer and railroad company executive, he served two brief tenures in the House of Representatives during the 1860s. Pruyn was elected to finish an uncompleted term in 1863, did not stand for reelection, was elected for a complete term in 1866, and did not stand for reelection again (Dodge and Koed 2005, 1769). He was also a regent of the University of the State of New York and the board's chancellor from 1868 until 1877.

Martin Kalbfleisch (1804–1873) was born in Holland and immigrated to the United States in 1826. He established a successful business manufacturing and selling paint in the independent city of Brooklyn, and rose rapidly in local politics. He was an alderman from 1855 to 1861 and mayor from 1862 to 1864 and afterward served one term in the House of Representatives, from 1863 to 1865 (Dodge and Koed 2005, 1358).

In June 1864, Wood, Pruyn, and Kalbfleisch helped stall the Thirteenth Amendment ending slavery in the United States by preventing the necessary two-thirds majority for passage (*Congressional Globe* 38/1 1864, 2939–62). Pruyn of Albany opened debate on the amendment by charging, "For the first time in our history it is now proposed to make a change in the Constitution which, if effected, will interfere with the reserved rights of the States." He blamed the devotion of the "Administration and its friends ... to questions of social reform in the condition of the slave population of the South" for "alienating thereby the friends of the Union in those States and embarrassing their return to their allegiance" (ibid., 2939). Wood, from Manhattan, challenged the extension of federal authority into "social interests" if the amendment were approved and the "tyrannical destruction of individual property" (ibid., 2940). He went on to defend both states rights and the institution of slavery itself as the "best possible condition to insure the happiness of the negro race" (ibid., 2942). Brooklyn's Kalbfleisch argued for the sanctity of the unamended Constitution and accused abolitionist "fanatics" of promoting "crazy delusion," "wicked and willful falsehood," and "unfairly exaggerating the evils of slavery" (ibid., 2945–46).

When the House reconvened and debate resumed in January 1865, Brooks and Chanler took the lead in defending slavery and the integrity of the City of New York against suggestions that it was disloyal (*Congressional Globe* 38/2 1865, 146–49). Brooks was furious when Glenni Scofield, a Republican from Pennsylvania, referring to the 1863 Draft Riots, charged that New York City was governed by "Five Points," and instead of worrying about emancipation, its elected representatives had "nothing to fear but its own mobs." After Brooks demanded the right to "defend the millions of people whom I represent," Scofield replied that he was only repeating accusations made in the city's own newspapers (ibid., 146). Chanler then accused Scofield of "low slander" and the federal government under Lincoln of interfering in New York City's 1864 congressional elections in an effort to intimidate his Democratic Party opposition (ibid., 146–47).

In an extended address to the House just before the constitutional amendment ending slavery was brought to a vote and approved, Kalbfleisch defended the "Constitution as it is and as it was when our country ... was marching with proud and stately step to empire and greatness." He argued that the "amendment you now propose to provide for may stand in the way of both peace and Union" at the moment when a negotiated end to the war was an actual possibility. He then paraphrased Lincoln's letter to Horace Greeley that "if he could save the Union he would do so, irrespective of slavery" and denounced the "famous note," the Emancipation Proclamation, as illegal and for initiating a policy "universally condemned by the true friends of the Union" (*Congressional Globe* 38/2 1865, 528).

Kalbfleisch's statement was wrought with deeply embedded racism and unfortunate prescience. He denounced the antislavery amendment as unenforceable and predicted that if abolition was forced on the South "without their consent and against their will ... the people of those States will not feel particularly anxious to aid in carrying the measure into practical effect" (*Congressional Globe* 38/2 1865, 529).

Kalbfleisch claimed he had always opposed slavery as "evil," but that "[m]y opposition to slavery does not permit me to aid in perpetuating gross wrong" or in supporting "wild fanaticism" violating the "rights and interests alike of the slave and the slaveholder" (ibid.); however, he did not explain how the rights of the formerly enslaved were being violated. Playing on racist fears, Kalbfleisch suggested that demands for emancipation were only "one step" away from calls for racial "amalgamation," and he predicted this "glorious and happy country, the home and asylum of millions of white men" will be "doomed to become the land of a race of hybrids" and destined to be "blotted out of existence in accordance with the immutable laws of nature" (ibid.). As he concluded, Kalbfleisch shifted away from race baiting to what was more likely the major concern of his supporters among New York's merchant and bankers and the main point of the entire diatribe. "How, sir, are the expenses of this war to be paid? ... Abolish slavery, and you destroy the ability on the part of the South to contribute a portion of what they should in justice be held to pay" (ibid.).

During congressional debate in January 1864 Representative Daniel Morris, a Republican-Unionist from rural Yates County in western New York State, demanded that Southern "traitors ... be punished for this wanton sacrifice of life" during the war and be forced to pay its costs. Morris charged that opponents of confiscation wanted to restore Confederate "real estate" to plantation owners, with "perhaps a group of human chattels to cultivate their lands and minister to their wants" (*Congressional Globe* 38/1 1864, 298). John Winthrop Chanler led the New York's anti–Radical Reconstruction opposition. In his rejoinder to Morris, Chanler demanded to know, "Under what law and in what spirit would the gentleman refuse, when peace is granted to this country by the Power which rules all nations, to grant to the offspring of a traitor the right to live in this country, to enjoy the protection of the law, to inherit property, and to carry on the system of creation? Under what law would he deny to the offspring the right of inheritance?" (ibid.).

On December 13, 1865, the House of Representatives debated a resolution introduced by Congressman John Farnsworth of Illinois, who served as a Union general during the Civil War, demanding full civil rights for African American veterans. Chanler took the Democratic Party lead in opposition to the proposal:

> These men, whom he and we all know to be yet in a condition of transition, he wishes to put upon a footing equal to those who not only in this war, but in every war, have carried the arms of this Government.... I will not attempt at this time to assail the motive of the gentleman in giving to the black soldier his right and claim to the admiration of the white man.... We know the service the black soldier has rendered to this Government, and when the time comes for rewarding him for his past services by those emoluments which are bestowed upon the brave and the suffering I will not be wanting in that hour. But there is, and undoubtedly will be, a difference between us as to the amount of the reward to be meted out.... He assumes ... that the black man is our equal.... I hope I am not using too strong language in saying that I deem it an insult to the white citizens of the United States (*Congressional Globe* 39/1 1865, 46).

Later in debate, Chanler charged that the Republicans were trying to "reduce this contest between the two races down to a legislative enactment." He, on the other hand, claimed to "draw no distinction of color" and accused Republicans of wanting to enflame "public passion and public prejudice," but in the very next sentence he casually used the word *nigger* (ibid., 47). According to Chanler, areas dominated by blacks were receding into "semi-barbarism" and "colored troops" were being used for the "purpose of putting the heel of central power upon that portion of the white race recently in rebellion, but now begging humbly for readmission to the protection of this Government" (ibid.). For Chanler, the goal of the federal government should be to protect "the purity of the white race, the representation of the white race, and the sovereignty of this people" (ibid.).

In extended remarks on January 12, Chanler explicated the political agenda and ideology of the antiwar Democrats. First, he challenged congressional efforts by Republicans in the House of Representatives to enfranchise African Americans in the District of Columbia (*Congressional Globe* 39/1 1866, 216–17). He opened his remarks by incorrectly citing and misquoting a passage from the *Federalist Papers*. Chanler believed he was quoting from #5 written by Alexander Hamilton (it was written by John Jay), when he was actually paraphrasing #51 written by James Madison. Chanler had Hamilton declare that "[i]n a society in which the stronger faction can readily unite to oppress the weaker, anarchy may as truly be said to reign as in a state of nature, where the weaker individual is not secured against the violence of the stronger" (ibid., 216). For Chanler, the weaker faction that needed to be defended against majority rule was Southern whites.

Chanler also believed that by opposing black enfranchisement he was defending fundamental constitutional principles:

> But by the principle of negro suffrage, if once established by the national Congress, the term "the people" will be made to include the negro race throughout the Union, and thereby pervert the intention of the framers of the Constitution.... "The people," therefore, who framed the Constitution of the United States were of the white race exclusively.... The only consideration given to the negro was as a slave in those sections regulating the slave trade and establishing the three-fifths rule of representation. To claim for the negro the position of a citizen of the United States is to violate the whole spirit of the preamble to the Constitution which made the United States a nation.... The negro should never be allowed to vote in this District until the majority of the whole people of this Union shall have passed their judgment upon his fitness to hold so great a power at the seat of Government.... Why bring a new and inexperienced race into the new compact and homogeneous people by extending the right to vote to the colored man? (*Congressional Globe* 39/1 1866, 216–17).

During the speech, Chanler declared that "enlisting the slave as a soldier in the armies of the Union was ... unnecessary and unwise," especially "on an equality with the white man." But although it was done by Lincoln and the Republicans, it "does not follow that the negro is entitled to vote as an inalienable right.... The right to vote carries with it too many and too weighty responsibilities to be ranked in the same class with pensions and bounty money.... I deny that any obligation rests against this Government to do anything more for the negro than has already been done" (*Congressional Globe* 39/1 1866, 217).

Chanler then launched into a defense of what he called "white democracy," a concept at the core of Democratic Party opposition to racial equality and congressional Reconstruction and its defense of slavery and the "Union as it was." For Chanler,

> The dominion over the different races on this continent belongs to the white man by right of conquest. That dominion is secured to us by the elective franchise.... [T]his is a white man's Government, founded by white men to preserve and perpetuate the laws and customs of their race, and to extend the blessing of their civilization to the humblest creature.... The negro race has been civilized, slave though he was, by the benign character of those laws.... If the ruling race hold dominion by just, constitutional law, they commit no injustice toward those who by that law

are excluded from the right to vote.... The fact that all but the white male citizens are excluded from voting in the municipal affairs of the District, the seat of Government, is a crowning proof, first, that this is a white man's Government, and second, that there is a ruling race recognized in the practice of that Government (*Congressional Globe* 39/1 1866, 218).

Once again, Chanler rooted his arguments in what he believed to be the intentions of the nation's founders. "[T]he statesmen of the revolutionary era ... knew what the inalienable rights of men were, but they never surrendered the material advantage of slave labor to the inalienable right of the negro. Why? Because they knew by stern experience that the negro did not himself know what his inalienable rights were.... White democracy makes war on every class, caste, and race which assails its sovereignty or would undermine the mastery of the white working man, be he ignorant or learned, strong or weak" (ibid., 219–20).

In Chanler's and the New York Democratic Party's vision for the nation's future, blacks were not entitled to participate in governing.

Black democracy does not exist.... Not one act of theirs has prove the capacity of the black race for self-government.... I admit that they have made successful insurrections, but my argument was not to the effect that the negro race was not capable of the bloodiest deeds.... I assert there is no record of the black race having proved its capacity for self-government as a race.... [T]hey are a race to be kept under.... I assert that if, through the fanatical efforts of the radicals of this country, the negroes be raised to a position of *quasi* political equality with the whites, I do not believe that they will be able to maintain that position (*Congressional Globe* 39/1 1866, 220–22).

On March 19, 1867, Congressman Thaddeus Stevens defended a confiscation bill and argued for a more forceful role for Congress in rebuilding the South. This time Stevens claimed that President Johnson's Reconstruction program was not "carrying out the policy of Mr. Lincoln." "In the midst of the war Mr. Lincoln had but little time or little occasions to examine into the question of reconstruction. Until the enemy was conquered everything was made subservient to that great objective." However, according to Stevens, "three days before his death" Lincoln acknowledged that his lenient plan, proposed in December 1863, was "not the only plan which might possibly be acceptable" and conceded that the "Executive claimed no right to say when or whether the members should be admitted to seats in Congress from such States" (*Congressional Globe* 40/1 1867, 207–208).

Stevens admitted "some apprehension that Mr. Lincoln" would have been "beguiled into a course," reconciliation, that would have "tarnished his well-earned fame," but fortunately he was spared from this by his death. "It was better that his posthumous fame should be unspotted than that he should ensure a few more years of trouble on earth."

Congressman Chanler rose to respond to Stevens and defend Lincoln, Andrew Johnson, and presidential Reconstruction, but discussion was tabled until the second session of the Fortieth Congress in December. When Chanler finally did get to speak on December 10, he laid out what was essentially a New York City Democrat's anti-Reconstruction manifesto (*Congressional Globe* 40/2 1867, 108–109).

Chanler called confiscation a "method by which a conqueror robs his foes and rewards his friends. Two distinct acts are done by it, and two distinct motives actuate it. One result is sought by it, namely, security to the state established by the conqueror. All confiscation is robbery; it is the tool of the tyrant and the oppressor, who under the law of might create his title to that which was another's.... Confiscation is one of the hideous monsters chained to the ear of grim-visaged war and never should be let loose to raven far its prey. It legitimately is only an instrument of terror and should not let loose to destroy. In time of peace it should be nowhere seen or heard; savage, cruel, destroying, it has no place among civilized, humane and law-abiding men in times like these."

Chanler accused Stevens and the Radical Republicans of seeking "blood for blood. Eye for an eye, life for life" with the "fierce spirit of vengeance.... Justice has no voice in such hue and cry after the vanquished in a time of profound peace and above all at a time when reconstruction of the Union is the known wish of this whole nation and the avowed object of our present legislation."

As the martyred president, Lincoln certainly had a peculiar legacy in congressional debate. Stevens, who attacked the idea of the "union as it was," felt the late president was better off dead than having his memory tarnished by acquiescence to Southern whites and Northern Copperheads. Chanler, who as an antiwar New York Democrat had fought to defeat Lincoln in his 1864 reelection campaign, now evoked him. "It is strange that by such acts as these the party which has carried this government through the war of the rebellion should so dim the brightness of its fame and so lower its high standard of 'good will toward all, and malice toward none' " (*Congressional Globe* 40/2 1867, 109).

The New York Times again dismissed Stevens's extremism. It saw the confiscation bill as vindictive and as having virtually no chance of passing, with little support in the Republican Party, even among its most radical members (*New York Times* 1867, 4). As a Republican paper, it offered no coverage of Chanler's response or discussion of the New York delegation's role in opposition to congressional Reconstruction. It seems that the *Times*, like most of the rest of the nation, was getting ready to move on from the Civil War and its aftermath.

The *New-York Tribune*, whose founder and editor Horace Greeley had pressured Lincoln in 1862 to use the power of the presidency to end slavery and who was a strong supporter of black rights including enfranchisement, also rejected Stevens's call for confiscation of rebel land (*New-York Tribune* 1867b, 4). Editorials written between 1865 and

1867 repeatedly called for reconciliation with the Confederate states and between the Republican-controlled Congress and President Andrew Johnson (*New-York Tribune* 1865c, 4; 1865d, 4; 1865e, 4; 1867a, 4). The *Tribune* also largely ignored the New York delegation's role in opposition to congressional Reconstruction.

During the next decade, New York Democrats continued to dominate a gravely wounded national party, which nominated New Yorkers former Governor Horatio Seymour, newspaper editor Horace Greeley, and former Governor Samuel Tilden for president in 1868, 1872, and 1876, although each candidate was defeated in the national election. Eventually the Fourteenth and Fifteenth Amendments were passed by Congress and approved by three-fourths of the states that remained in the Union. Approval of the three Reconstruction amendments ending slavery (Thirteenth), granting citizenship rights (Fourteenth), and enfranchising black men (Fifteenth) was made a condition for read-mission to the Union for rebel states (Foner 2006, 271–80). But in the newly readmitted states economic threats, white political ascendancy, legal discrimination, and Ku Klux Klan terror combined to gradually strip blacks of their rights. With the abandonment of Reconstruction in 1877 and the establishment of Redeemer governments in the South, almong with Jim Crow, the United States was condemned, as Thaddeus Stevens had warned in the House of Representatives, to the "execration of history," a curse the nation is still trying to address today (Degler 1984, 228–57; Foner 2006, 189–213).

TEACHING NOTES

Slavery and Abolition in Books and Movies

There have been a number of works of fiction, in books and on screen, as well as documentaries exploring slavery and abolition in the United States. Most do not specifically or extensively focus on New York State. Many have sections that are very valuable for teaching. In this Teaching Notes I review some more recent contributions, starting with movies, both documentaries and historical fiction, and then shifting to literature, including young adult and juvenile fiction. The list is a bit eclectic, but I think it is a useful guide for general readers.

Recommended Documentaries

Slavery and the Making of America (2005) remains the best overall documentary about slavery in the United States. The first episode opens with a reenactment of slavery in the Dutch New Amsterdam colony and discussion of the evolution of slavery as a work and legal system. Episode 3 includes sections on New York abolitionists Sojourner Truth, Amy Post, and Frederick Douglass (continues on page 156)

(*continued from page 155*)

and freedom seeker Harriet Jacobs, who lived in New York City and Rochester after escaping enslavement. A PBS website aligned with the documentary contains lesson plans and primary source documents.

There are two very useful documentaries on the history of the New York City African Burial Ground and the battle by the city's African American community to have it preserved and recognized as a national monument. *Then I'll Be Free to Travel Home* (2001) is a two-part video by independent filmmaker Eric Tait. The first part (86 minutes) is on the history of the burial ground that was rediscovered when a new federal office building was being excavated in Lower Manhattan and the second part (56 minutes) documents the struggle against government bureaucracy to protect the site. *The African Burial Ground: An American Discovery* (1994) is a more official production made for United States General Services Administration and narrated by Ossie Davis and Ruby Dee.

I was involved in two projects documenting the history of slavery in New York City. *New York's History of Slavery* (2015) is a 20-minute "walking tour" of Lower Manhattan slavery sights by Susan Modaress. *Slavery and the Law* (2011) is an overview of slavery and Jim Crow by Paula Heredia that was produced for the Office of the District Attorney of Kings County (Brooklyn).

The Abolitionists (2013), produced by PBS as part of its *American Experience* series, is an excellent reenactment of the role played by five abolitionists, Frederick Douglass, William Lloyd Garrison, Angelina Grimké, Harriet Beecher Stowe, and John Brown, in the struggle to end slavery in the United States. *13* (2016) is not about slavery in the pre–Civil War era. Directed by Ava DuVernay, it looks at the way a clause in the Thirteenth Amendment ending slavery other than as punishment for a crime contributed to Jim Crow segregation in the aftermath of the war and has produced a criminal injustice system with the largest imprisoned population in the world, one-third of whom are black men.

Movies Based on History

Social Studies and history teachers are always looking for movies to help bring the past alive for students. Many movies look as if they have potential, but questionable historical validity and outright misrepresentation make them less than useful. I believe the best movie depiction of slavery in the United States continues to be the original Gordon Parks version of Solomon Northup's story, *Solomon Northup's Odyssey* (1984). Parks's

movie (later released as *Half Slave, Half Free*) and Northup's book *Twelve Years a Slave* include a focus on work and community on Southern cotton and sugar plantations and not just the horror of enslavement. *Twelve Years a Slave* (2013), also based on Solomon Northup's book, was a box office success and won many major awards including Oscars for Best Picture and Best Supporting Actress. The movie is generally authentic to the book, however for dramatic affect some characters are collapsed and it leaves out scenes of work and community that Parks included.

The Birth of a Nation, about the life of Nat Turner, was overwhelmed by controversy surrounding its director and star. It is a beautifully filmed and emotionally powerful movie, but I could not identify useful scenes to show in a high school or college class. Part of the problem is that much of what we believe we know about Turner's life and rebellion against slavery were filtered by a white lawyer who originally published Turner's "confession."

Free State of Jones is a recent entry in the category "Movies You Should Not Show in History Classes." The movie purports to tell the "true story" of a Confederate deserter who organized an interracial militia in Mississippi swamp country. A review in *Variety* described the lead character as "Kevin Costner in 'Dances with Wolves' crossed with a saintly Marxist professor crossed with a white version of Malcolm X" and a "little too good to be true" (Gleiberman 2106). Charles Blow (2016, A23) in the *New York Times* dismissed the movie as an act of distortion.

Adult Fiction

The Underground Railroad (Doubleday, 2016) is an award-winning novel by Colson Whitehead. It is an imaginative and powerful book about the human desire for freedom, but despite its title, it is not about the historic Underground Railroad. Initially I read the book as a historian and was constantly correcting Whitehead in my head until I accepted that he was not really concerned with how historians understand and explain the past. The Underground Railroad, in the novel an actual railroad that runs under the ground, and even slavery were metaphors used to explore racism in the United States, the condition of black life, people's hopes, and people's struggles, in the past and present. At a time when police violence against black men seems to be almost a daily occurrence, this book is a statement that Black Lives Matter. It is an excellent addition to a curriculum where a history class is paired with an English class.

A fictional character resembling Frederick Douglass makes an appearance in the novel as Elijah Lander, the son of a white father and black mother from Boston, who travels the nation risking his life to speak out against slavery. Eugene Wheeler is a William Lloyd Garrison-like character, although this time he is an abolitionist lawyer in New York City. Mingo is the accommodationist Booker T. Washington and Royal is a male Harriet Tubman figure. It is Royal who explains to readers how the Underground Railroad works. "The underground railroad is bigger than its operators—it's all of you, too. The small spurs, the big trunk lines. We have the newest locomotives and the obsolete engines, and we have handcars like that one. It goes everywhere, to places we know and those we don't" (Whitehead 2016, 267).

Kindred (Doubleday, 1979) is a novel by science fiction writer Octavia E. Butler. Its central (*continues on page 158*)

(*continued from page 157*)

character is Dana Franklin, an African American writer, who mysteriously time travels from Los Angeles in the 1970s to Maryland in the early 1800s. In Maryland, Dana meets her ancestors, a white plantation owner named Rufus Weylin, and Alice Greenwood, a free black woman raped by Weylin. To remain hidden, Dana takes on the role of an enslaved African. Dana's husband, Kevin, is white. He accompanies her on some of her trips to the past where he pretends to be her owner in an effort to help her survive.

The Good Lord Bird (Riverhead, 2013), like *The Underground Railroad*, was a National Book Award winner for fiction. Its author, James McBride, imagines the memoirs of Henry Shackleford, an enslaved African boy in the Kansas territory during the 1850s who encounters a fictional John Brown and joins his abolitionist band. Shackleford, who often passes as a girl, later meets Harriet Tubman and Frederick Douglass and joins Brown at Harpers Ferry. Some critics, me included, dismiss the book because of its comic elements and its negative depiction of important historic figures, especially Douglass.

Sacred Hunger (Norton, 1993), by Brian Unsworth, is a Booker Award–winning novel about the brutality of the transatlantic slave trade. The *Liverpool Merchant* is wracked by epidemic disease and the captain wants to throw its human cargo overboard so that he can collect insurance. There is a rebellion on board, the captain is killed, and the ship is beached on the coast of Florida. There, the enslaved blacks and surviving white sailors form a maroon community where they live in relative harmony until they are captured or killed by agents of the original owner of the ship. Unsworth was a magnificent writer and this is an excellent work of historical fiction.

Homegoing (Knopf, 2016), by Yaa Gyasi, traces the history of sisters and their descendants from a fictional Fante family on the Gold Coast of Africa through enslavement in the Americas and colonialism in Africa into the modern era. The early part of the book focuses heavily on the role of some African nations in the enslavement of other tribes. While reviews of the book were generally good, it was not my favorite book and I don't recommend it for classroom use.

Forever: A Novel (Little, Brown, 2002), by Pete Hamill, is the story of an Irishman, Cormac O'Connor, who arrives in colonial New York City in 1740. O'Connor aids an enslaved African shaman and is rewarded with eternal life as long as he remains on the island of Manhattan. While I did not like the overall book that much, the early depictions of colonial New York are done well.

Young Adult and Juvenile Fiction

Chains (Atheneum, 2010), by Laurie Halse Anderson, is set in New York City during the American Revolution. Thirteen-year-old Isabel is enslaved. She and her sister had been promised emancipation but when their "master" dies they are sold. Isabel eventually becomes a spy for the revolutionary forces hoping to finally obtain freedom, but this dream is betrayed. As the story ends, Isabel is poised to escape. The book is widely used in middle school classrooms.

In *Anthony Burns: The Defeat and Triumph of a Fugitive Slave* (Knopf 1988), Virginia Hamilton tells a fictionalized account of the true story of a freedom seeker who is captured in Boston under the Fugitive Slave Act. Abolitionists and the Boston Vigilance Committee rally to secure his release. Federal troops are eventually brought into Boston to suppress riot and rebellion. The city was placed under martial law and Burns was forcefully transported to Virginia, but his freedom was then purchased by Boston abolitionists. The book is intended for students in upper elementary and middle school grades.

Like *Homegoing*, Walter Dean Myers's *The Glory Field* (Scholastic, 1994) is a multigenerational story. It opens in the 1750s when a young boy is captured in Sierra Leone and sent to the Americas on a slave ship. Through his descendants, we learn of the African American experience in the plantation South and from the Civil War through the civil rights era. It is recommended for middle school students.

47 (2005), by Walter Mosley, has some of the same science fiction and magical qualities as *Kindred* and *The Underground Railroad*. It is the story of a fourteen-year-old boy enslaved on a Southern plantation who meets a self-emancipated former slave named Tall John who helps him achieve freedom. It is recommended for middle school students, but at times the story is confusing as Mosley weaves together time travel, shape-shifting, intergalactic conflict, along with slavery in the American South.

Jip, His Story (Dutton, 1996), by Katherine Paterson, is the story of a twelve-year-old orphan in the 1850s who lives on a poor farm for the mentally ill. While the setting is Vermont, it could just as well be Upstate New York. Jip learns that his mother was an escaped slave and he is being sought as property by her owner, who is also his biological father. Fearful of being captured and enslaved, Jip escapes on the UGRR into Canada. As an adult, Jip returns to the United States and joins a negro regiment from New York State to fight in the Civil War. This book is intended for students in the upper elementary grades.

11

POLITICS OF HISTORICAL MEMORY

ARTHUR AND LEWIS TAPPAN OPERATED A SILK IMPORTING FIRM AND WERE THE LEAD-
ing white abolitionists in New York City during the 1830s and 1840s. They are probably
best remembered for organizing a committee of the city's leading abolitionists to aid in
defense of the kidnapped Africans on the *Amistad*. The brothers secured lawyers for the
Amistad captives, raised money for their defense, mobilized public support for their cause,
recruited tutors to teach them English, and arranged for their return home after they were
freed. After the passage of the Fugitive Slave Act in 1850, Lewis Tappan declared it was
legitimate to disobey laws promoting the slave system and he became an active supporter
of the Underground Railroad.

In 1834, Arthur Tappan invited the Reverend Samuel Cornish, a black man who
was the co-founder of *Freedom's Journal*, the first African American newspaper in the
United States, to sit in his pew at the Laight Street Church. White parishioners were outraged and anti-abolitionist groups began to circulate rumors that the abolitionists were
promoting, among other things, interracial marriage. Later that year, when an interracial
group met at the Chatham Street Chapel to commemorate New York's Emancipation Day,
an angry white mob broke up the meeting. Another meeting was disrupted by a white mob
on July 7. This time, the police interceded. After the July 7 riot, they arrested six African
Americans who were trying to defend themselves.

There was more extensive rioting two nights later, and pro-abolitionist churches
and businesses and African American institutions, including the African school on
Orange Street, were either damaged or destroyed (Burrows and Wallace 1999, 556–59;
Jackson 1995, 627). On July 10, the city's *Journal of Commerce* blamed the abolitionists
for the rioting by their white opponents, charging, "Their business is, not *defence* [*sic*]
but *attack*. They set the whole community in a blaze by their violence,—call men pirates,
thieves, kidnappers, knaves, villains, &c.—encourage the blacks to rescue slaves from the
hands of the Police" (Thompson 1850, 189). A few days later, an editorial declared the
number one cause of the rioting was the "indiscreet zeal of the abolitionists" (*Journal of
Commerce* 1834, 1).

A century and a half after the Emancipation Proclamation, political disagreement about slavery and abolition, perhaps tinged with a hint of racism, still touches a raw nerve. In the last few years there has been sharp political conflict over state-sponsored displays of the Confederate battle flag, buildings and institutes at major universities named after slaveholders, and streets and statues across the United States celebrating racists. Battles over how we understand the past help define who we are in the present and the possibilities for our future.

A major step in examining the history of slavery and of race in the United States was the 2016 opening of the Smithsonian's National Museum of African American History and Culture on the Mall in Washington, D.C. Founding director Lonnie Bunch calls it a "space where Americans can debate issues, come together, and maybe find common ground" (Capps 2016). One of the things that makes the museum so powerful is the way it is organized. Artifacts are used to illustrate the historical narrative, but the narrative remains primary. The museum groups displays into five exhibitions; Slavery and Freedom, 1400–1877; The Era of Segregation, 1877–1968; A Changing America, 1968 and Beyond; and Community Galleries and Cultural Expressions. The historical exhibits are below ground level; visitors climb from past to present; from slavery to freedom. The history of African Americans in New York City is prominent in each of the exhibits.

The slavery-era exhibit has plaques highlighting New York laws regulating and oppressing enslaved Africans in the city. Exhibit artifacts include early photographs, a copy of *Freedom's Journal*, and Harriet Tubman's shawl and gospel hymnal. While the museum is not about slavery, the history of slavery and its continuing impact on American society is prominent. The Slavery and Freedom section opens with "The Paradox of Liberty." Text from the Declaration of Independence, the Constitution, and the Bill of Rights is on a high wall behind a statue of Thomas Jefferson, author of the Declaration and a Virginia planter and slaveholder. Behind Jefferson are bricks with the names of the hundreds of people he claimed to own. He stands surrounded by statues of prominent opponents of slavery including Toussaint Louverture, Benjamin Banneker, and Phyllis Wheatley.

I visited the Museum of African American History and Culture with high school students and teachers from the Minneapolis-St. Paul region participating in a "Civil Rights Research Experience" sponsored by the West Metro Educational Program. The students were focused on discovering historical patterns, the role of institutions in the oppression and liberation of people, and the way language conveys meaning. Visiting the museum with these students helped me understand its impact and importance. I was especially impressed with the connections these young people drew between the exhibit on Emmett Till and the death of Trayvon Martin, and how the treatment of the Scottsboro Boys in Alabama in the 1930s was eerily similar to the treatment of five black teenagers in New York City in 1989 who were accused of rape and rampaging in Central Park.

Why do real historical memories so important

I have not received the same positive reaction to every effort I have made to explain slavery and race to the American public. Over the years, I have had a series of disagreements with the New-York Historical Society (N-YHS) and the Gilder Lehrman Institute of American History that controls its board of directors (Singer 2008, 119). My "battles" with the N-YHS are not just about accuracy or interpretation, but about the way historical memory defines a nation.

Between 2005 and 2012, N-YHS produced three major exhibitions on slavery and its historic connection with New York City, along with curriculum materials and a comprehensive history, including "Slavery in New York" (October 2005–March 2006); "New York Divided: Slavery and the Civil War" (November 2006–September 2007); and "Revolution! The Atlantic World Reborn!" (November 2001–April 2012). While the physical exhibitions have long been closed, they remain accessible on the historical society's website.

The exhibits were generally well received, but I was always bothered by what I saw as an underlying ideological bias—Gilder and Lehrman are major donors to the Republican Party and conservative groups—and occasional historical "flaws." The N-YHS also has a tendency to organize exhibits around the availability of artifacts rather than the significance of events and actors and to include a bit of sensationalism in their displays and advertisements (Pogrebin and Collins 2004, E1; Berlin and Harris 2005; Rothstein 2005, E43; Collins 2005, E1).

On a Saturday in January 2012, I took students from a teacher education class to the N-YHS exhibition "Revolution! The Atlantic World Reborn!" I had visited the exhibit before, and although I was critical of it in reviews published by the *History News Network* and the *Huffington Post*, I thought it important that teachers and future teachers see the exhibit and draw their own conclusions (Singer 2011e; Singer 2012a). Artifacts on display included a surviving copy of Haiti's Declaration of Independence from 1804; material used by British abolitionist Thomas Clarkson as part of lectures opposing the transatlantic slave trade; a ca. 1789 wooden model of the slave ship *Brookes*; antislavery pamphlets; and implements of the slave trade. Also included, and I am not sure why, was a copy of Thomas Paine's *Common Sense* and a desk from the original federal capitol building in lower Manhattan, both part of the N-YHS's permanent collection.

Visitors to the N-YHS museum at the corner of Central Park West and Seventy-Seventh Street in Manhattan are greeted by statues of Abraham Lincoln and Frederick Douglass placed at entryways outside the building. According to Louise Mirrer, the N-YHS's president, "Lincoln and Douglass quintessentially point to the story we tell through our exhibitions, programs and extraordinary collections about the open-ended history of American freedom, and our nation and city's accomplishments, as well as failures to make good on the promise of liberty and equality for all" (Dunlap 2011b, B1). In the reviews, including one titled "You Don't Own Frederick Douglass," I suggested that

Lincoln and Douglass, if they were alive, would probably be picketing the exhibit because of its historical inaccuracies (Singer 2012b). When I returned to the N-YHS with my class, I hung a sign on the Frederick Douglass statue warning, "The exhibits at the New-York Historical Society are ideologically driven and plagued by historical inaccuracy. View critically and use at your own risk. Be suspicious when White men tell the story about how they made the world better for Black people."

David Ruggles, secretary of the New York Committee of Vigilance, and Charles Ray, editor of New York City's *Colored American*, would have agreed with my warning. An 1839 editorial in the *Colored American* declared, "As long as we let them think and act for us, as long as we will bow to their opinions, and acknowledge that their word is counsel, and their will is law; so long they will outwardly treat us as men, while in their hearts they still hold us as slaves" (Bacon 2007, 272). In an unsigned article published in the June 27, 1840, edition of the *Colored American* that was probably written by Ruggles, the author insists that "[a]s long as we attend the Conventions called by our white friends we will be looked upon as playing second fiddle to them. They will always form the majority at such Conventions, and the sentiments and opinions thus promulgated will go forth as the sentiments and opinions of white men, but when we act then they will see that the worm is turning.... We should enter upon the work with the honest conviction that we are doing what no others can do for us, and what cannot be effected under any other circumstances" (Harding 1981, 139).

Samuel Ringgold Ward would also have agreed with my sign. Ward became a major proponent of the independent Negro Convention movement because white opponents of slavery rarely supported equal rights and full citizenship for black Americans. He challenged white abolitionists who "have not so much regard for the rights of colored men as they think they have.... I know not how else to account for their strong and determined action in defence [*sic*] of their own rights, while now they are comparatively mute concerning ours" (Ripley 1991, 341).

As a teacher and a historian I agree that the transatlantic slave trade and New World slavery as well as the revolutionary movements at the end of the nineteenth century played major roles in shaping the modern world. I was pleased that the slave rebellion in Santo Domingue that led to the creation of an independent Haiti received prominent place along with revolutions in British North America, France, and Great Britain. However, other than the coverage of the struggle in Haiti, I was very disappointed when I visited the exhibit.

Many of the panels offered broad simplifications in the form of platitudes about the past two hundred years rather than an accurate account or historical analysis, while other panels were more focused but equally misleading. An area I found particularly inaccurate was the exhibit's discussion of the British campaign to end, first, the transatlantic slave trade, and then slavery in the British Empire. I had to copy the text quoted below from the exhibit panels in a notepad so I apologize for any errors.

But then would every thing be eg.?

A major theme of the exhibit was that "[t]he Age of Revolution made us all citizens of the world as well as our own nation, loyal to global ideals as well as local and group bonds." I only wish this were true. If it were, slavery in the United States might not have continued into the 1860s until it ended after a bloody Civil War; European imperialists might not have subdivided and colonized Africa and Asia in the nineteenth century; the United States and other countries might not have virtually exterminated their indigenous populations; and the world might have avoided World War I, World War II, a series of genocides, and the nuclear arms race.

A second theme was, "Remaking law rather than remaking society has been the nation's strongest instrument of change for more than two centuries." I think this represents a fundamental misunderstanding about the relationship between law and society. Laws are generally a reflection of a society rather than instruments for change. The American legal system has frequently codified social injustice. Fugitive slave laws, Black Codes, Jim Crow segregation laws, and numerous Supreme Court decisions, the most infamous being *Dred Scott* and *Plessy*, have supported the enforcement of slavery and racism. As I have documented in earlier chapters of this book, the "strongest instrument of change" has been social movements to extend liberty and democracy that forced changes in the law. These include the abolitionist, labor, civil rights, women's, and gay rights movements, and more recently Black Lives Matter. *[margin: laws represent changes in society]*

The New-York Historical Society exhibit maintained that "gradually during and after the Revolution, and particularly in the Bill of Rights" rights were defined as "universal." Actually, the Bill of Rights, which placed limits on the ability of Congress to interfere with religious practice, speech, assembly, and the press, placed no similar restrictions on state governments, hence the question of the legality of slavery, which is unmentioned in the Constitution, remained subject to the judgment of individual states. It was not until the Fourteenth Amendment, approved after the Civil War in 1868, that states were forced to respect the rights of citizens of the United States and it was not until 1920 that American women were ensured the right to vote. Prior to the Civil War, the rights protected by the Bill of Rights were limited to a few and could be abridged by the states; they clearly were not universal.

The exhibit concluded with the statement about what the modern world owes to the Age of Revolution. It claims that the Age of Revolution "created several 'new normals,'" among them that "slavery was fundamentally inhuman and had to be abolished"; "Nations should have the right to govern themselves"; and "Even the poor and weak should be treated with dignity." But of course, these were not "normals" for much of the nineteenth and twentieth centuries and are still not "normals" in much of the world today. If they were, how do we explain British policy during the Great Irish Famine of the 1840s and the famine in India in the 1940s, when food was shipped overseas while people starved, and recurrent famine in Africa during the last three decades; colonized indigenous people in *[margin: Not an accurate representation]*

Latin America driven off of their homelands in the name of profit or progress; civil wars in Africa financed by outside corporate interests; control over the economies of many of the world's nominally independent nations by banking interests based in the economically developed nations and supragovernmental multinational agencies; and the more than twenty million who live in bondage today, more than half of whom are children.

While these criticisms can be dismissed as responses to the underlying themes, interpretations, and conclusions that shaped the exhibit and as a question of point of view, I was also disturbed by ordinary misstatements that good historical work would have avoided. According to the exhibit, "With the signing of this treaty [Treaty of Paris, 1763, ending the Seven Years' War], the stage was set for a secure period of peace. George III and Louis XV could settle into the business of managing empires." At best, this statement is misleading on two counts. The Treaty of Paris was not a permanent solution to conflicts between expanding British and French empires. It was only a temporary settlement of colonial boundaries, and the war between the two superpowers quickly resumed in 1778 when France supported the American revolutionaries seeking independence. It was the French fleet that trapped Cornwallis at Yorktown in 1781 and brought the American Revolution to a successful end. It is also unclear how much King George and King Louis actually governed their empires. Great Britain was governed by Parliament, which George attempted to influence but could not control. If anything, Louis XV was best noted for political incompetence, prolific spending on his court, and sexual affairs rather than affairs of state.

The exhibit also minimized the extent of racism in what would become the United States during and after the Revolution. One panel states, "Despite early misgivings, the Continental Army also began recruiting enslaved men with offers of liberty." However, twice as many African Americans fought on the British side during the War for Independence. While some New England militias and regiments made efforts to recruit black soldiers from the start of the war, and Alexander Hamilton advocated for the enlistment of freed blacks, George Washington ordered recruiters for the Continental Army not to enroll any deserters from the British army, vagabonds, or negroes.

According to another panel, in *Notes on the State of Virginia*, Thomas Jefferson expressed his "fundamental opposition to slavery and his fear of what emancipation would bring." I think it would be more accurate to say Jefferson expressed his total antipathy toward people of African ancestry. Jefferson postulated that emancipation would only be practical if the freed black population were expelled and replaced by new white immigrants. Freed blacks could not remain in the United States because of the "[d]eep rooted prejudices entertained by the whites; ten thousand recollections, by the blacks, of the injuries they have sustained; new provocations; *the real distinctions which nature has made*; and many other circumstances, will divide us into parties, and produce convulsions which will probably never end but in the extermination of the one or the other race" (Countryman 2012, 147–48). Jefferson goes on to use pseudoscience to "document" all aspects of the racial inferiority of the African when compared to the white European.

Later in the exhibit, it states, "President Jefferson, more attentive to southern fears of slave revolt, would embargo trade with Saint Domingue." While this statement is accurate, it tells a very small part of the relationship between the United States and Haiti or the attitudes of Thomas Jefferson. Thomas Jefferson feared that Haiti's revolt would inspire similar slave rebellions in the United States. In a letter written in 1797 about events in Haiti, Jefferson argued, "If something is not done, and soon done, we shall be the murderers of our own children" (Danticat 2004). During Jefferson's presidency, the United States offered to help the French defeat the Haitian revolutionary forces. After independence was secured in 1804, Haiti sought closer ties with the United States because of what its leaders saw as their shared revolutionary heritage. Haitian leader Jean-Jacques Dessalines wrote directly to Jefferson, who ignored the letter (Fleming 2004).

Unfortunately, Jefferson's prejudices were shared by later American political leaders, and the government of an independent Haiti was not recognized by the United States until 1862, after it had repaid French planters for the cost of their lost slaves, and at a time when the United States and Abraham Lincoln were considering shipping millions of freed American slaves to the black nation (Wesley 1917, 369–83; Matthewson 1996, 22–48).

While "Revolution! The Atlantic World Reborn" claimed to be about the revolutions in British North America, France, and Saint-Domingue (Haiti), it actually treated British antislavery campaigns as a fourth "revolution." Its interpretation here was largely drawn from Adam Hochschild's *Bury the Chains* (2005). In this case, I think Hochschild and the exhibit gave too much credit for the end of slavery in the British Empire to idealists, religious dissenters, and parliamentary reformers. According to the exhibit, "Britain's economic interests weighed against abolition. But culturally and politically, slavery became objectionable to large segments of the British public." In addition, "Eradicating the slave trade, and ultimately emancipating all the empire's slaves, would assure Britons … were a people loyal to a principle as well as a homeland…. Abolition wrapped British nationhood in both moral and imperial glory."

These statements are debatable. With the withdrawal of Saint-Domingue from the international sugar trade, British Caribbean colonies dominated the sugar market. The continuing importation of slaves from Africa would have benefited Britain's competitors, allowing them to put more land into production and challenge Britain's market dominance. It would also have increased the possibility of slave rebellions.

Great Britain ended slavery because of the cost of suppressing slave rebellions and fear that sooner or later a British colony would become the next Haiti. In the early nineteenth century, there were major slave rebellions in the British colonies of Barbados, Guyana, and Jamaica. In Barbados, in 1816, twenty thousand Africans from more than seventy plantations drove whites off the plantations during "Bussa's Rebellion." In Guyana, in 1823, the East Coast Demerara Rebellion was fueled by the belief among enslaved Africans that the planters were deliberately withholding news of the impending freedom of the slaves.

Orlando Patterson, a sociologist and historian originally based at the University of the West Indies in Jamaica, argued that "with the possible exception of Brazil, no other slave society in the New World experienced such continuous and intense servile revolts as Jamaica" (Patterson 1969, 273). Patterson argued that this was attributable to a number of factors, including an inaccessible mountainous interior, the high proportion of Africans to Europeans, and the large number of enslaved people who had been born free in West Africa. Patterson also credited what he saw as the general ineptitude of the planter caste and their high rate of absenteeism. Significantly, these were very similar to conditions in Haiti prior to its revolution.

The 1831 slave rebellion in Jamaica that shook the British Empire and led to the abolition of slavery in British colonies was in the area around Montego Bay in the northwest portion of the island (Craton 1982, 291–322; Singer 2011a, 108–10). It is generally called either the Baptist War, because of the church affiliation of its leaders, or the Christmas Uprising, because the rebellion took place following the Christmas holiday break from work. While as many as twenty thousand enslaved Africans participated in attacks on more than two hundred plantations in the Montego Bay area, causing over a million pounds worth of damage, their actions were contained, and the rebellion was largely suppressed within two weeks. Hundreds of rebels were captured, more than 750 were convicted of insurrection, and 138 were sentenced to death, either by hanging or firing squad. Sharpe was captured and publicly executed in May 1832 in Market Square at Montego Bay. Before he was hanged, Sharpe is reported to have said, "I would rather die in yonder gallows, than live for a minute more in slavery" (Olajide 2013, 59).

Two parliamentary inquiries were launched to determine the causes of the insurrection and a week after Sharpe's execution the British Parliament appointed a committee to consider ways of ending slavery in the colonies. In August 1833, the Slavery Abolition Act was approved, formally ending slavery in British America. A provision of the act was that plantation owners would receive compensation for the loss of their slaves. No provision was made to compensate enslaved Africans for years of bondage and unpaid work (House of Commons 1837).

The main thrust of "Revolution! The Atlantic World Reborn," as it had been in previous exhibits at the N-YHS on slavery and the slave trade, is that slavery was an evil, but because of its commitments to liberty (rights) and democracy (popular rule) the United States overcame this evil. My view is that the history of the United States is much more complex. For example, the exhibit presented the free press in the British American colonies as a major part of the democratizing process. However, it did not mention that early American publishers, including John Peter Zenger, supported their newspapers and pamphlets by printing advertisements for the recapture of escaped slaves (Hodges and Brown 1994, 30).

The exhibit also neglected the role played by ordinary people such as sailors, slaves, and commoners, what historians Peter Linebaugh and Marcus Rediker call the "many-headed hydra," in defining the culture of the revolutionary Atlantic (Linebaugh and Rediker 2000). Lastly, while the exhibit and the New-York Historical Society cele-brated the triumph of liberty, they completely ignored the continuing impact of racism and imperialism on shaping the United States and the world.

It is worth noting Frederick Douglass's view of the founders and the American independence movement. In his 1852 Fourth of July address in Rochester, New York, Douglass demanded to know:

> What to the American slave is your Fourth of July? I answer, a day that reveals to him more than all other days of the year, the gross injustice and cruelty to which he is the constant victim. To him your celebration is a sham; your boasted liberty an unholy license; your national great-ness, swelling vanity; your sounds of rejoicing are empty and heartless; your denunciation of tyrants, brass-fronted impudence; your shouts of liberty and equality, hollow mockery; your prayers and hymns, your ser-mons and thanksgivings, with all your religious parade and solemnity, are to him mere bombast, fraud, deception, impiety, and hypocrisy—a thin veil to cover up crimes which would disgrace a nation of savages. There is not a nation of the earth guilty of practices more shocking and bloody than are the people of these United States at this very hour (Aptheker 1973, 330–34).

TEACHING NOTES

*Public History Projects on Slavery
and Abolition in New York*

QUESTIONS TO CONSIDER

1. What public history projects can bring to light the history
of slavery and the struggle to end it in your community?

2. Do projects such as these have a value beyond
their effort to correct the historical record?

As a postscript to this chapter, I want to highlight some important efforts to teach the public about the history of slavery and abolition in New York.

In 1992, during the excavation of a federal office building, an eighteenth-century African Burial Ground was rediscovered two blocks from New York City Hall (Smalls 1997, WC21). Following a campaign by the local African American community, there is now a national park with exhibits and a monument to enslaved Africans who built the infrastructure of the colonial city. Journalist and videographer Eric Tait, formerly of ABC News, produced a documentary history of slavery in New York centered on the burial ground, "Then I'll Be Free to Travel Home," with an introduction by Lena Horne. Anthropologist Dr. Sherril Wilson served as the projects academic consultant.

More recently, elementary school children and their teachers from PS 48 in the Bronx uncovered evidence of a slave burial ground in their Hunts Point neighborhood (Foderaro 2015, A14). The project originated when Phil Panaritis, formerly the local coordinator of Teaching American History grants, showed teachers a 1910 photograph labeled "Slave burying ground" on a no longer existing road in the area that he located in the archives of the Museum of the City of New York. Local politicians are now supporting student efforts to get the site recognized and preserved. The Burial Database Project of Enslaved Africans, originally based at Fordham University, has identified more than 350 African American burial grounds dating from slavery days, including eleven in New York State. Many are unmarked, waiting to be adopted by an elementary school class or community group (Arnold 2016).

In June 2015, New York City mayor Bill de Blasio unveiled a plaque on the corner of Wall and Water Streets in lower Manhattan, the site of the eighteenth-century New York City slave market (Chayes 2015). It was a small step toward recognizing the city's deep historic ties to slavery and the transatlantic slave trade. In response to the dedication, independent filmmaker Susan Modaress produced an Inside Out report on "New York's History of Slavery" that is available for viewing online at https://www.youtube.com/watch?v=t0R9tbHnHnU&feature=youtu.be. At the same time, as part of a program

"Listen for a Change: Sacred Conversations for Racial Justice," Trinity Church on Wall Street produced a video history examining the relationship of the church and its parishioners to slavery in early New York. It is also available for viewing online at https://www.trinitywallstreet.org/video/shadow-slavery.

The Office of Brooklyn District sponsored a fifty-five minute documentary on *Slavery and the Law* (Singer 1911d) with funding from the Kellogg Foundation. *Slavery and the Law* followed the creation of a mural by Brooklyn teenagers, interweaving their journey of discovery through art with an examination of the legal status of enslaved Africans in Colonial America up until the American civil rights movement. The film chronicles struggles to transform the law and create a more just society in the United States. One of its goals was to provide young people with knowledge of the past to empower them to become active citizens committed to racial healing and social justice. The video was produced and directed by documentary filmmaker Paula Heredia. Participating historians and educators include former New York State regent Adelaide Sanford, Ira Berlin of the University of Maryland, a former president of the Organization of American Historians, Deborah Gray White and Clement Price of Rutgers University, and Gloria Browne-Marshall of John Jay College of Criminal Justice-CUNY. At the end of the film a panel of community-based religious leaders discuss possibilities for unity and racial healing.

Another project involved efforts by local anthropologists to resurrect Seneca Village in New York City's Central Park (Dunlap 2005a, B1). Seneca Village was located between what are now Eighty-Second and Eighty-Ninth Streets and Seventh and Eighth Avenues (Burrows and Wallace 1999, 480; Singer 2011c). The village existed from 1825 to 1857, when it was destroyed to make way for Central Park. The origin of the village's name remains unclear. According to the New-York Historical Society, it could have been named for the Seneca tribe of Native Americans, or was a distortion of the word *Senegal*. Many streets and towns in New York State bear Roman names, so it might refer to the Roman philosopher Seneca, known for his writings about morals. During the 1850s, local newspapers, including what would become the *New York Times*, derisively described the settlement as "Nigger Village" (*New York Times* 1856, 3). In 1825, parcels of land were sold to members of the African Methodist Episcopal Zion Church. They included a former bootblack named Andrew Williams, who purchased six lots of land for $125, and laborer named Epiphany Davis, who bought twelve lots for $578. Land in Seneca Village was considerably less expensive than in the main downtown areas of the city. It was important for African American males to be landowners because under the New York State Constitution of 1821, ownership of property valued at $250 or over entitled men to vote.

The New York State Census of 1855 reported that 264 people, largely African Americans but also Irish and German immigrants, lived in Seneca Village. There were three churches, Colored School No. 3 was located in the basement of the African Union Methodist Church, and several cemeteries. All Angels' Church, built in 1849, had a (*continues on page 172*)

(*continues from page 171*)

racially integrated congregation of African American, Irish, and German parishioners. The congregation is currently an affiliate of St. Michael's Episcopal Church on Broadway at Ninety-Ninth Street.

In 1853, the New York state legislature set aside land for the construction of Central Park and authorized the use of "eminent domain" to confiscate private property between Fifty-Ninth and 106th Streets (later extended to 110th Street) for public purposes. The residents of Seneca Village received final eviction notices during the summer of 1856. Although property holders were compensated, many protested in the courts. An article in the *New York Times* reported, "The policemen find it difficult to persuade them out of the idea which has possessed their simple minds, that the sole object of the authorities in making the Park is to procure their expulsion from the homes which they occupy." After eviction, the community was never reestablished.

On August 24, 2011, the Institute for the Exploration of Seneca Village exhibited its findings about the village on a hillside in Central Park, where the original All Angel's Episcopal Church had been located. There were presentations by student interns from nine local universities. Their work on the archeological dig was funded by a National Endowment for the Humanities grant and supervised by local archeologists Jenna Coplin and Meredith Linn and project co-director Cynthia Copeland.

A number of New York State regions have organized Underground Railroad or Freedom Trail self-guided tours and exhibits. In the Buffalo area, the tour includes UGRR safe houses, a "Negro Burial Ground," a "Follow the North Star" exhibit at the St. Catharines Museum on the Canadian side of the Niagara River, and "Freedom Crossing: The Underground Railroad in Greater Niagara" at the Castellani Art Museum. In Auburn and Cayuga Counties, the tour includes the homes of Harriet Tubman and William and Frances Seward. In Ausable Chasm, about thirty-six miles from the Canadian border, there is a North Star Underground Railroad Museum that tells the story of freedom seekers who passed through on their way to Canada.

I continue to be impressed with the public education and historical preservation done by the Underground Railroad History Project of the Capital Region based in Troy, New York, and the National Abolition Hall of Fame in Peterboro, New York. The UGRR History Project hosts an annual conference, produces teaching materials, publishes a newsletter, and maintains a website. I have spoken at their conferences and have been an excited participant in their tours. They are also continually restoring the Stephen and Harriet Myers Residence in Albany, New York. The Myerses were conductors at a key location on the Underground Railroad.

The Hall of Fame, which shares a small town crossroads with the Gerrit Smith National Historic Landmark, held its first induction ceremony in 2005 and selected as honorees Frederick Douglass, William Lloyd Garrison, Gerrit Smith, Harriet Tubman, and Lucretia Mott. As of 2016, it had honored seventeen other participants in the fight to end slavery in the United States.

REFERENCES

The Abolitionists. 2013. http://www.pbs.org/wgbh/americanexperience/films/abolitionists/; accessed February 21, 2016.

Albany Evening Journal. 1859. "The Harper's Ferry Outbreak," October 27.

Amherst College, Department of American Studies. 2009. *The Compromise of 1850*. Rockville, MD: Wildside Press.

Aptheker, H. 1989. *Abolitionism*. Boston: Twayne.

———, ed. 1973. *A Documentary History of the Negro People in the United States, Vol. 1*. Secaucus, NJ: Citadel.

Arnold, S. 2016. *Memory and Landmarks, Report of the Burial Database Project of Enslaved Americans*. Ithaca, NY: Periwinkle Initiative.

Bacon, J. 2007. *Freedom's Journal: The First African American Newspaper*. Lanham, MD: Lexington Books.

Bailey, T. 1966. *The American Pageant: A History of the Republic*. Boston: DC Heath.

———, and D. Kennedy. 1983. *The American Pageant: A History of the Republic, Seventh Edition*. Lexington, MA: DC Heath.

Bailyn, B. 1973. "The Central Themes of the American Revolution: An Interpretation." In *Essays on the American Revolution*, edited by S. Kurtz and J. Hutson, 3–31. Chapel Hill: University of North Carolina Press.

Baptist, E. 2014. *The Half Has Never Been Told: Slavery and the Making of American Capitalism*. New York: Basic Books.

Barton, D. 2011, July. "The Founding Fathers and Slavery." *Wall Builders*. http://www.wall builders.com/libissuesarticles.asp?id=122); accessed January 20, 2016.

Basker, J., ed. 2012. *American Antislavery Writings: Colonial Beginnings to Emancipation*. Washington, DC: Library of Congress.

Bass, J. 2010. "History Shows Secession was about Slavery." *Charleston, South Carolina Post and Courier*, December 26. http://www.postandcourier.com/article/20101226/ARCHIVES/312269943; accessed April 18, 2012.

Bayard, J. 1858. *Speech of Hon. James A. Bayard, of DEL. In the Senate of the United States, March 22, 1858, on the Bill for the Admission of Kansas into the Federal Union Under the LeCompton Constitution*.

Beckert, S. 2015. *The Empire of Cotton: A Global History*. New York: Knopf.

Beecher, W., and S. Scoville. 1888. *A Biography of Rev. Henry Ward Beecher*. New York: Webster.

Benton, J., ed. 1891. "Greeley's Estimate of Lincoln." *The Century Magazine*, XLII. New York: The Century Co., 371–82.

Berlin, I. 2015. *The Long Emancipation: The Demise of Slavery in the United States*. Cambridge: Harvard University Press.

———, and L. Harris, eds. 2005. *Slavery in New York*. New York: New Press.

Bernstein, I. 1990. *The New York City Draft Riots*. New York. Oxford University Press.

Bickford, J. 2015. "Assessing and Addressing Historical Misrepresentations within Children's Literature about the Civil Rights Movement." *The History Teacher* 48 (4): 693–736.

Black, L. 1847. *The Life and Sufferings of Leonard Black, a Fugitive from Slavery*. New Bedford, MA: Benjamin Lindsey.

Blackburn, R. 2011. *The American Crucible, Slavery, Emancipation, and Human Rights*. New York: Verso.

Blight, D. 1989. *Frederick Douglass' Civil War*. Baton Rouge: Louisiana State University Press.

Blow, C. 2016. "White Savior, Rape and Romance?" *New York Times*, June 27.

Boritt, G. 2005. *The Gettysburg Gospel: The Lincoln Speech That Nobody Knows*. New York: Simon and Schuster.

Bradford, S. 1869. *Scenes in the Life of Harriet Tubman*. Auburn, NY: W. J. Moses.

———. 1886. *Harriet Tubman, The Moses of Her People*. New York: George R. Lockwood and Son.

Branch, T. 1988. *Parting the Waters: America in the King Years 1954–1963*. New York: Simon and Schuster.

Brooklyn Eagle. 1863a. "Our Colored 'Bredren,'" January 2.

———. 1863b. "Mr. Everett at Gettysburg," November 20.

———.1865a. "Inaugural Addresses of the President and Vice President," March 6.

———. 1865b. "Let Us Honor the Dead by Imitating His Example," April 17.

———. 1865c. Account of Harriet Tubman Speaking at the Bridge Street African Wesleyan Methodist Episcopal Church, October 23.

———. 1872. "Mentionable Men," November 13.

———. 1873. "Ex-Mayor Kalbfleisch," February 12.

Brooks, N. 1896. *Washington in Lincoln's Time*. New York: The Century Co.

Brown, C. 1971. *William Cullen Bryant*. New York: Scribner's.

Brown, W. 1847. *Narrative of William W. Brown, Fugitive Slave*. Boston: Anti-Slavery Office.

Brown, W., ed. 1848. *The Anti-Slavery Harp: A Collection of Songs for Anti-Slavery Meetings*. Boston: Bela Marsh.

Brummer, S. 1911. "Political History of New York State during the Period of the Civil War." *Studies in History, Economics and Public Law* XXXXIX (2). New York: Columbia University Press.

Burrows, E., and M. Wallace. 1999. *Gotham: A History of New York City to 1898*. New York: Oxford University Press.

Byrd, R., ed. 1995. *Senate, 1789–1989: Classic Speeches, 1830–1993, Volume 3*. Washington, DC: Government Printing Office.

Calmes, J. 2016. "Harriet Tubman Ousts Andrew Jackson in Change for a $20." *New York Times*, April 21, A1.

Campbell. S. 1968. *The Slave Catchers*. Chapel Hill: University of North Carolina Press.

Capps, K. 2016. "Don't Call It the Blacksonian." *Atlantic City Lab*, December 30. http://www.citylab.com/design/2016/12/dont-call-it-the-blacksonian-lonnie-bunch-on-americas-best-new-museum/511934/; accessed March 7, 2017.

Chait, J. 2017. "Elizabeth Warren Violates Republican Gag Rule by Criticizing Jeff Sessions." *New York*, February 8. http://nymag.com/daily/intelligencer/2017/02/eliza-beth-warren-violates-gag-rule-by-criticizing-sessions.html; accessed February 24, 2017.

Chayes, M. 2015. "Mayor Bill de Blasio Dedicates Plaque marking Wall Street Slave Market." *Newsday*, June 27. http://www.newsday.com/news/new-york/bill-de-blasio-dedicates-plaque-marking-wall-street-slave-market-1.10586817; accessed April 6, 2016.

Chernow, R. 2005. *Alexander Hamilton*. New York: Penguin.

Chesebrough, D. 1998. *Frederick Douglass: Oratory from Slavery*. Westport CT: Greenwood.

Chittenden, L. 1864. *A Report of the Debates and Proceedings in the Secret Sessions of the Conference Convention*. New York: Appleton.

Christianson, S. 2010. *Freeing Charles: The Struggle to free a Slave on the Eve of the Civil War*. Urbana: University of Illinois Press.

Clarke, L. H. 1821. *Report of the Debates and Proceedings of the Convention of the State of New-York: Held at the Capitol, in the City of Albany on the 28th Day of August, 1821*. New York: Seymour.

Clinton, C. 2004. *Harriet Tubman, The Road to Freedom*. Boston: Little, Brown.

Coates, T. 2014. "This Town Needs a Better Class of Racists." *The Atlantic*, May 1. http://www.theatlantic.com/politics/archive/2014/05/This-Town-Needs-A-Better-Class-Of-Racist/361443/; accessed January 14, 2015.

Cohen, R. 2008. "Was the Constitution Pro-Slavery? The Changing View of Frederick Douglass." *Social Education* 72 (5): 246–50.

Collins, G. 2005. "A 'Main Event' in Old New York." *The New York Times*, September 27.

Congressional Globe, 24th Congress, 1st Session. December 7, 1835–July 4, 1836. Washington, DC.

Congressional Globe, 28th Congress, 2nd Session. December 2, 1844–March 3, 1845. Washington, DC.

Congressional Globe, 29th Congress, 1st Session. December 1, 1845–August 10, 1846. Washington, DC.

Congressional Globe, 38th Congress, 1st Session. December 7, 1863–July 4, 1864. Washington, DC.

Congressional Globe, 38th Congress, 2nd Session. December 5, 1864–March 3, 1865. Washington, DC.

Congressional Globe, 39th Congress, 1st Session. December 4, 1865–July 28, 1866. Washington, DC.

Congressional Globe, 39th Congress, 2nd Session. December 3, 1866–March 3, 1867. Washington, DC.

Congressional Globe, 40th Congress, 1st Session. March 4, 1867–December 1, 1867. Washington, DC.

Congressional Globe, 40th Congress, 2nd Session. December 10, 1867–November 10, 1868. Washington, DC.

Conrad, E. 1942. *Harriet Tubman*. New York: International Publishers.

Cook, J. 1999. "Fighting with Breath, Not Blows: Frederick Douglass and Anti-Slavery Violence." In *Anti-Slavery Violence*, edited by J. McKivigan and S. Harrold. Knoxville: University of Tennessee Press.

Countryman, E. 2012. *Enjoy the Same Liberty*. Lanham, MD: Rowman and Littlefield.

Craton, M. 1982. *Testing the Chains: Resistance to Slavery in the British West Indies*. Ithaca: Cornell University Press.

Croly, D. 1864. *Miscegenation: The Theory of the Blending of the Races, Applied to the American White Man and Negro*. New York: H. Dexter, Hamilton.

Crummell, A. 1882. *The Eulogy on Henry Highland Garnet, D. D.* Washington, DC: Union Bethel Literary and Historical Association.

Damico, J., M. Baildon, and D. Greenstone. 2010. "Examining How Historical Agency Works in Children's Literature." *Social Studies Research and Practice* 5 (1): 1–12.

Danticat, E. 2004. "Thomas Jefferson: The Private War: Ignoring the War Next Door." *Time*, July 5. http://content.time.com/time/magazine/article/0,9171,994563,00. html; accessed April 6, 2016.

Davis, R., and D. Wilson. 2014. *The Lincoln-Douglas Debates: The Lincoln Studies Center Edition*. Champaign: University of Illinois Press.

Degler, C. 1983. *Out of Our Past: The Forces that Shaped Modern America*. 3rd edition. New York: Harper Perennial.

Dew, C. 2001. *Apostles of Disunion*. Charlottesville: University Press of Virginia.

Dickinson College House Divided. n.d. http://hd.housedivided.dickinson.edu/node/9639.

Dodge, A., and B. Koed, eds. 2005. *Biographical Directory of the United States Congress, 1774–2005 (House Document 108–222).* Washington, DC: Government Printing Office.

Donald, D. 2003. *"We Are All Lincoln Men": Abraham Lincoln and his Friends.* New York: Simon and Schuster.

Douglas, S. 1858. "The Lincoln/Douglas Debates of 1858." *Lincoln/Net.* http://lincoln.lib. niu.edu/lincolndouglas/nhdebate.html; accessed February 14, 2009.

Douglass, F. 1863, February. "Rejoicing Over the Proclamation." *Douglass' Monthly.* http:// www.civilwar.org/education/hitory/primarysources/rejoicing-over-the.html ?referrer=http://historynewsnetwork.org/article/149938; accessed January 20, 2016.

———. 1962. *Life and Times of Frederick Douglass.* New York: Collier.

———. 1968. *Narrative of the Life of Frederick Douglass.* New York: New American Library.

———, and J. McKivigan. 2012. *The Frederick Douglass Papers: Series Two: Autobiographical Writings, Volume 3.* New Haven: Yale University Press.

Douthat, R. 2006, December. "The Made America." *The Atlantic.* http://www.theatlantic. com/magazine/archive/2006/12/they-made-america/305385/; accessed February 4, 2016.

Du Bois, W. E. B. 1903/2007. *The Souls of Black Folk.* New York: Cosimo Classics.

Dummond. D. 1931. *The Secession Movement 1860–1861.* New York: Macmillan.

———, ed. 1964. *Southern Editorials on Secession.* Gloucester, MA: Peter Smith.

Dunlap, D. 2005. "Ghosts on the Radar Screen, Scientists Seek 19th Century Black Village Under the Park." *New York Times,* August 10.

———. 2011. "No Debate: It's Lincoln and Douglass." *The New York Times,* November 1.

Durkin, E. 2015. "Yay for My Yale Son's Cause: Blaz." *New York Daily News,* November 24.

Eakin, S., and D. Logsdon, eds. 1967. *Twelve Years a Slave.* Baton Rouge: Louisiana State University Press.

Edmonds, J., ed. 1869. *Statutes at Large of the State of New York, 2nd edition, vol. IV.* Albany: Weed, Parsons.

Ellis, C., and S. Smith, eds. 2010. *Say It Loud: Great Speeches on Civil Rights and African American Identity.* New York: The New Press.

engageNY. 2013. "Text List for P-12 ELA." New York State Education Department. https:// www.engageny.org/resource/text-list-for-p-12-ela; accessed online February 15, 2017.

———. 2016. "New York State K-12 Social Studies Framework." New York State Education Department. https://www.engageny.org/resource/new-york-state-k-12-soc ial-studies-framework; accessed online February 15, 2017.

Fernandez, M., and C. Hauser. 2015. "Texas Mother Teaches Textbook Company a Lesson on Accuracy." *The New York Times,* October 6.

Ferrell, C. 2006. *The Abolitionist Movement*. Westport, CT: Greenwood.

Finkelman, P. 1994. "Thomas Jefferson and Antislavery: The Myth Goes." *The Virginia Magazine of History and Biography* 102 (2).

———. 2102. "The Appeasement of 1850." In *Congress and the Crises of the 1850s*, edited by P. Finkelman and D. Kennon. Athens: Ohio University Press.

Fiske, D. 2016. *Solomon Northup's Kindred: The Kidnapping of Free Citizens before the Civil War*. Santa Barbara, CA: Praeger.

———, C. Brown, and R. Seligman. 2013. *Solomon Northup: The Complete Story of the Author of Twelve Years a Slave*. Santa Barbara, CA: Praeger.

Flanders, H. 1855. *The Lives and Times of the Chief Justices of the Supreme Court of the United States, Volume 1*. Philadelphia: Lippincott.

Fleming, T. 2004. "Why We Are Partly Responsible for the Mess That is Haiti." *History News Network*, February 26. http://historynewsnetwork.org/article/3694; accessed April 6, 2016.

Fleming, W. 1906). *Documentary History of Reconstruction: Political, Military, Social, Religious, Educational and Industrial, 1865 to the Present Time, Vol. 1*. Cleveland: Clark.

Foderaro, L. 2015. "South Bronx May Have Found Site of Slave Burial Ground." *New York Times*, January 25.

Fogel, R., and S. Engerman. 1974. *Time on the Cross: The Economics of American Negro Slavery*. Boston: Little, Brown.

Foner, E. 1970. *Free Soil, Free Labor, Free Men: The Ideology of the Republican Party before the Civil War*. New York: Oxford University Press.

———. 1988. *Reconstruction: America's Unfinished Revolution, 1863–1877*. New York: Harper and Row.

———. 2006. *Forever Free: The Story of Emancipation and Reconstruction*. New York: Vintage.

———. 2010. *The Fiery Trial, Abraham Lincoln and American Slavery*. New York: Norton.

———. 2015. *Gateway to Freedom, The Hidden History of the Underground Railroad*. New York: Norton.

Foner, P. 1941. *Business and Slavery: The New York Merchants and the Irrepressible Conflict*. Chapel Hill: University of North Carolina Press.

———, and Y. Taylor, eds. 2000. *Frederick Douglass: Selected Speeches and Writings*. Chicago: Chicago Review Press.

Franklin, J. 1974. *From Slavery to Freedom, 4th edition*. New York: Knopf.

Freehling, W. 2007. *The Road to Disunion*. New York: Oxford University Press.

———, and C. Simpson. 1992. *Secession Debated, Georgia's Showdown in 1860*. New York: Oxford University Press.

Funnell, W. 1937. "Many Nassau Families Owned Slaves in Late 18th Century." *Nassau Democrat Review-Star*, February 17.

Garrison, W. 1832. *Thoughts on African Colonization*. Boston: Garrison and Knapp.

———. 1832. "The Great Crisis!" *The Liberator* II, 52.

———. 1981. "To Edmund Quincy, Samuel E. Sewall, etc, Boston, March 17, 1873." In *The Letters of William Lloyd Garrison, Volume VI: To Rouse the Slumbering Land: 1868–1879*, edited by W. Merrill and L. Ruchames. Cambridge, MA: Belknap Press.

Gellman, D., and D. Quigley, eds. 2003. *Jim Crow New York: A Documentary History of Race and Citizenship 1777–1877*. New York: New York University Press.

Genovese, E. 1965. *The Political Economy of Slavery: Studies in the Economy and Society of the Slave South*. New York: Pantheon.

———. 1974. *Roll, Jordan, Roll: The World the Slaves Made*. New York: Pantheon.

George, J. 1978. " 'A Catholic Family Newspaper' Views the Lincoln Administration: John Mullaly's Copperhead Weekly." *Civil War History* 24 (2) (June).

Gershman, J. 2015. "Harvard Law Students Want School's Link to Slaveholder Scrubbed from Official Seal." *Wall Street Journal*, November 3. http://blogs.wsj.com/law/2015/11/03/harvard-law-students-want-schools-link-to-slave-owner-scrubbed-from-official-seal/; accessed January 20, 2016.

Gleiberman, C. 2016. "Film Review: 'Free State of Jones.'" *Variety*, June 20. http://variety.com/2016/film/reviews/free-state-of-jones-review-matthew-mcconaughey-1201799222/; accessed February 10, 2017.

Goodman, P. 1998. *Of One Blood: Abolitionism and the Origins of Racial Equality*. Berkeley: University of California Press.

Goodwin, D. 2005. *Team of Rivals: The Political Genius of Abraham Lincoln*. New York: Simon and Schuster.

Greeley, H. 1866. *The American Conflict: A History of the Great Rebellion in the United States of America, 1860–'64, Volume 2*. Hartford, CT: Case.

Grinspan, J. 2015. "Was Abolitionism a Failure?" *The New York Times*, February 1.

Guelzo, A. 2004. *Lincoln's Emancipation Proclamation: The End of Slavery in America*. New York: Simon and Schuster.

Haley, A. ed. 1965. *The Autobiography of Malcolm X*. New York: Grove.

Hamilton, V. 1985. *The People Could Fly: American Black Folktales*. New York: Knopf.

———. 2004. *The People Could Fly: The Picture Book*. New York: Random House.

Harding, V. 1981. *There is a River: The Black Struggle for Freedom in America*. New York: Houghton Mifflin.

Herbert, B. 2005. "Impossible, Ridiculous, Repugnant." *The New York Times*, October 6.

Higginson, M., ed. 1921. *Letters and Journals of Thomas Wentworth Higginson, 1846–1906*. Boston: Houghton Mifflin.

Higginson, T. 1899. *Contemporaries*. Boston: Houghton Mifflin.

Hochschild, A. 2005. *Bury the Chains: Prophets and Rebels in the Fight to Free an Empire's Slaves*. Boston: Houghton Mifflin.

Hodges, G. 1999. *Root and Branch: African Americans in New York and East Jersey 1613–1863*. Chapel Hill: University of North Carolina Press.

⸻. 2010. *David Ruggles: A Radical Black Abolitionist and the Underground Railroad in New York City*. Chapel Hill: University of North Carolina Press.

⸻, and Brown, A., eds. 1994. *"Pretends to Be Free": Runaway Slave Advertisements from Colonial and Revolutionary New York and New Jersey*. New York: Garland.

Holt, M. 2003. *The Rise and Fall of the American Whig Party: Jacksonian Politics and the Onset of Civil War*. New York: Oxford University Press.

Holzer, H. 2014. *Lincoln and the Power of the Press: The War for Public Opinion*. New York: Simon and Schuster.

Hopkins, J. 1863. "Bible View of Slavery." *Papers from the Society for the Diffusion of Political Knowledge, no. 8*.

Horton, J. 1993. *Free People of Color*. Washington, DC: Smithsonian Institution Press.

House of Commons. 1837. *Slavery Abolition Act Amendment. A Bill, [as Amended in the Committee, and on the Report] entitled, an Act to Amend the Act for the Abolition of Slavery in the British Colonies, Session 1837–38*. London: House of Commons.

Humez, J. 2003. *Harriet Tubman: The Life and the Life Stories*. Madison: University of Wisconsin, 2003.

Jackson, K. ed. 1995. *The Encyclopedia of New York City*. New Haven: Yale University Press.

Jay, W. 1833. *The Life of John Jay, Volume I*. New York: J. and J. Harper.

Jefferson, T. 2010. *The Works of Thomas Jefferson: Correspondence 1771–1779, the Summary View, and the Declaration of Independence*. New York: Cosimo.

Johnson, C., and P. Smith. 1999. *Africans in America: America's Journey through Slavery*. New York: Houghton Mifflin Harcourt.

Jones, M. 2013. "History and Commemoration: The Emancipation Proclamation at 150." *Journal of the Civil War Era* 3 (4) (December).

Jones, R., D. Cox, J. Navarro-Rivera, E. Dionne, and W. Galston. 2014. *What Americans Want from Immigration Reform*. Washington, DC: Public Religion Research Institute.

Journal of Commerce. 1834. "Causes of the Late Riots," July 15.

Kaplan, S. 1991. *American Studies in Black and White*. Amherst: University of Massachusetts Press.

Katz, J. 1974. *Resistance at Christiana, The Fugitive Slave Rebellion, Christiana, Pennsylvania, September 11, 1851*. New York: Thomas Y. Crowell.

Katz, W. 1995. *Eyewitness: A Living Documentary of the African American Contribution to American History*. New York: Simon and Schuster.

Katznelson, I. 2005. *When Affirmative Action Was White: An Untold History of Racial Inequality in Twentieth-Century America*. New York: Norton.

Kennedy, D. 2015. *The American Spirit: United States History as Seen by Contemporaries*. New York: Cengage.

Kirschke, J. 2005. *Gouverneur Morris: Author, Statesman, and Man of the World*. New York: Macmillan.

Kleiser, G. 1911. *Great Speeches and How to Make Them*. New York: Funk and Wagnalls.

Kommers, D., J. Finn, and G. Jacobsohn, eds. 2004. *American Constitutional Law: Essays, Cases, and Comparative Notes, 2nd edition*. Lanham, MD: Rowan and Littlefield.

Kraditor, A. 1969. *Means and Ends in American Abolitionism; Garrison and his Critics on Strategy and Tactics, 1834–1850*. New York; Pantheon.

Lander, M., and M. Shear. 2013. "President Offers a Personal Take on Race in U.S." *The New York Times*, July 20, A1.

Landis, M. 2015. "These Are Words Scholars Should No Longer Use to Describe Slavery and the Civil War." *History News Network*, September 4. http://historynews network.org/article/160266; accessed January 17, 2016.

Lanning, M. 2005. *African Americans in the Revolutionary War*. New York: Citadel.

Larson, K. 2004. *Bound for the Promised Land, Harriet Tubman, Portrait of an American Hero*. New York: Ballantine.

Lee, S. 1992. "Malcolm X, 1992." http://www.imdb.com/title/tt0104797/. accessed October 19, 2011.

Library of Congress. *The Frederick Douglass Papers*. https://www.loc.gov/collection/ frederick-douglass-papers/about-this-collection/; accessed June 22, 2016.

Libresco, A., J. Balantic, and J. Kipling. 2011. *Every Book Is a Social Studies Book: How to Meet Standards with Picture Books, K-6*. Santa Barbara, CA: ABC-CLIO.

Lincoln, A. 1858. "House Divided Speech." *Abraham Lincoln Online*. http://showcase. netins.net/web/creative/lincoln/speeches/house.htm; accessed February 14, 2009.

———. 1862/1895. *State of the Union Address*. United States Congressional serial set, Issue 6; Issue 3265. Washington, DC: Government Printing Office.

———. 1894. *Abraham Lincoln: Complete Works, Comprising His Speeches, Letters, State Papers, and Miscellaneous Writings, Volume 2*. Edited by J. Nicolay and J. Hay. New York: Century.

———. 1989. *Speeches and Writings, 1832–1858: Speeches, Letters, and Miscellaneous Writings, the Lincoln-Douglas debates*. Washington, DC: Library of Congress.

———. 1989. *Lincoln: Speeches and Writings, 1859–1865*. New York: Library of America.

———. 2008. *The Collected Works of Abraham Lincoln, Volume 7*. Rockville, MD: Wildside Press.

Lincoln. 2012. http://www.imdb.com/title/tt0443272/; accessed February 20, 2016.

Lindgren, J., S. Calabresi, L. Leo, and C. D. Smith. 2000. "Rating the Presidents of the United States, 1789–2000," *The Federalist Society*, November 16. http://www.fed-soc.org/publications/detail/rating-the-presidents-of-the-united-states-1789-2000-a-su rvey-of-scholars-in-history-political-science-and-law; accessed February 9, 2017.

Linebaugh, P., and M. Rediker. 2000. *The Many-Headed Hydra: Sailors, Slaves, Commoners, and the Hidden History of the Revolutionary Atlantic*. Boston: Beacon.

Litwack, L. 1961. *North of Slavery*. Chicago: University of Chicago Press.

———. 1965. "The Emancipation of the Negro Abolitionist." In *The Antislavery Vanguard*, edited by M. Duberman. Princeton: Princeton University Press.

Lloyd. 1927. *Papers of the Lloyd Family of the Manor of Queens Village, Lloyd's Neck, Long Island, NY, 1654–1826*. The New York Historical Society, Collections.

Loguen, J. 1859. *The Rev. J. W. Loguen, as a Slave and as a Freeman. A Narrative of Real Life*. Syracuse: J. G. K. Truair.

Lowance, M. 2003. *A House Divided: The Antebellum Slavery Debates in America, 1776–1865*. Princeton: Princeton University Press.

Lowry, B. 2007. *Harriet Tubman: Imagining a Life*. New York: Doubleday.

MacEwan, A. 2013. "Black-White Income Differences: What's Happened?" *Dollars & Sense*, July/August.

Madison, J., ed. 1901. *The Debates in the Several State Conventions on the Adoption of the Federal Constitution, as Recommended by the General Convention at Philadelphia in 1787, Volume II*. Philadelphia: Lippincott.

Marable, M. 2011. *Malcolm X, A Life of Reinvention*. New York: Viking, 2011.

———, and L. Mullings, eds. 2009. *Let Nobody Turn Us Around: Voices of Resistance, Reform, and Renewal*. Lanham, MD: Rowman and Littlefield.

Marcus, G. 1988. *A Forgotten People: Discovering the Black Experience in Suffolk County*. Setauket, NY: Society for the Preservation of Long Island Antiquities.

Matthewson, T. 1996. "Jefferson and the Nonrecognition of Haiti." *Proceedings of the American Philosophical Society* 140 (1): 22–48.

May, S. 1869. *Some Recollections of Antislavery Conflict*. Boston: Fields, Osgood.

McGowan, J., and W. Kashatus. 2011. *Harriet Tubman: A Biography*, Westport, CT: Greenwood.

McManus, E. 1966. *A History of Negro Slavery in New York*. Syracuse: Syracuse University Press.

McPherson, J. 1964. *The Struggle for Equality: Abolitionists and the Negro in the Civil War and Reconstruction*. Princeton: Princeton University Press.

Miranda, L-M. 2015. *Hamilton*. http://www.hamiltonbroadway.com; accessed January 24, 2016.

Moss, R. 1993. *Slavery on Long Island: A study in Local Institutional and Early African-American Communal Life*. New York: Garland.

Mushkat, J. 1990. *Fernando Wood: A Political Biography*. Kent, OH: Kent State Press.

Myers, G. 1917. *The History of Tammany, 2nd ed*. New York: Boni and Liveright.

National Constitution Center. 2015. "Looking at 10 Great Speeches in American History." *National Constitution Center*, August 28. http://blog.constitutioncenter. org/2015/08/looking-at-10-great-speeches-in-american-history/; accessed February 9, 2017.

Nesbit, J. 2015. "The White Vote and the GOP." *U.S. News and World Report*, September 8. http://www.usnews.com/news/blogs/at-the-edge/2015/09/08/the-white-vote-the-rise-of-donald-trump-shows-it-may-be-returning; accessed January 14, 2016.

New Orleans Daily Crescent. 1860. "The Constitution—The Union—The Laws," November 13.

New York Committee of Vigilance. 1837. *The First Annual Report of the New York Committee of Vigilance for the Protection of People of Color*. New York: Piercy and Reed.

New York Times. 1851a. "Of a Fugitive Slave," October 1.

———. 1851b. "Topics of the Day," October 4.

———. 1852. "The Slave Case," November 15.

———. 1853a. "The Kidnapping Case," January 19.

———. 1853b. "The Kidnapping Case," January 20.

———. 1856. "NEW-YORK CITY: The Present look of our Great Central Park," July 9.

———. 1859a. "The Fugitive Slave Law," March 4.

———. 1859b. "Northern Sentiment," December.

———. 1860a. "Report of an Anti-slavery Meeting in Boston, Massachusetts, on Saturday June 2, 1860," June 5.

———. 1860b. "The Fugitive Slave Law," December 10.

———. 1860c. "The Copperhead Council," December 17.

———. 1861. "Message of the Mayor," January 8.

———. 1863a. "Grand Emancipation Jubilee," January 1.

———. 1863b. "The Edict of Emancipation," January 6.

———. 1863a. "The Crisis in New-York," May 19.

———. 1863b. "The Peace Party," June 4.

———. 1863c. "Brooklyn Democracy on Free Speech," June 12.

———. 1863d. "The National Cemetery at Gettysburg," November 18.

———. 1863e. "The Heroes of July," November 20.

———. 1864a. "More Trouble for the Country—Another First-Class Crisis," March 21.

———. 1864b. "What We Are Coming To, and When Shall We Reach It?" March 26.

———. 1864c. "Victims of Misplaced Confidence," March 26.

———. 1864d. "The Presidential Election," August 10.

———. 1864e. "The Editor of the Metropolitan Record Arrested for Inciting Gov. Seymour to Resist the Draft," August 20.

———. 1864f. "Democratic Ratification Meeting in Union Square," September 18.

————. 1864g. "Victory!: Glorious Union Triumph," October 12.

————. 1864h. "The Election; The Result in New-York," November 13.

————. 1865a. "The Inauguration," March 6.

————. 1865b. "From Washington," December 19.

————. 1867. "Minor Topics," March 20.

————. 1873. "Obituary: Martin Kalbfleisch," February 13.

————. 2015. "The Case Against Woodrow Wilson at Princeton," November 25.

New-York Tribune. 1863. "The National Cemetery at Gettysburg," November 18.

————. 1865a. "The Inaugural," March 6.

————. 1865b. "The Nation's Loss," April 17.

————. 1865c. "An Outside Congress," December 13.

————. 1865d. "Suggestions," December 14.

————. 1865e. "The President and Congress," December 20.

————. 1867a. "Progress of Reconstruction," March 11.

————. 1867b. "Untitled," March 11.

Niven, S. 2016. "Ona Judge Staines: She Challenged George Washington and Won Her Freedom." *The Root*, March 7. http://www.theroot.com/ona-judge-staines-she-challenged-george-washington-and-1790854513; accessed February 28, 2017.

Northup, S. 1853. *Twelve Years a Slave: Narrative of Solomon Northup, A Citizen Of New-York, Kidnapped In Washington City in 1841 and Rescued in 1853, From a Cotton Plantation Near the Red River in Louisiana*. Auburn, NY: Derby and Miller.

NYSED. 2012. "Common Core Exemplar for High School ELA: Lincoln's Gettysburg Address." *engageNY*, October 18. https://www.engageny.org/resource/common-core-exemplar-for-high-school-ela-lincoln-s-gettysburg-address; accessed February 9, 2017.

Oakes, J. 1986. "The Political Significance of Slave Resistance." *History Workshop* 22: 89–107.

————. 2008. "Frederick Douglass Changed My Mind about the Constitution." *Social Education* 72 (5): 251–52.

Ofari (Hutchinson), E. 1972. *"Let Resistance Be Your Motto": The Life and Thought of Henry Highland Garnet*. Boston: Beacon.

Olajibe, O. 2013. *The Complete Concise History of the Slave Trade*. Bloomington, IN: AuthorHouse.

Ondaatje, M. 2011. *Black Conservative Intellectuals in Modern America*. Philadelphia: University of Pennsylvania Press.

Patterson, O. 1969. *The Sociology of Slavery: An Analysis of the Origins, Development, and Structure of Negro Slave Society in Jamaica*. Rutherford, NJ: Fairleigh Dickinson.

Phillips, U. 1918. *American Negro Slavery: A Survey of the Supply, Employment, and Control of Negro Labor as Determined by the Plantation Régime*. New York: Appleton.

Pogrebin, R., and G. Collins. 2004. "Shift at Historical Society Raises Concerns." *The New York Times*, July 19.

Pohlmann, M. 2003. *African American Political Thought: Capitalism vs. collectivism, 1945 to the present*. New York: Taylor and Francis.

Quarles, B. 1969. *Black Abolitionists*. New York: Oxford University Press.

Rael, P. 2002. *Black Identity and Black Protest in the Antebellum North*. Chapel Hill: University of North Carolina Press.

————. ed. 2008. *African-American Activism before the Civil War*. New York: Routledge.

Rava, R., and C. Matthews. 2013. "An Archaeological View of Slavery and Social Relations at Rock Hall, Lawrence, New York." *Long Island History* 23 (2). https://lihj. cc.stonybrook.edu/2013/articles/an-archaeological-view-of-slavery-and-soc ial-relations-at-rock-hall-lawrence-new-york/; accessed February 28, 2017.

Register of Debates in Congress, The First Session of the Twenty-Fourth Congress, Part II of Volume 12. Washington, DC: Gales and Seaton, 1836.

Ripley, C., and R. Finkenine, eds. 1986. *The Black Abolitionist Papers, Vol II Canada, 1830–1865*. Chapel Hill: University of North Carolina Press.

Ripley, C. ed. 1991. *The Black Abolitionist Papers, Vol III, 1830–1846*. Chapel Hill: University of North Carolina Press.

Ripley, C. P., ed. 1992. *The Black Abolitionist Papers, Volume V, The United States, 1859–1865*. Chapel Hill: University of North Carolina Press.

Roberts, J. 2007. "Parents Involved in Community Schools v. Seattle School District No. 1." http://www.supremecourt.gov/opinions/06pdf/05-908.pdf); accessed January 14, 2016.

Root, E. 2008. *All Honor to Jefferson?: The Virginia Slavery Debates and the Positive Good Thesis*. Lanham, MD: Lexington Books.

Rossiter, C., ed. 1961. *The Federalist Papers*. New York: New American Library.

Rothstein, E. 2005. "The Peculiar Institution as Lived in New York." *The New York Times*, October 7.

————. 2012. "Life, Liberty and the Fact of Slavery." *New York Times*, January 27.

Rottinghaus, B., and J. Vaughn. 2015. "New Ranking of U.S. Presidents puts Lincoln at No. 1, Obama at 18." *The Washington Post*, February 16. https://www.washingtonpost.com/ news/monkey-cage/wp/2015/02/16/new-ranking-of-u-s-presidents-puts-lin coln-1-obama-18-kennedy-judged-most-over-rated/?utm_term=.db47b442fafe; accessed February 9, 2017.

Ruchmames, L., ed. 1969. *John Brown, The Making of a Revolutionary*. New York: Grossett and Dunlap.

Scarry, R. 2001. *Millard Fillmore*. Jefferson, NC: McFarland.

Schor, J. 1979. "The Rivalry between Frederick Douglass and Henry Highland Garnet." *Journal of Negro History* 64 (1): 30–38.

SCNHC. 2014. "A Revolutionary Profile; Henry Laurens." *South Carolina Traveler*. South Carolina National Heritage Corridor. http://www.scnhc.org/story/a-revolution ary-profile-henry-laurens; accessed February 24, 2017.

Sernett, M. 1999. *African American Religious History: A Documentary Witness*. Durham: Duke University Press.

———. 2002. *North Star Country: Upstate New York and the Crusade for African American Freedom*. Syracuse: Syracuse University Press.

———. 2007. *Harriet Tubman: Myth, Memory, and History*. Durham: Duke University Press, 2007.

Siebert, W. 1898. *The Underground Railroad: From Slavery to Freedom*. New York: The Macmillan Company.

———. 1937. *Vermont's Anti-slavery and Underground Railroad Record*. Columbus, OH: Spahr and Glenn.

Simon, R. 2015. "The GOP and Willie Horton: Together Again." *Politico*, May 19. http://www.politico.com/story/2015/05/jeb-bush-willie-horton-118061); accessed January 14, 2016.

Singer, A. 2007. "Venture Smith's Autobiography and Runaway Ad: Enslavement in Early New York." *MLL, middle level learning supplement to Social Education* 28 (January/February).

———. 2008. *New York and Slavery, Time to Teach the Truth*. Albany: State University of New York Press.

———. 2011a. *Teaching Global History: A Social Studies Approach*. New York: Routledge.

———. 2011b. "Michelle Bachmann was Half-Right: New York's Founding Fathers Worked to End Slavery." *History News Network*, July 17. http://hnn.us/articles/140711.html; accessed January 20, 2016.

———. 2011c. "The Resurrection of Seneca Village." *Huffington Post*, August 25. http://www.huffingtonpost.com/alan-singer/the-resurrection-of-senec_b_935566.html; accessed April 6, 2016.

———. 2011d. "*Slavery and the Law* Takes an Honest Look at Our History." *Huffington Post*, November 8. http://www.huffingtonpost.com/alan-singer/slavery-and-th e-law-premi_b_1079669.html; accessed April 6, 2016.

———. 2011e. "Fairy Tale History at New York's (un)Historical Society." *History News Network*, November 29. http://historynewsnetwork.org/article/143282; accessed April 6, 2016.

———. 2012a. "Lincoln and Douglass Would Be Angry." *Huffington Post*, January 5. http://www.huffingtonpost.com/alan-singer/historical-society-revolution-exhib it_b_1179397.html; accessed April 6, 2016.

———. 2012b. "You Don't Own Frederick Douglass." *Huffington Post*. http://www.huffing tonpost.com/alan-singer/ny-historical-society-exhibit_b_1192337.html; accessed January 24, 2016.

———. 2014. "Common Core and the End of History." *Huffington Post*, October 27. http://www.huffingtonpost.com/alan-singer/common-core-history-exams_b_6050456.html; accessed January 24, 2016.

———. 2015. "Instead of Honoring Slaveholders, Slave Traders, and Racists." *Huffington Post*, December 21. http://www.huffingtonpost.com/alan-singer/instead-of-honoring-slave_b_8852766.html); accessed January 20, 2016.

———, ed. 2001. "Runaway Slave Ads from New York State." *Social Science Docket* 1 (2) (Summer-Fall).

———, ed. 2004. *New York and Slavery: Complicity and Resistance Curriculum Guide*. New York: Gateway to the City Teaching American History Grant.

Sinha, M. 2000. "Revolution or Counterrevolution?: The Political Ideology of Secession in Antebellum South Carolina." *Civil War History* 46 (3): 205–26.

———. 2013. "The Strange Victory of the Palmetto State." In *The New York Times Disunion: Modern Historians Revisit and Reconsider the Civil War from Lincoln's Election to the Emancipation Proclamation*, edited by T. Widmer, with C. Risen and G. Kalogerakis. New York: Black Dog and Leventhal.

———. 2016. *The Slave's Cause: A History of Abolition*. New Haven: Yale University Press.

Smalls, F. R. 1997. "African Burial Ground Is Documented in Film." *New York Times*, March 16.

Smedley, R. 1883/1969. *History of the Underground Railroad*, New York: Arno Press.

Smith, G. 1844. "Letter to John G. Whittier." *The Liberator*, July 18.

Smith, V. 1896. *A Narrative of the Life and Adventures of Venture, a Native of Africa: But Resident above Sixty Years in the United States of America. Related by Himself.* New London: C. Holt.

Sotomayer, S. 2014. *Schuette, Attorney General Of Michigan v. Coalition To Defend Affirmative Action, Integration And Immigration Rights And Fight For Equality By Any Means Necessary (Bamn) et al.* https://www.law.cornell.edu/supct/pdf/12-682.pdf; accessed January 14, 2016.

Stack, L. 2016. "Publisher Halts Children's Book on Slave." *The New York Times*, January 25.

Stahr, W. 2012. *Seward: Lincoln's Indispensable Man*. New York: Simon and Schuster.

Staples. B. 2014. "X-Men, Not All Fiction." *The New York Times*, May 31, A18.

Stephanopoulos, G. 2011. "John Quincy Adams a Founding Father? Michele Bachmann Says Yes." ABC News, August 6. http://blogs.abcnews.com/george/2011/06/john-quincy-adams-a-founding-father-michele-bachmann-says-yes.html; accessed January 25, 2016.

Still, W. 1872. *The Underground Rail Road*. Philadelphia: Porter and Coates.

Stowe, H. 1852. *Uncle Tom's Cabin or, Life among the Lowly*. Boston: Jewett.

Strausbaugh. 2016. *City of Sedition: The History of New York City during the Civil War*. New York: Grand Central.

Sumner, C. 1865. "The Promises of the Declaration of Independence: Eulogy on Abraham Lincoln." Boston: Farwell.

Syracuse Daily Journal. 1852. *Trial of Henry W. Allen, U. S. Deputy Marshal, For Kidnapping, With Arguments of Counsel & Charge of Justice Marvin on the Constitutionality of The Fugitive Slave Law, In the Supreme Court of New York.* Syracuse: Power Press of the Daily Journal Office.

Tagg, L. 2009. *The Unpopular Mr. Lincoln: The Story of America's Most Reviled President.* New York: Savas Beatie.

Takaki, R. 1965. "The Movement to Reopen the African Slave Trade in South Carolina." *The South Carolina Historical Magazine* 66 (1) (January): 38–54.

Tappan, L. 1837. *The Slave's Friend, Volume II.* New York: Anti-Slavery Office.

———. 1850. *The Fugitive Slave Bill: Its History and Unconstitutionality.* New York: Harned.

Taylor, E. 2012. *A Slave in the White House: Paul Jennings and the Madisons.* New York: Macmillan.

Thomas, J., ed. 1965. *Slavery Attacked: The Abolitionist Crusade.* Englewood Cliffs, NJ: Prentice-Hall.

Thompson, J. 1850. *Memoir of David Hale: Late Editor of the Journal of Commerce.* New York: J. Wiley.

Thompson, M. 1999. "The Only Unavoidable Subject of Regret." Conference paper, "George Washington and Alexandria, Virginia: Ties that Bind." http://www.mountvernon. org/george-washington/slavery/the-only-unavoidable-subject-of-regret/; accessed February 28, 2017.

Tilly, C. 1999. "From Interactions to Outcomes in Social Movements." In *How Social Movements Matter*, edited by E. Giugni, D. McAdam, and C. Tilly. Minneapolis,: University of Minnesota Press.

———. 2004. *Social Movements 1768–2004.* Boulder: Paradigm.

Tise, L. 1990. *Proslavery: A History of the Defense of Slavery in America, 1701–1840.* Athens: University of Georgia Press.

de Tocqueville, A. 1839. *Democracy in America*, vol. 1. New York: Adelard.

Trescott, J. 2012. "Closer Look at Jefferson's Slaves." *The Washington Post*, January 27.

Underground Railroad. n.d. "National Newspaper Reaction to the Christiana Resistance." https://beta.fold3.com/page/1342_underground_railroad/stories/#5135/; accessed January 19, 2016.

Urofsky, M., ed. 2000. *The American Presidents: Critical Essays.* New York: Garland.

Von Holst, H. 1888. *The Constitutional and Political History of the United States, Volume II.* Chicago: Callaghan.

Wald, A. 2005. "Between Insularity and Internationalism: The Lost World of the Jewish Communist 'Cultural Workers.' In *America in Dark Times, Dire Decisions: Jews and Communism, Studies in Contemporary Jewry, Volume XX*, edited by Jonathan Frankel. New York: Oxford University Press.

Walker, D. 1830. *Walker's Appeal*. Boston: David Walker.

Washington Post. 2017. "Yale's Smart Choice in Renaming Calhoun College," February 19. https://www.washingtonpost.com/opinions/yales-smart-choice-in-renam ing-calhoun-college/2017/02/19/fd391418-f235-11e6-b9c9-83fce42fb61_story. html?utm_term=.1f0d34a991e6; accessed March 4, 2017.

Washington, G. 1797. "Letter from George Washington to Tobias Lear." https://founders. archives.gov/documents/Washington/06-01-02-0019; accessed February 28, 2017.

Waugh, J. 1997. *Reelecting Lincoln: The Battle for the 1864 Presidency*. New York: Crown.

Webster, D. 1914. *The Speeches and Orations of Daniel Webster*. Boston: Little, Brown.

Wesley, C. 1917. "The Struggle for the Recognition of Haiti and Liberia as Independent Republics." *Journal of Negro History* 2 (4): 369–83.

West. C. 1993. *Race Matters*. New York: Vintage.

White, R. 2006. *Lincoln's Greatest Speech: The Second Inaugural*. New York: Simon and Schuster.

Whitehead, C. 2016. *The Underground Railroad*. New York: Knopf Doubleday.

Wilder, C. 2000. *In the Company of Black Men: The African Influence on African American Culture in New York City*. New York: New York University Press.

———. 2013. *Ebony and Ivy: Race, Slavery, and the Troubled History of America's Universities*. New York: Bloomsbury.

Wills, G. 1992. *Lincoln at Gettysburg: The Words That Remade America*. New York: Simon and Schuster.

Wilson, C. 1994. *Freedom at Risk: The Kidnapping of Free Blacks in America, 1780–1865*. Lexington: University of Kentucky Press.

Wilson, W. 1978. *The Declining Significance of Race: Blacks and Changing American Institutions*. Chicago: University of Chicago Press.

———. 1987. *The Truly Disadvantaged: The Inner City, the Underclass, and Public Policy*. Chicago: University of Chicago Press.

———. 1996. *When Work Disappears: The World of the New Urban Poor*. New York: Vintage.

———. 2009. *More than Just Race: Being Black and Poor in the Inner City*. New York: Norton.

Wood, F. 1968. *Black Scare: The Racist Response to Emancipation and Reconstruction*. Berkeley: University of California Press.

Wootson, C. 2017. "Trump Implied Frederick Douglass was Alive." *The Washington Post*, February 2. https://www.washingtonpost.com/news/post-nation/wp/2017/02/02/ trump-implied-frederick-douglass-was-alive-the-abolitionists-family-of- fered-a-history-lesson/?utm_term=.c9e02452d8e2; accessed February 15, 2017.

INDEX

44418562R00128

Made in the USA
Middletown, DE
06 May 2019